IMAGES
of America

THE OSSIPEE VALLEY

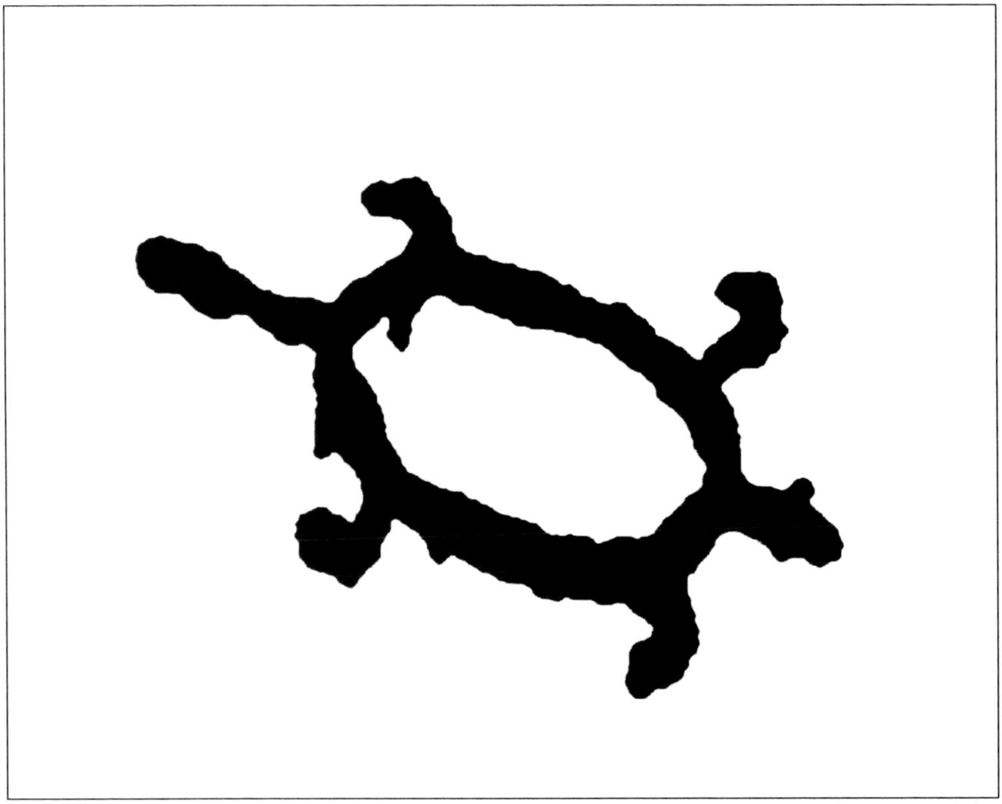

Chief Wesumbe of the Newichewanock tribe conveyed the Ossipee Lands when he executed the ancient deed on November 28, 1668, with the Sign of the Turtle. This deed may be seen at the Maine Historical Society in Portland, Maine. The Sign of the Turtle is used today as the logo for the Francis Small Heritage Trust. The trust serves the five Ossipee towns by holding in public trust hundreds of acres of forest, in its natural state, for the people of the area to enjoy. (Used with the permission of The Maine Historical Society.)

IMAGES
of America

THE OSSIPEE VALLEY

Cornish, Limerick, Limington, Newfield, and
Parsonsfield-Porter Historical Societies

ARCADIA
PUBLISHING

ISBN 978-0-7385-3905-8

Published by Arcadia Publishing
Charleston, South Carolina

Printed in the United States of America

Library of Congress Catalog Card Number: 2005930998

For all general information contact Arcadia Publishing at:
Telephone 843-853-2070
Fax 843-853-0044
E-mail sales@arcadiapublishing.com
For customer service and orders:
Toll-Free 1-888-313-2665

Visit us on the Internet at www.arcadiapublishing.com

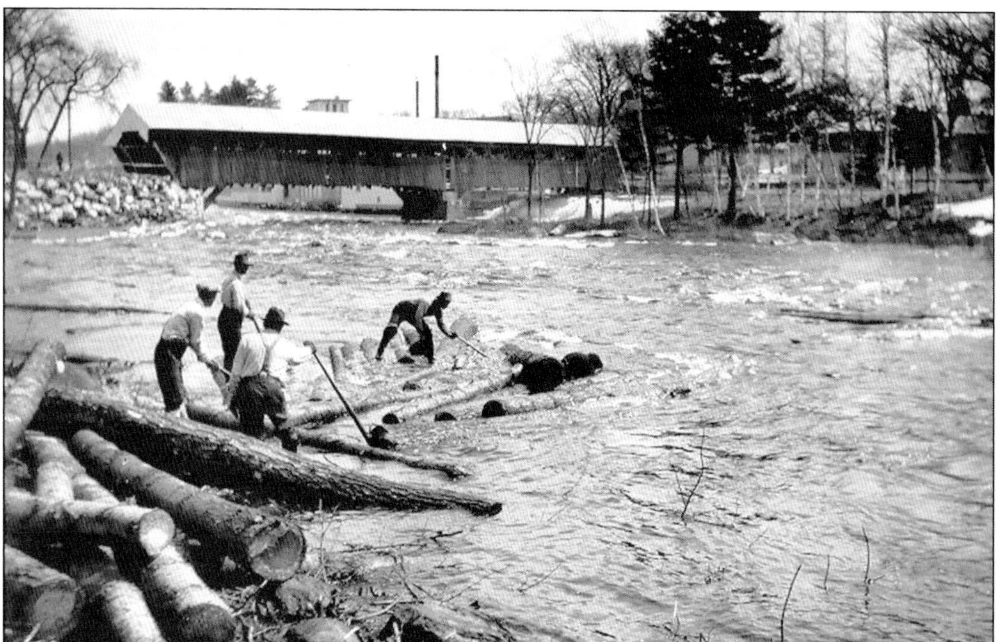

Loggers are diligently working at the Great Ossipee River above the covered bridge at Parsonsfield-Porter. The word Ossipee means "River of Pine."

Contents

Acknowledgments

The Historical Societies of Cornish, Limerick, Limington, Newfield, and Parsonsfield would like to express their deep appreciation to those who have gifted their fine collections of photographs, postcards and research materials over the years.

We would also like to thank the many individuals who graciously shared their memories, personal photographs, and knowledge that filled in the gaps for this publication. Your contributions are truly priceless.

Our special thanks to those committee members who worked tirelessly in the pursuit of images and the tasks of searching, sorting, authenticating, and finding just the right words for this effort. And also, our sincerest thank you, to the staff of Arcadia Publishing in Portsmouth, New Hampshire for their act of faith in placing this in our hands.

The committee for the Cornish chapter consists of the following: Steven Dibiaso, Jack and Diane Barnes, O. B. Denison, Highland Farms, and author Gary Mason.

The contributors for the Limerick chapter consist of the following: Glen Taylor, David Chase Carpenter, Marguerite and David Hayes, Joan Carroll, William Lanoue, Thurland Ricker, George Carroll, Sarah Lessard, Ester Gochie, Colleen Berry, Mildred Libby, Doris Smith, Hilary Wallis, George Wilson, Florette Whiteley, Eleanor Watson, Harland Eastman, The Sanford Historical Committee, Stephanie and Ray Bishop, and Steve Libby. The committee for the Limerick chapter consists of the following: Adele Floyd, Candace Gooch, Jane Lougee Bryant, and author Gail Libby.

The committee for the Limington chapter consists of the following: Mona Belle Braley, Louise Chick, Frank and Marion Foss, Phil Dearborn, Pat Dearborn, Maureen Calnan, Minot Holmes, Dot Haley, Peter Childs, and author Ann Dunbar.

The committee for the Newfield chapter consists of the following: Janet Colwell, Ruth Bridges Ayers, Lee Russell, and author Joyce Bond.

The contributors for the Parsonsfield chapter consist of the following: John Bunton, Patricia Campbell, Maxine Chadbourne, Janet Colwell, Merle Day, Robert Bruce Gordon, Linda Humphrey, Aleta Pease, James Stanley, Jean Stanley, Merrillyn Stanley, Earl Taylor, and Barbara VanPelt. As always, we are extremely grateful for access to the photographs of George French who documented our area and our state so beautifully. The committee for the Parsonsfield chapter consists of the following: Janice Burch, Madeline French, Merideth Shea, Sylvia Wilson, and author Janice Iler.

The village maps that appear throughout this publication are from the *1872 Atlas of York County, Maine*, published by Sanford, Everts, and Company.

INTRODUCTION

Intrepid Francis Small set the history of the Ossipee Valley in motion as early as 1666, when he ventured through the wilderness from Kittery and set up a trading post within sight and sound of the Great Ossipee River, a short distance from the Newichawanock Indian village and stockade located at the confluence of the Ossipee and Saco Rivers. Instead of trading him furs, the local American Indians in the summer of 1668 burned his trading post (said to have been located near the present Clifford house in Cornish) to the ground. Small, having been warned, made his way safely back to Kittery. However, the Newichawanock chief, referred to as Captain Sandy by the British, pursued Small to Kittery where he granted him a deed to "all the land between the Ossipee Rivers" in exchange for blankets, beads, rum, and other sundry items.

Because the American Indians had sold the Ossipee Valley more than once, ownership of the land was in contention. The ancient deed was declared genuine by two Boston experts, William P. Upham, of Suffolk County Court, and Robert B. Swan, commissioner of public records for Massachusetts, and the land was determined to be owned by the Small family. Once the issue of ownership was settled, over 100 years after the deed conveyance between Francis Small and Chief Wesumbe, the communities of Francisborough, Limerick Plantation, Ossipee, Washington Plantation, and Parsonsfield emerged. These communities would someday become the towns of Cornish, Limerick, Limington, Newfield, and Parsonsfield, Maine.

The Ossipee Valley contains the Great Ossipee River, the Little Ossipee River, and the mighty Saco River. These bodies of water and their tributaries were significant to each of the Ossipee Valley town's development. The water motion provided sawmill and gristmill power, and eventually electric generation. The rivers provided a way to move products to market, sustenance, recreation, and were a means of transportation.

And, like the rivers, the histories of the towns within the Ossipee Valley have been "sparkling and gloomy, deep and shallow, and smooth and tumultuous," but they have always rolled on.

November 28, 2005

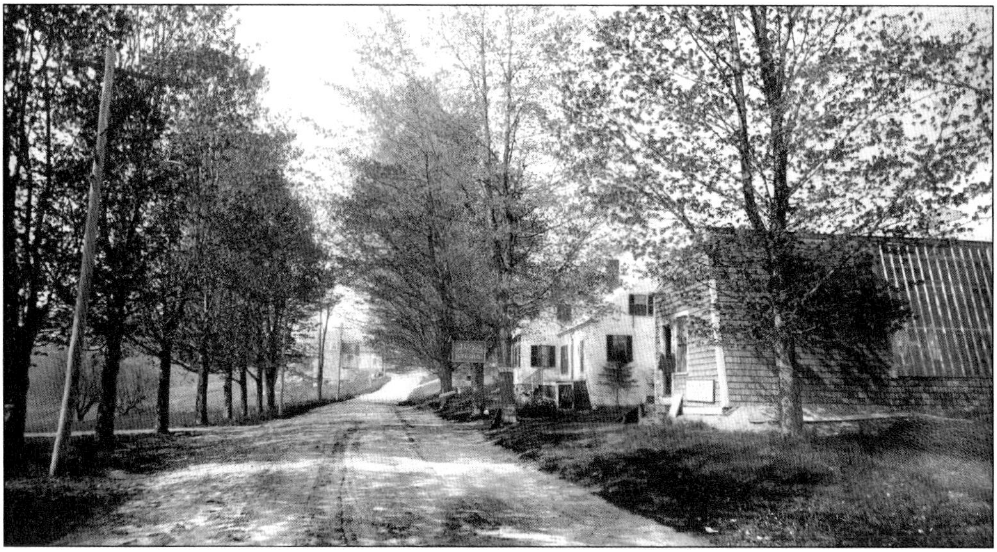

Fred C. Philpot hailed from Limerick, Maine. He photographed much of York County before 1900. Many of his photographs appear in the Limerick and Newfield chapters. His Limerick Studio was on Washington Street, located next to Norris L. Berry's farm.

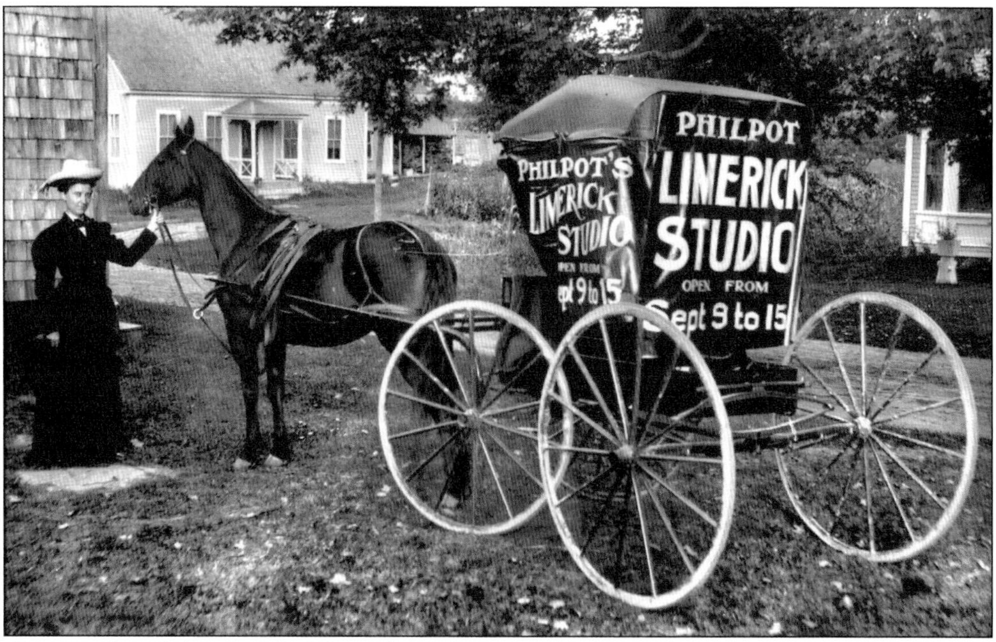

Photographer Philpot traveled throughout the Ossipee Valley with his portable studio. His sister, Catherine, is holding the reins of his horse, Pat. Fred Philpot advertised he had over 10,000 postcards available. Many of his glass negatives are in existence today.

One

CORNISH

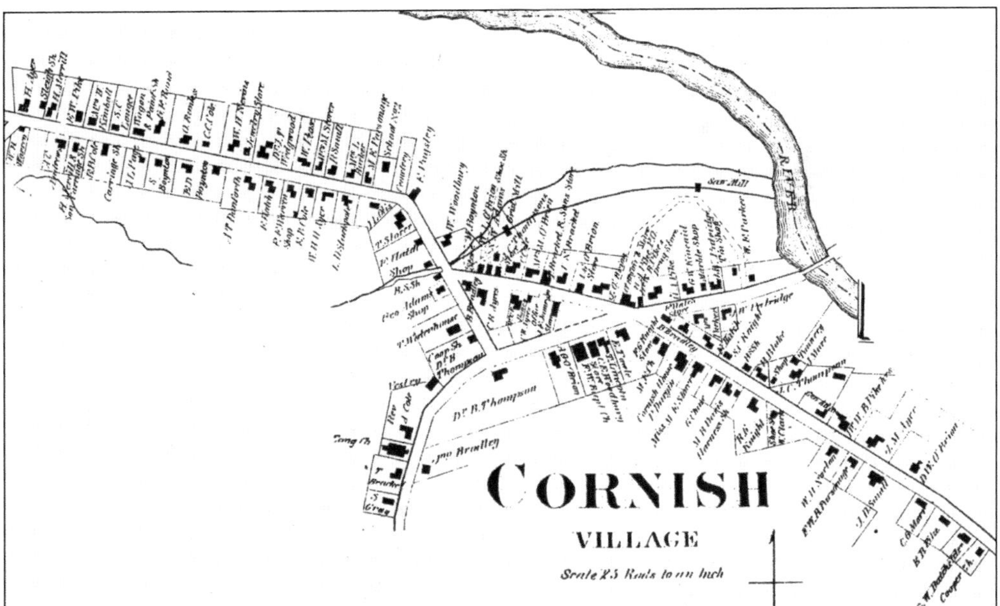

Eleven years after the Peace of Paris—ending the long series of Indian Wars that were particularly devastating to York County, Maine—settlers such as John Durgin, James Holmes, and Asahel Cole began clearing land and setting up the indispensable sawmill in the plantation of Francisboro. Townsfolk renamed their village Cornish, very likely after England's Cornish coast, and it was incorporated on February 26, 1794.

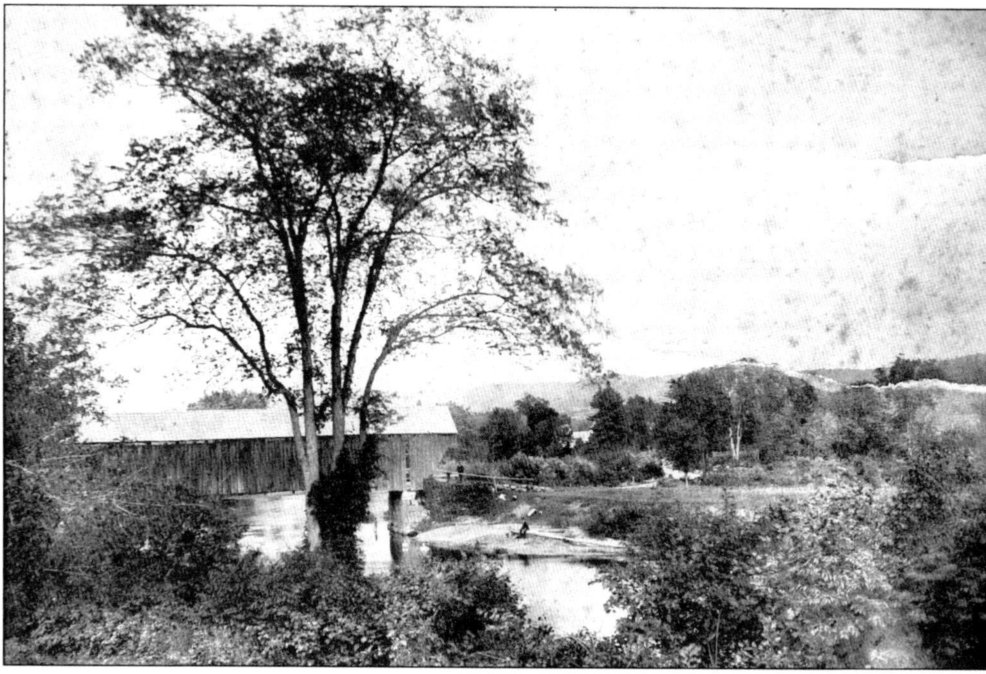

This covered Bridge (top) is between Cornish and Hiram on Bridge Street. It was replaced in 1933 by the cement bridge (bottom), which is only one of a handful of curved bridges in the state.

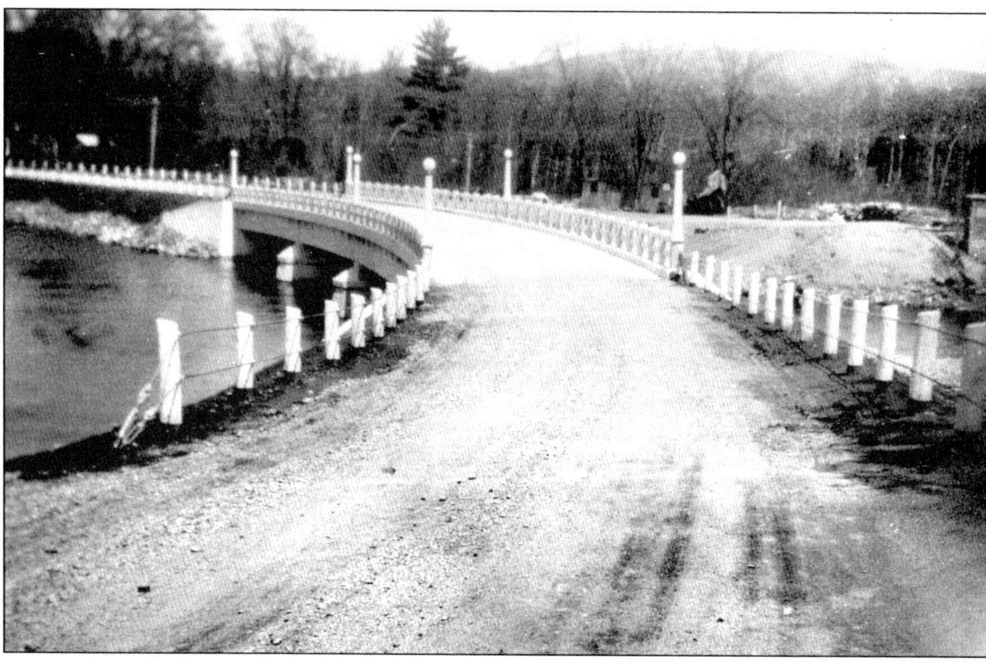

Dr. Benjamin Thompson lived a long life as a medical practitioner and was known for his eccentricities. His hair was always worn long, but he could not grow a beard, due to an incident with a poisoned razor. Flies were allowed in his home because he thought them to be healthy. He never asked a patient for payment, and everyone in town knew they could help themselves to his fields and orchards.

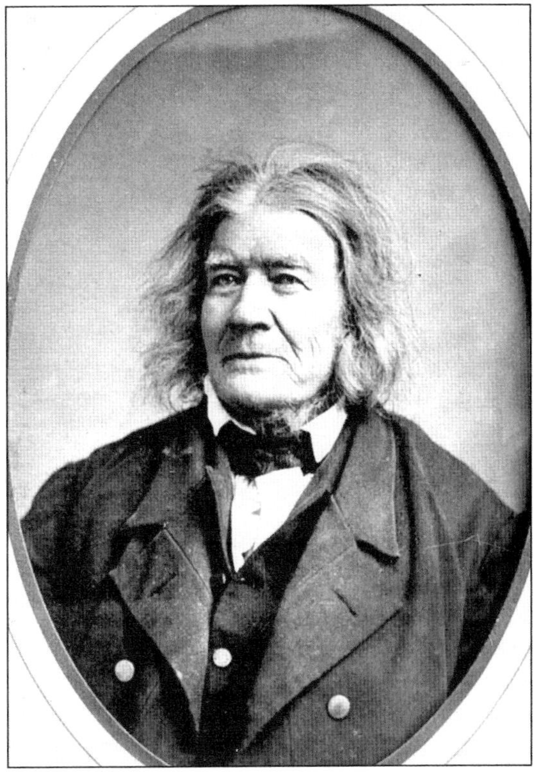

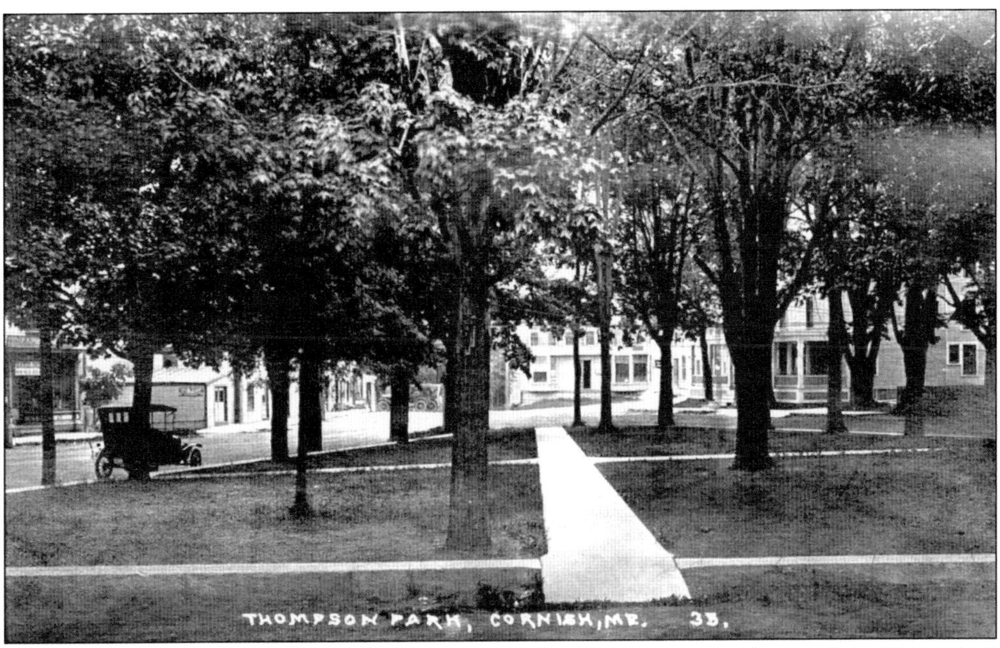

Thompson Park's land was donated to the town by Dr. Thompson after his death in 1874. It had been used as a dump and teamsters would graze their animals there. A few years later relatives had the land cleaned up and made into a park.

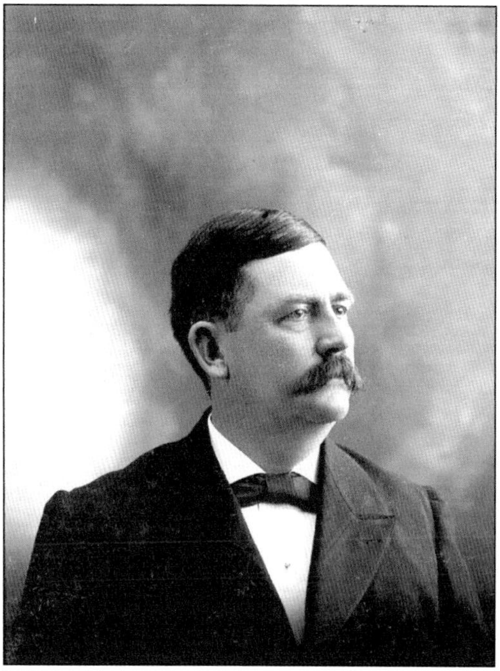

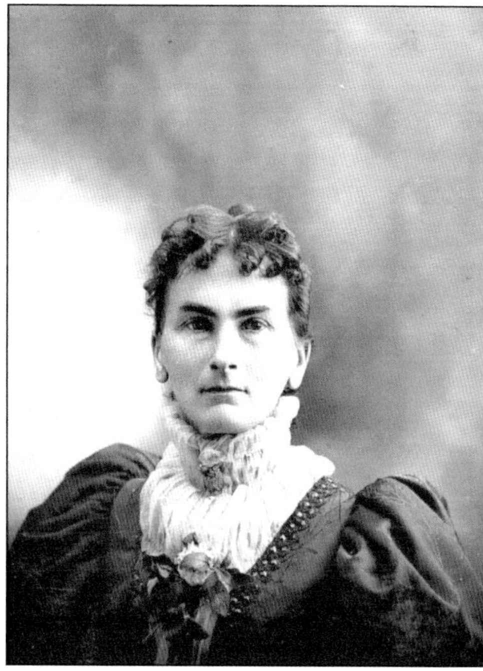

LeRoy F. Pike was born in Cornish in 1850. His wife, Jennie Guptill Pike, was born in 1851. He served the town in many capacities: tax collector, selectman, moderator, and constable, and was a state senator in 1897. On a trip with Jennie Pike to the West to visit the Panama-Pacific Exposition in 1915, he died of a heart attack. After her death in 1922, Jennie Pike left in her will the sum of $20,000 to construct a town hall (pictured below, center) in her husband's memory. Finished in 1924, it became the place in town where most functions were held. The building on the right, the Rose Window School, was deemed unsafe and was torn down in 1930.

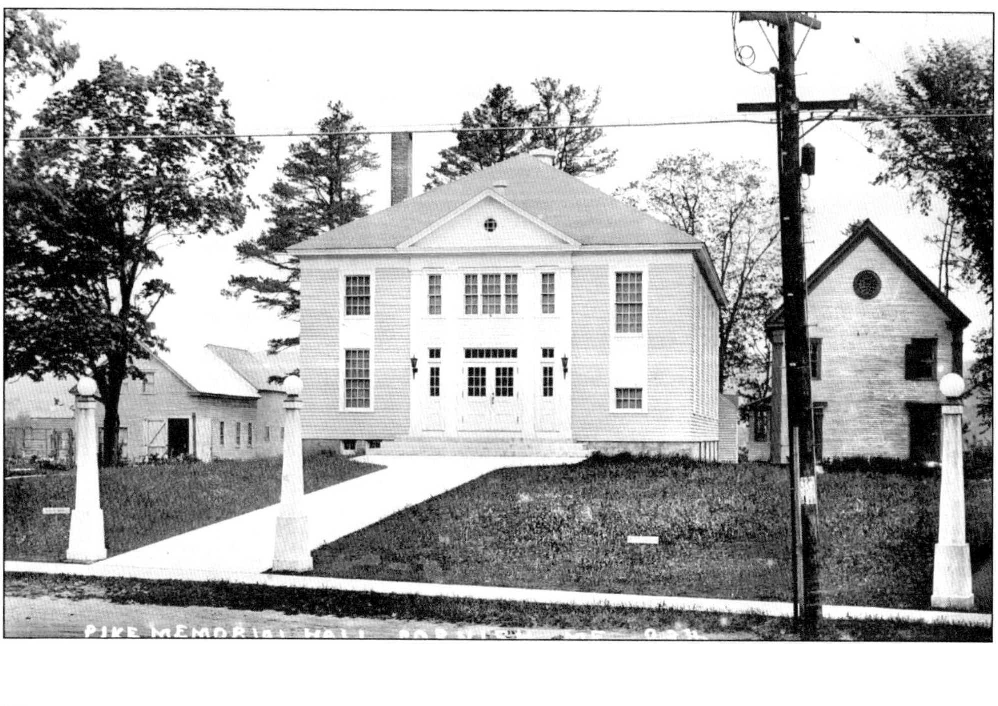

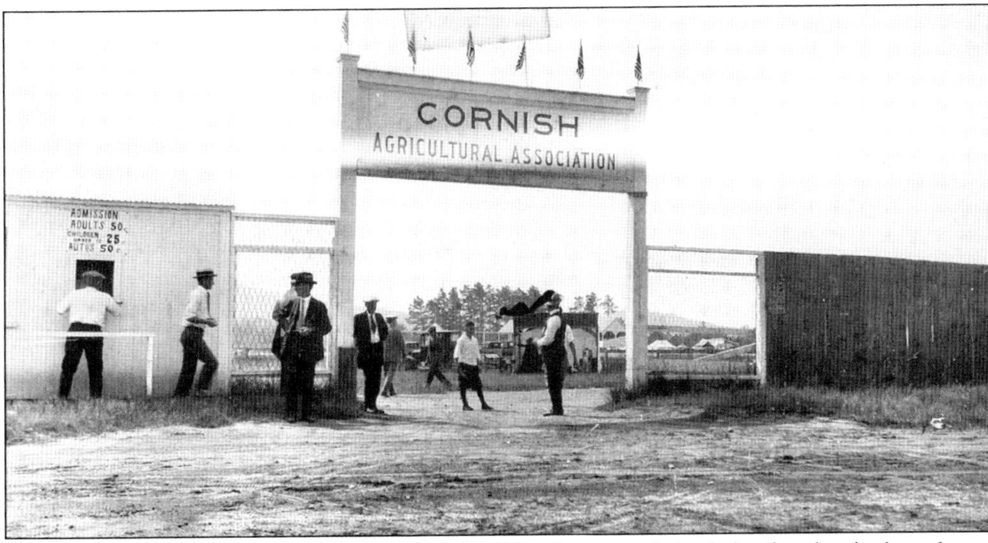

Horse racing was a major activity in Cornish. The fairgrounds had the first banked track and underpass in the state. In 1914, the railroad ran six trains a day from Portland hauling people to the Cornish Fair. During the fair week, locals would board fairgoers in their extra rooms. The grandstand was built in 1888 and it was replaced in 1904.

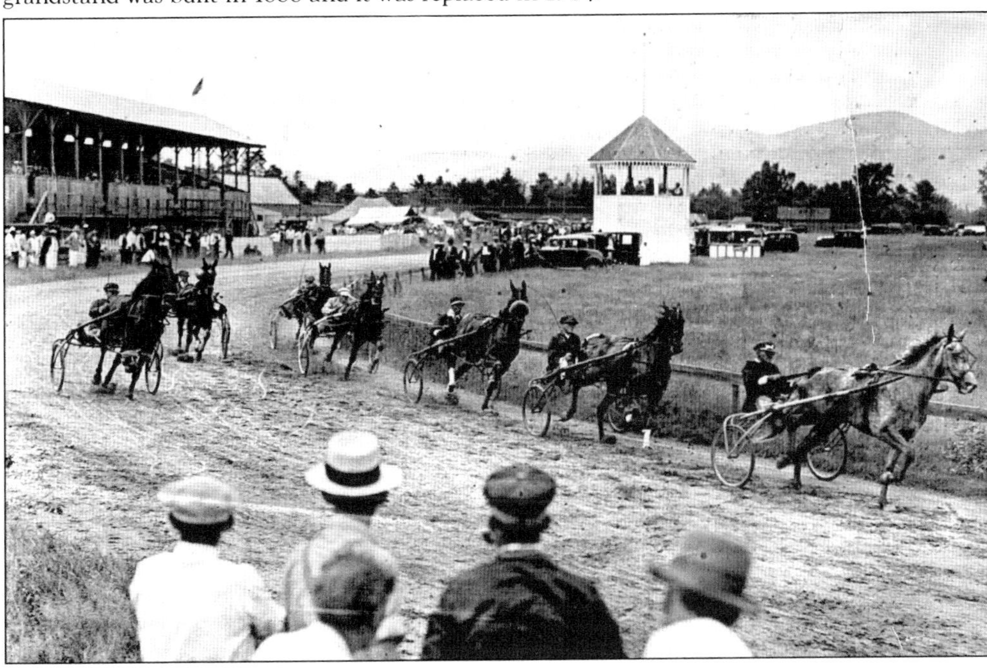

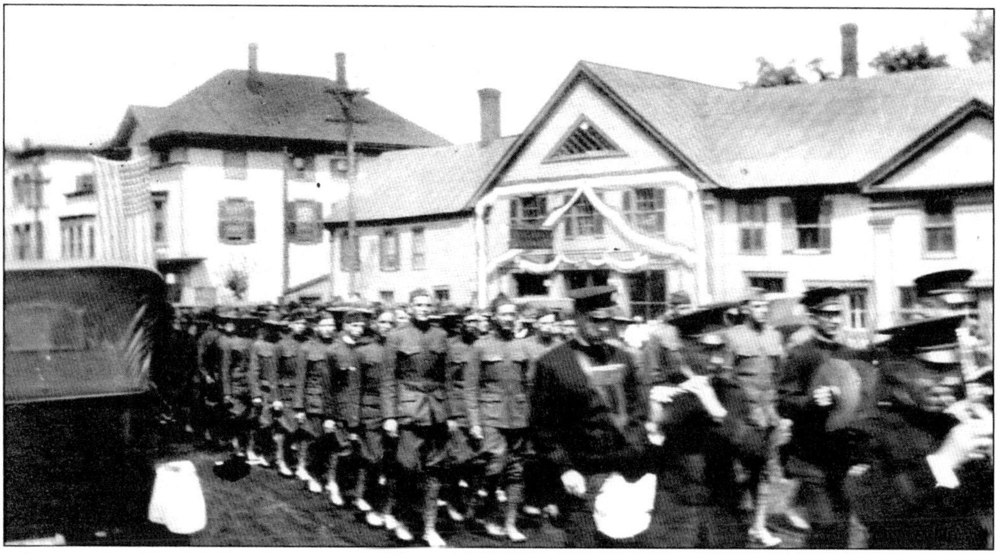

This was the World War I victory celebration held on July 4, 1919. The day was full of festivities capped off by splendid music and electric illumination at Thompson Park. The soldiers are from around the area.

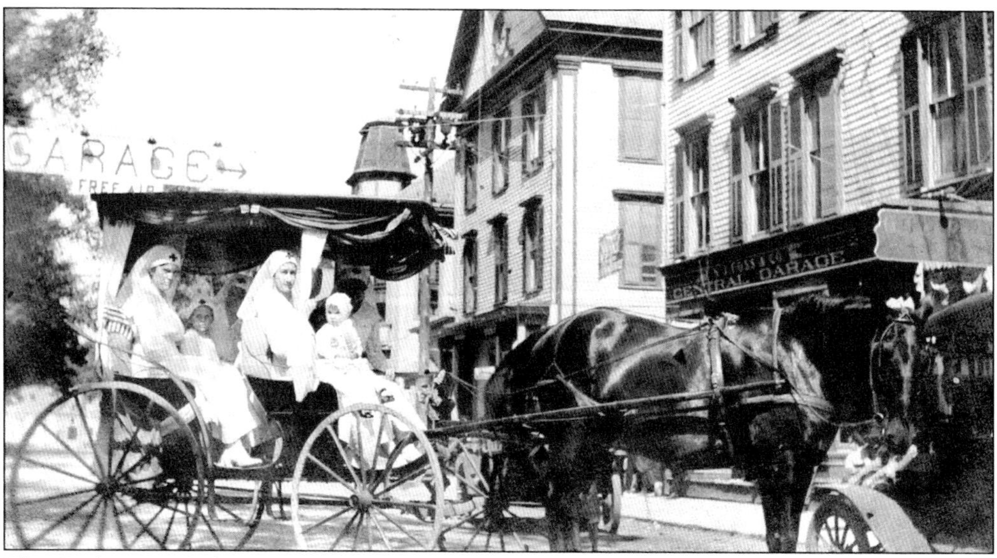

The Red Cross ladies are taking part in the Victory Parade. In the background is the Central Block.

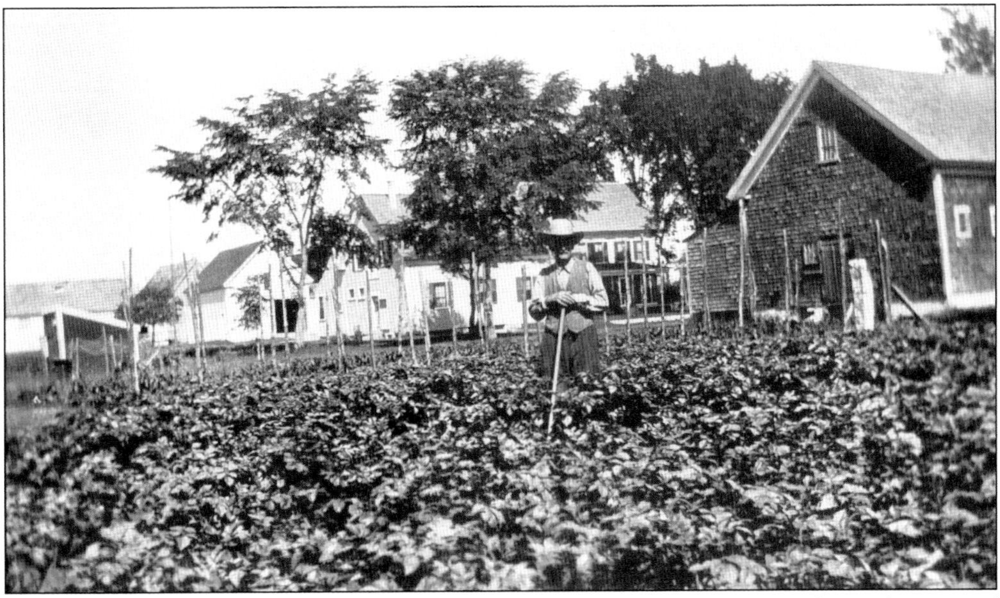

John Rounds was the last surviving Civil War veteran in Cornish. He fought at the siege of Petersburg, and died in 1930 at the age of 86.

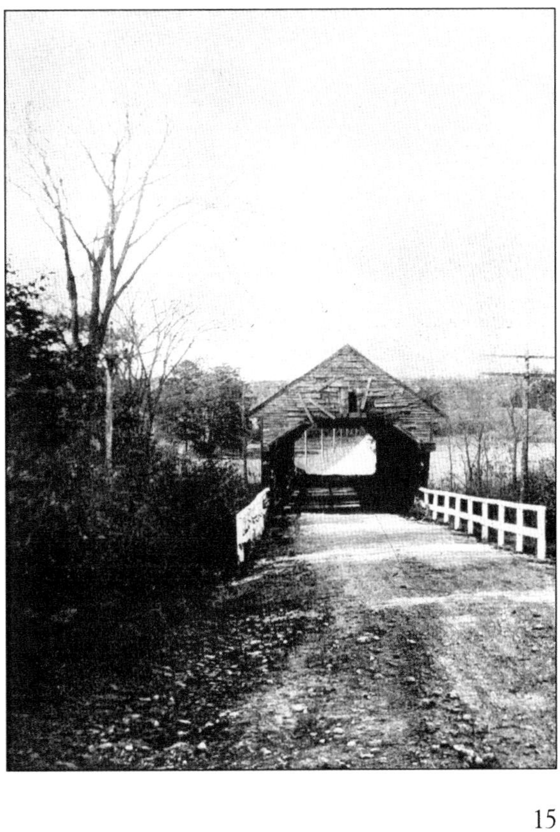

Warren's bridge was built by Col. John Warren. His father, Nathaniel, ran a tavern on the western side of the bridge. The bridge was torn down in 1930 and replaced by the current cement bridge.

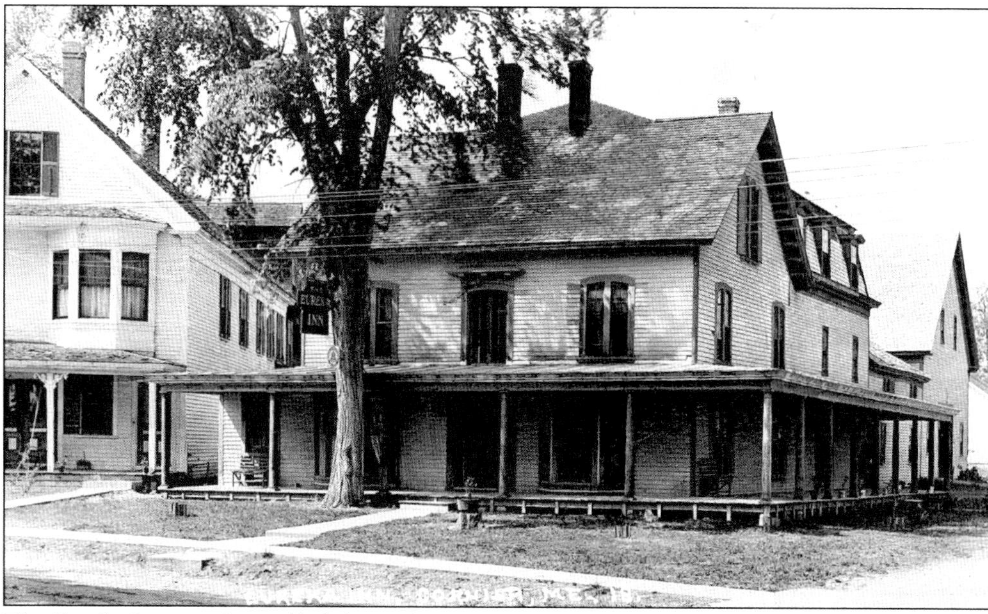

The Eureka Inn was first called the Park House. It was managed by Freeman Pugsley, who later became the proprietor of the Lincoln Hotel.

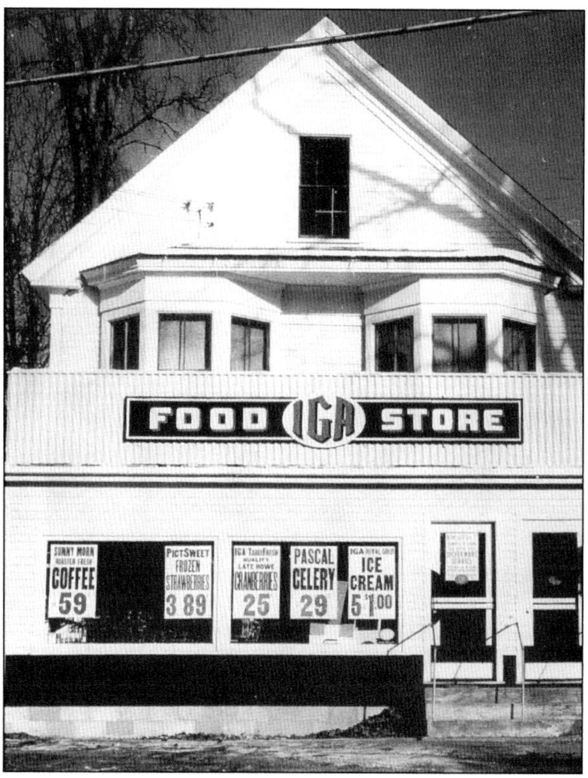

The IGA Grocery Store was located where the current Hardware Store's parking lot is, at Norton Street and Maple Street. Walter Rines was the owner.

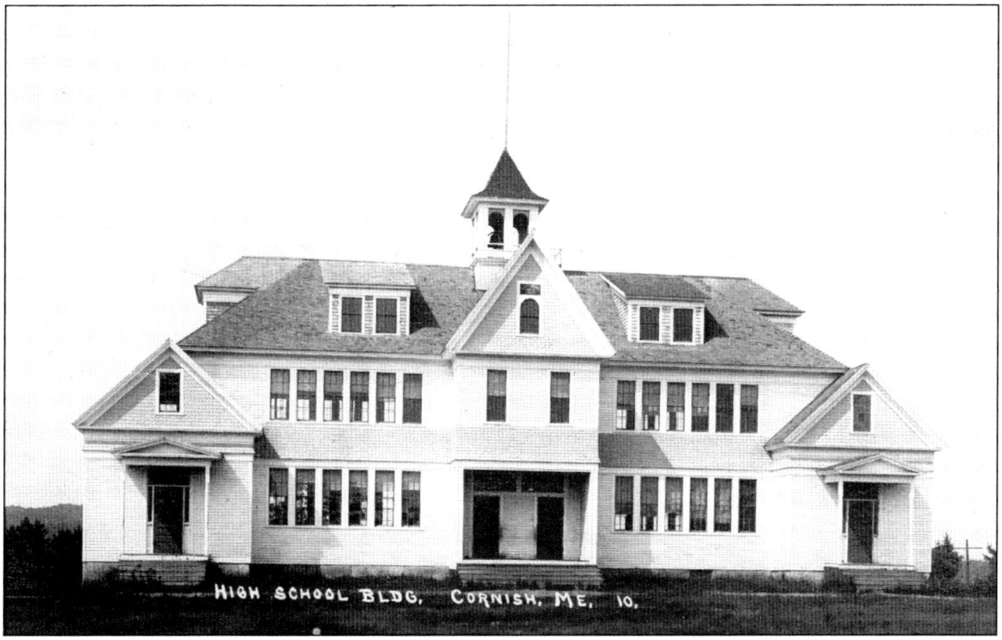

The Cornish School was built in 1878. There was a bell in the belfry that was rung by anyone who got there first after a sports event victory. The building was torn down in the 1970s to make room for a new school building.

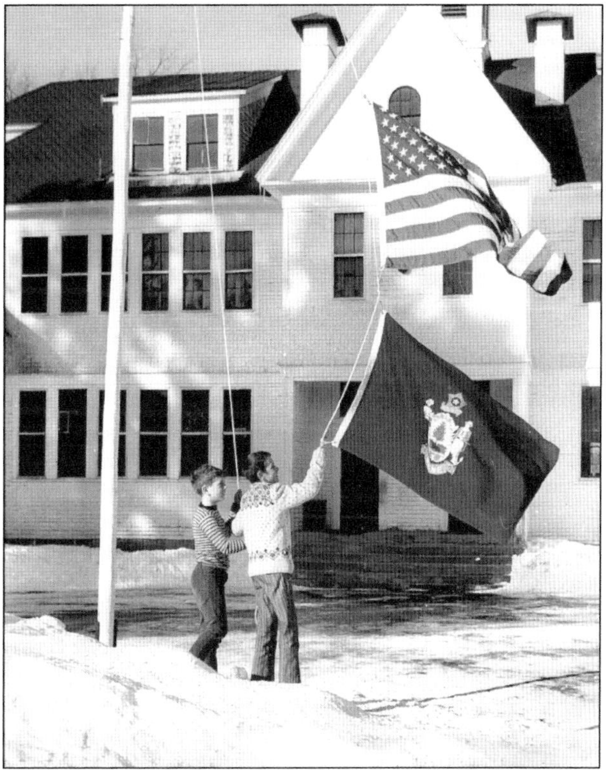

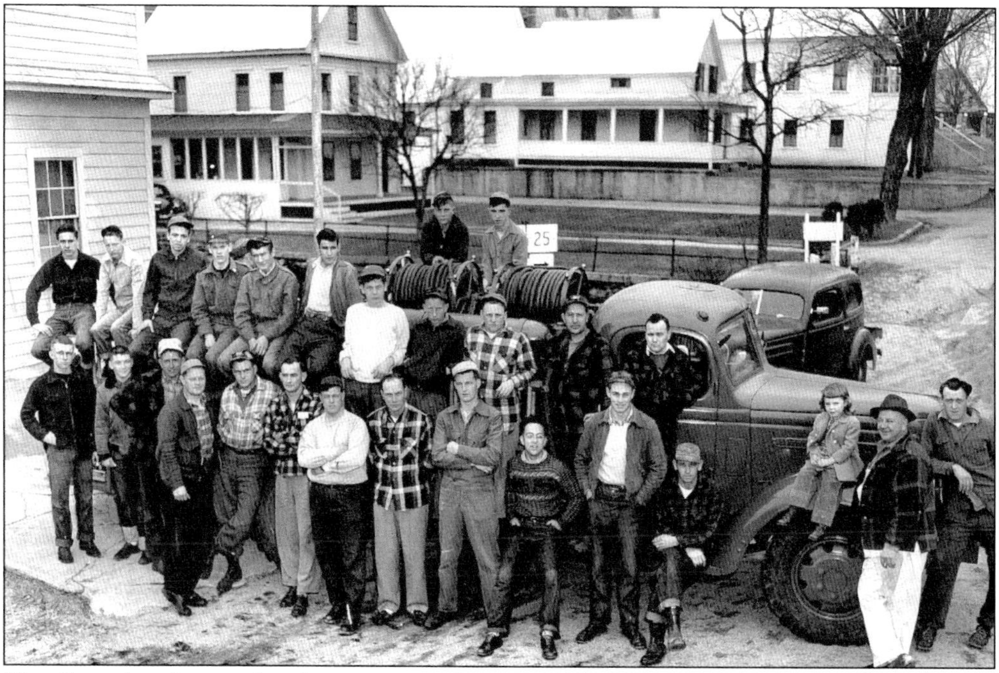

The Cornish volunteer fire department is shown *c.* 1950. Whenever there was a fire, whoever arrived first grabbed and wore the white fire cap and he automatically got to drive the truck.

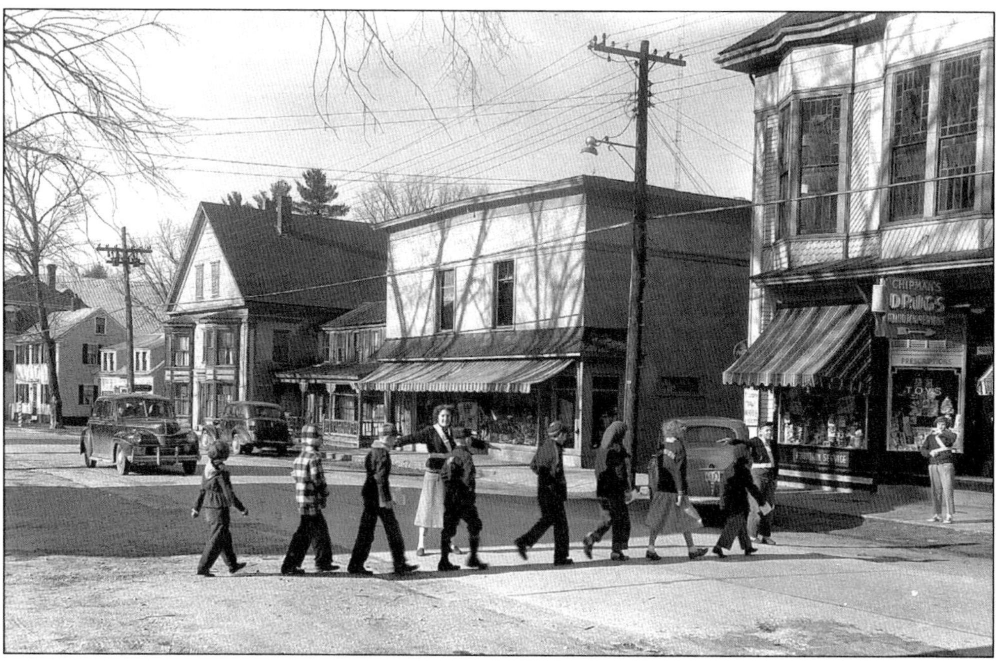

George Adams built Chipman's Drug in the early 1880s. It later became J. B. Watson's and then Boynton's Drug. The Morrison family ran it until the mid-1970s. Children would hang out at the soda fountain after school.

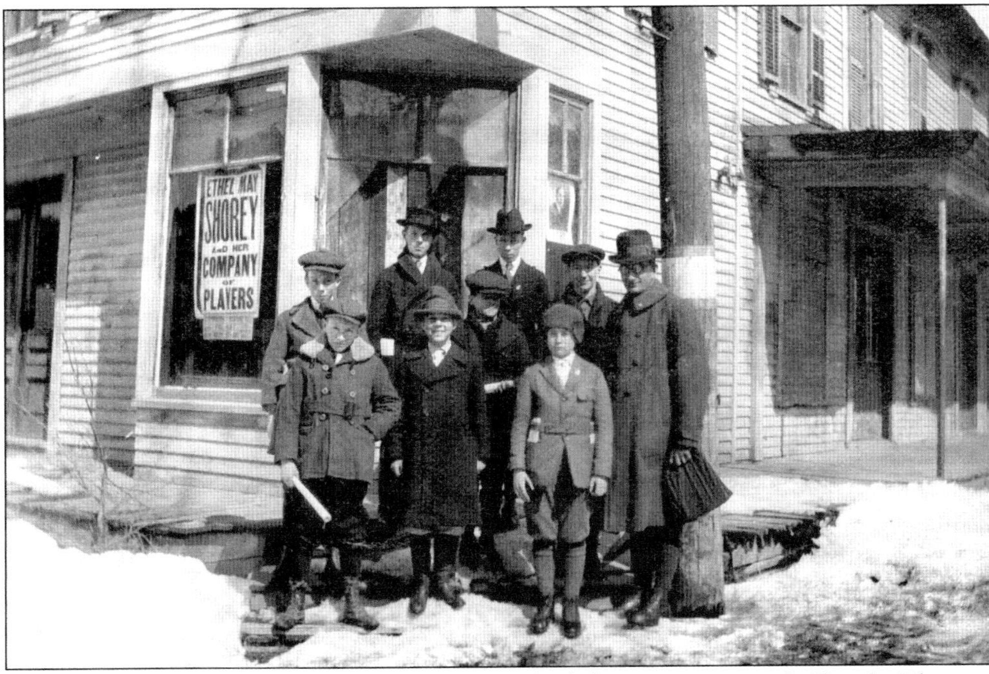

The Truth Seekers was the boy's Sunday school of the Congregational Church. They are standing in front of the Pendexter Store prior to 1927. Clarence Lord taught there from 1915 to 1953. They would meet in the kitchen of the church. Clarence was so popular that underage children would lie about their age so they could attend his class.

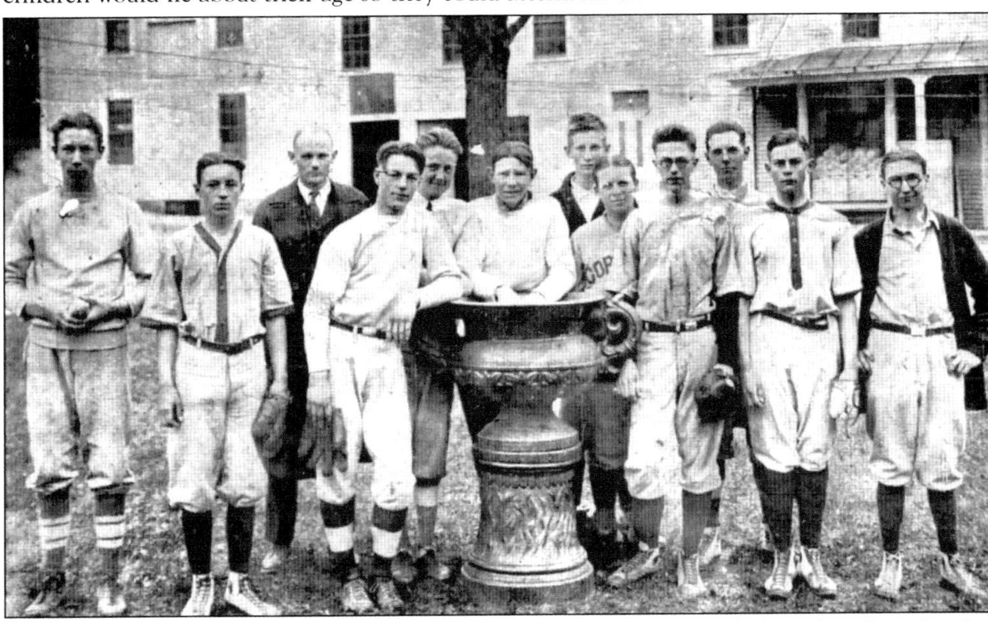

This is Cornish's baseball team in 1925. Every town had a team and they played on Sunday. They are standing in front of an urn in Thompson Park. The Masonic hall is in the background. Shown from left to right are Lawrence Sargent, Smith, Lester Harriman (coach), Scott Syphers, Stuart Chaplin, ? Harding, Raymond Day, Millard Dow, Leavitt Flint, Raymond Benson, Arthur Bucknell, and Charles Bradeen.

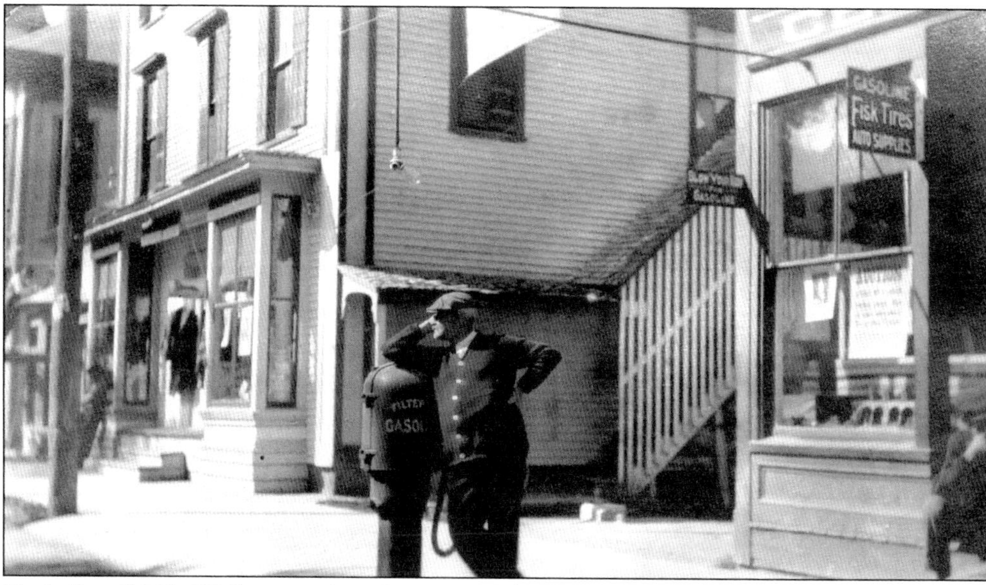

Noah Foss (1860–1930) is seen here leaning on the gas pump. Gas was hand pumped in those days. Noah owned the Central Garage which was located on the Central Block. He died in 1930 at age 70. This photograph was taken in the 1920s.

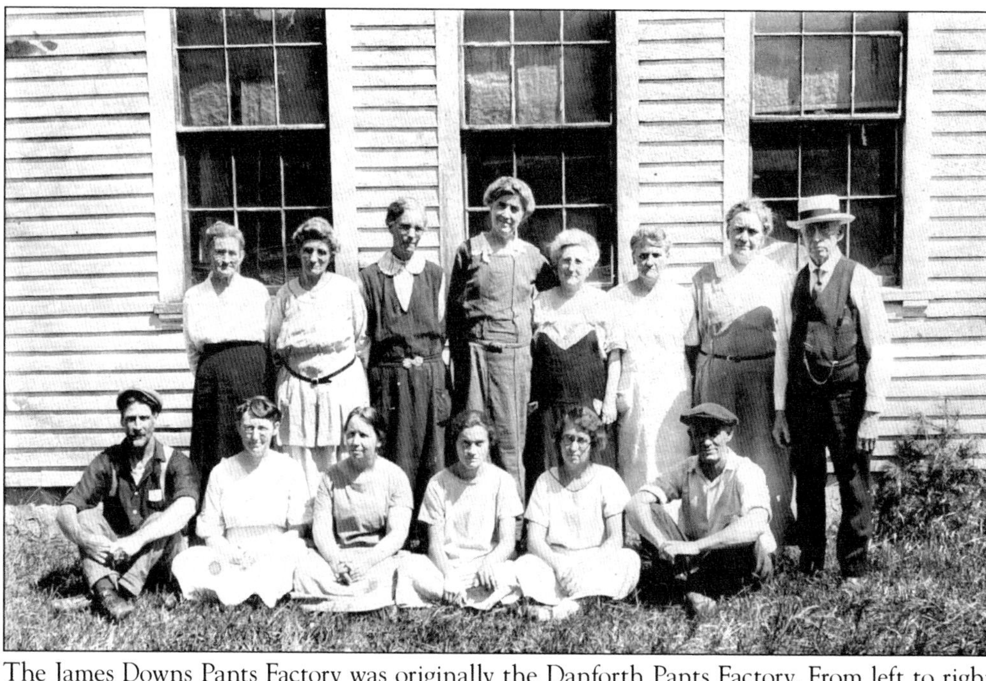

The James Downs Pants Factory was originally the Danforth Pants Factory. From left to right are (first row) Henry Pendexter, Minnie Smith, Lizzie Wentworth, Nellie Parker, Marguerite Goodwin, and Charles Goodwin; (second row) Amanda Clemmons, Mary Swan, Nellie Trafton, Jennie Ricker, Eva Marston, Lillian Parker, Etta Ricker, and James Downs.

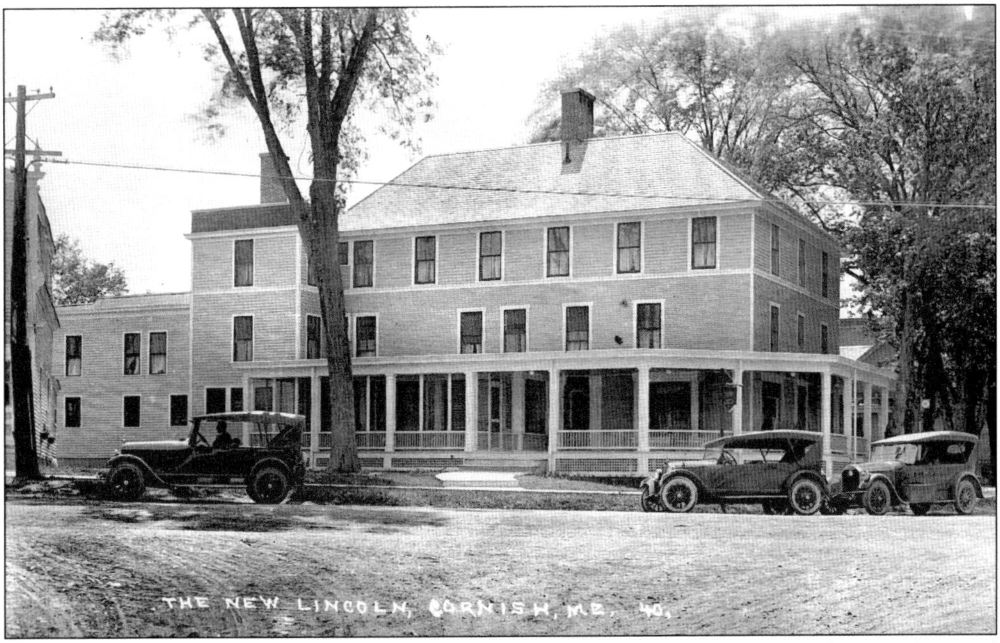

Cotton Lincoln built this building between 1816 and 1820 for his home. It became the Lincoln Hotel in 1888. Fred Small bought the hotel in the mid-1920s and remodeled it to how it looks today.

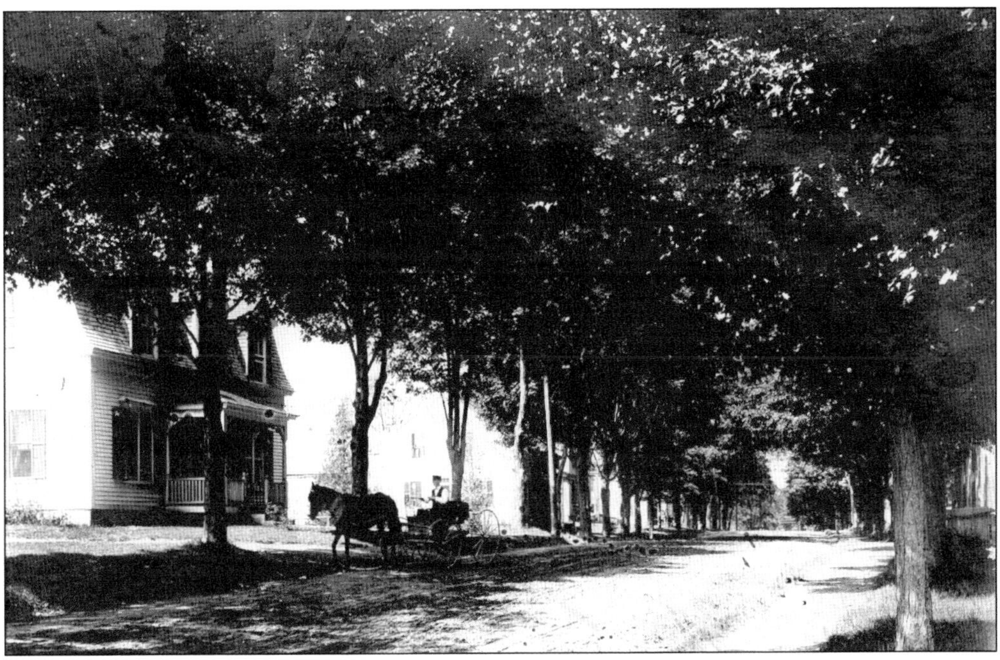

This is lower Main Street looking west at the top of the hill. The house to the left belonged to Ezra Pike, who had a shop next to the Park House. Next-door is the house of Cyrus Marr, a charter member of the Greenleaf Lodge.

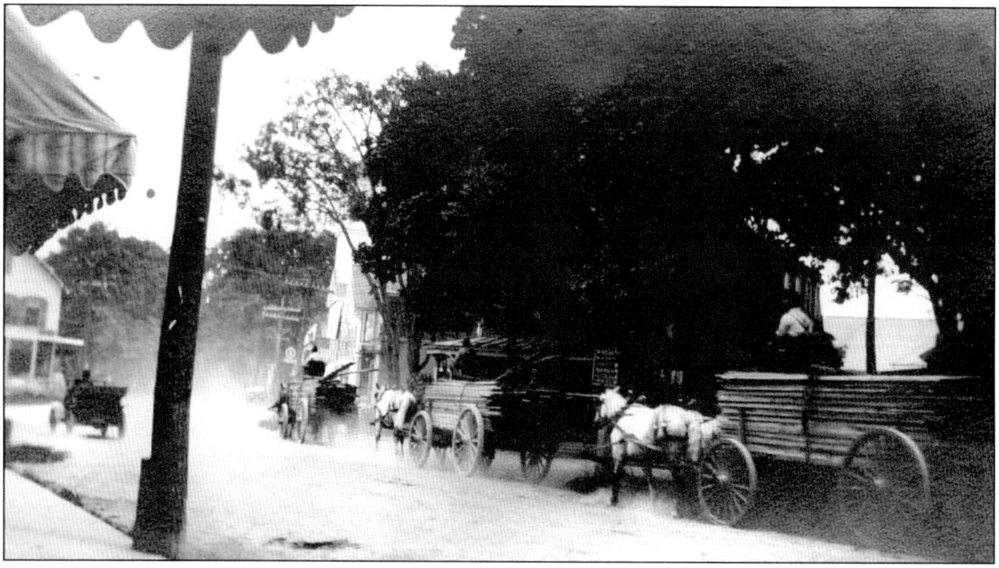

These wagons, hauling lumber in the 1920s, are going east in front of Thompson Park, heading for Cornish Railroad Station.

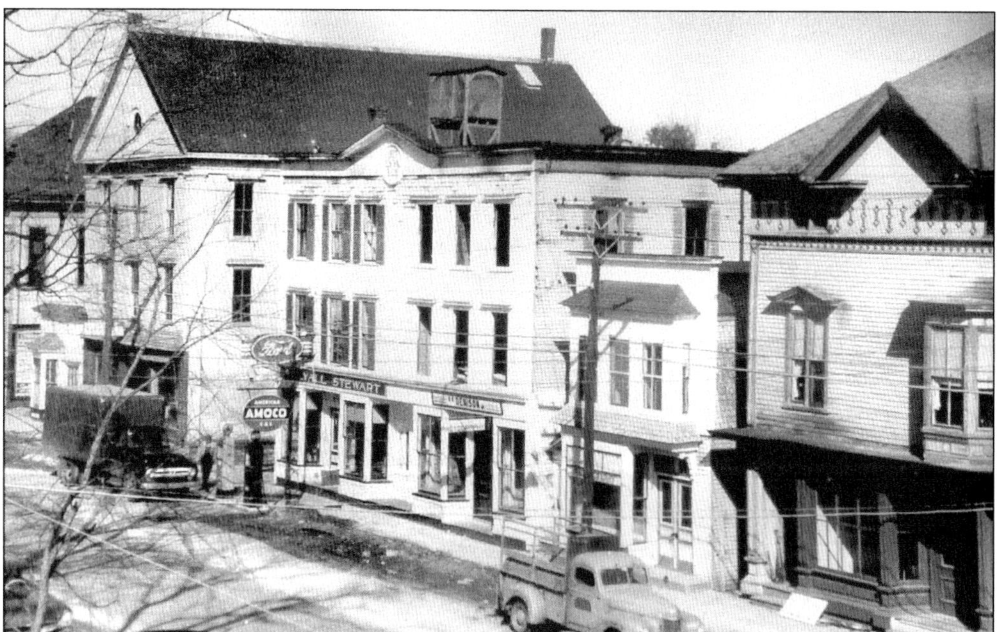

The building second from the left was built by Freeman Hatch and housed the drugstore. The third building is the Central Block, built in 1850. It housed Lyall Stewart's garage and O. B. Denison's photography shop, the man who took this picture. Originally it was the Parker drugstore, run by George Parker and his son Elmer. The Central Block burned on January 1, 1958.

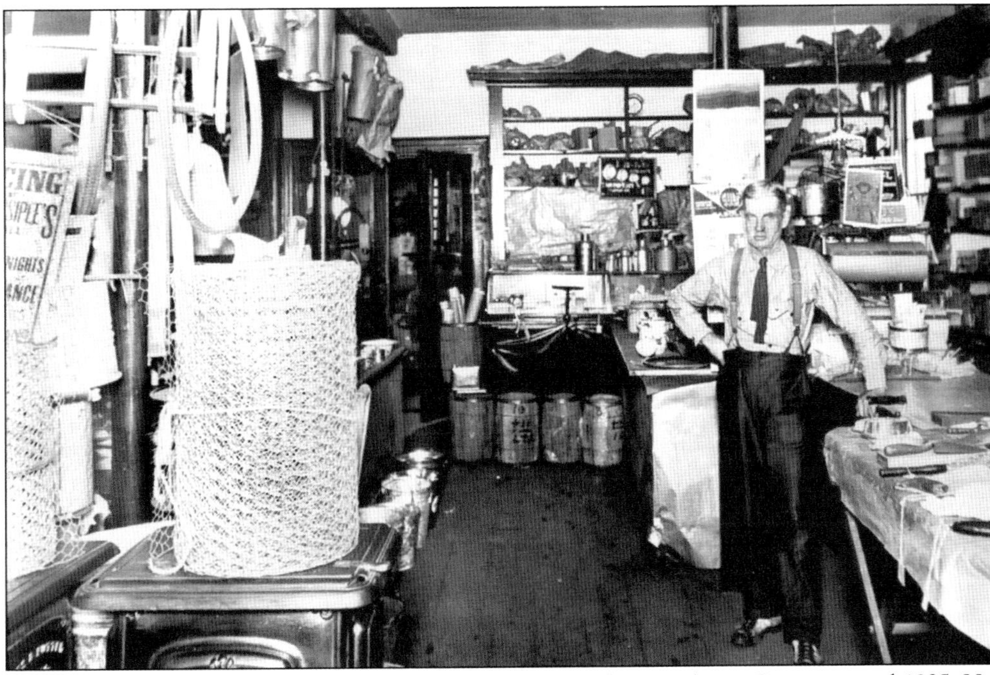

Fred Partridge is shown here at his store, the J. W. Partridge Hardware Store, around 1935. His father, John, erected the building in 1877. Fred was well known for his frugality.

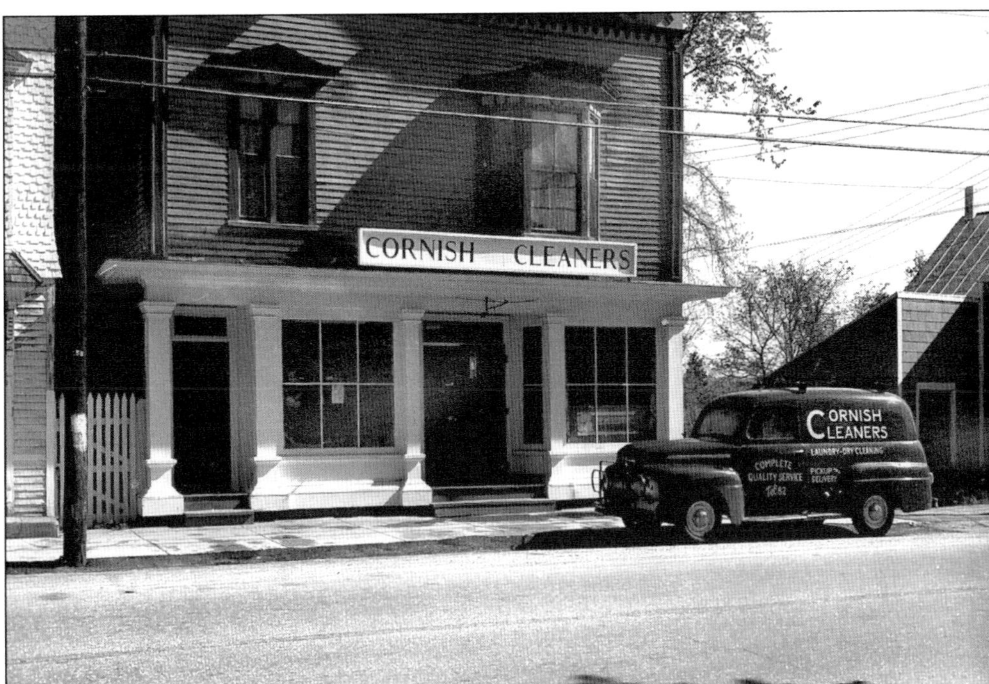

This building housed the Partridge Store, Cornish Cleaners, and later Thompson Park Grill, run by Richie Aaron.

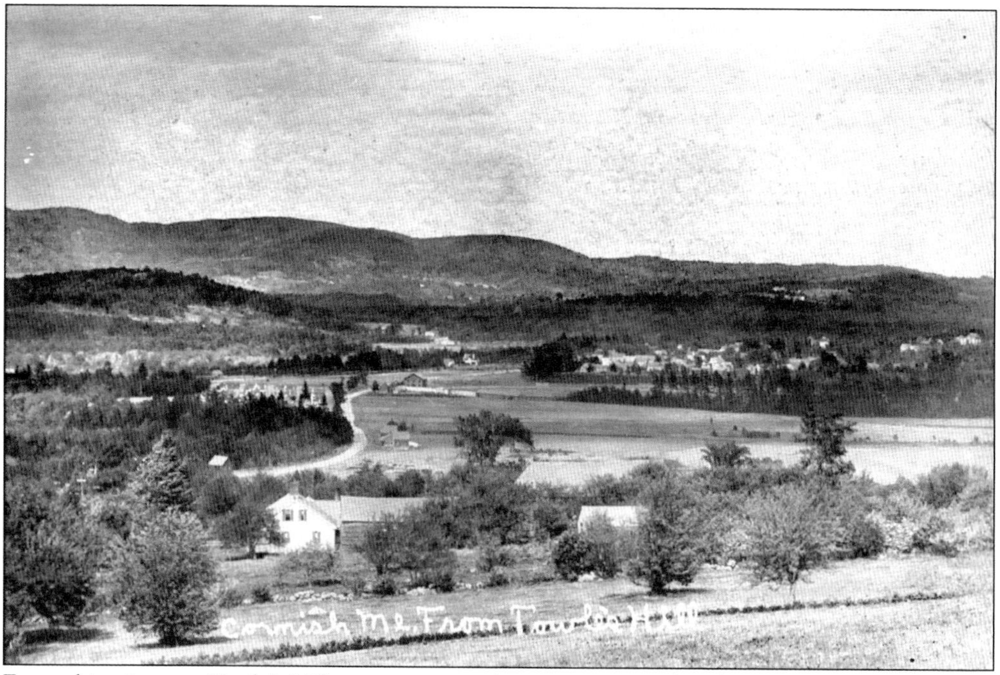

From this view on Towle's Hill, one can see the cemetery in the distance, the Jewell house, which is gone, and the exhibition hall. On the right are the buildings on upper Maple Street. This section of town was also known as Shapleigh.

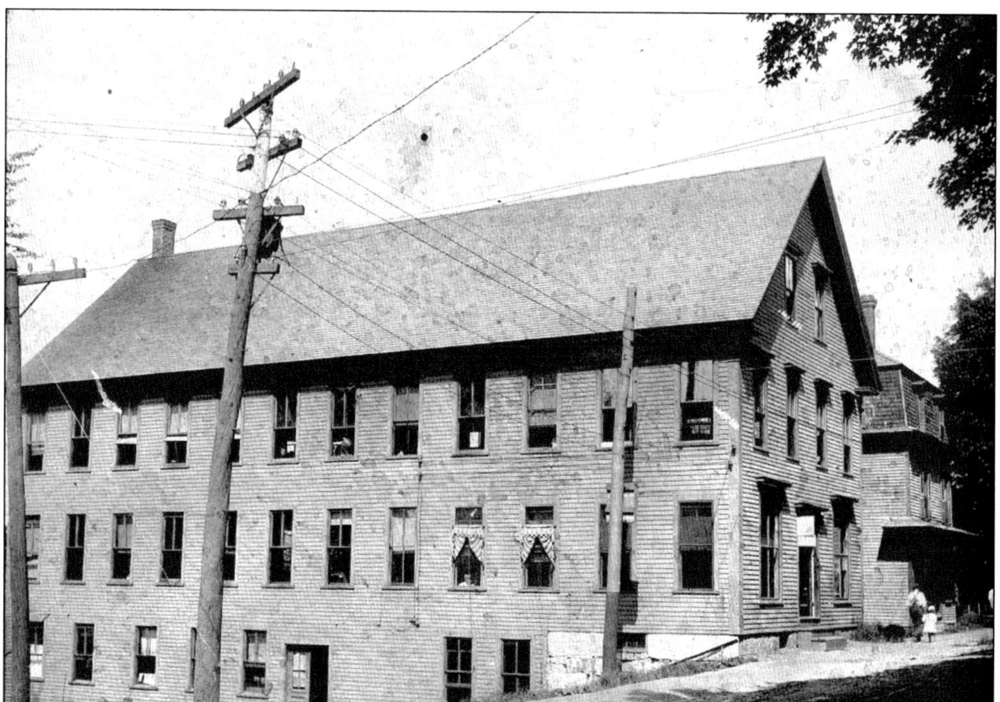

This is the Emery Milliken Factory located on Main Street near the mill pond. It was a clothing factory built in 1891. The building was also the home of the Webb-Smith Printing Company.

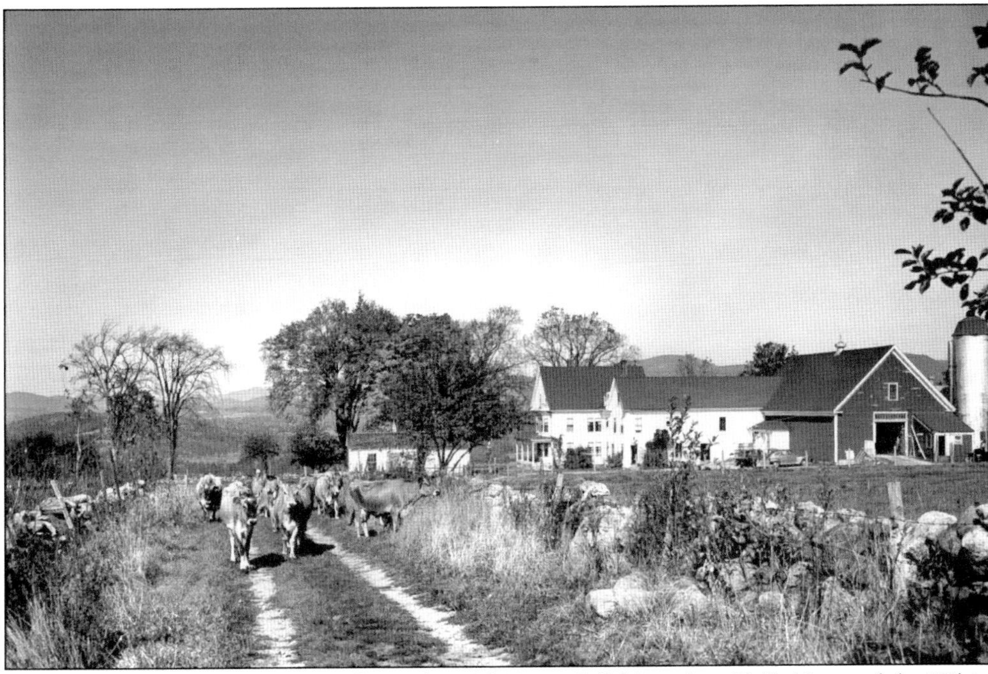

The Highland Farm cows are walking the "Ol' Kezar Falls" Road in 1943. Views of the White Mountains and Cornish can be seen from this hill (Towle's Hill). The Jersey dairy herd is bred for international commerce, even today. In this picture, Robert Pike is driving the cows.

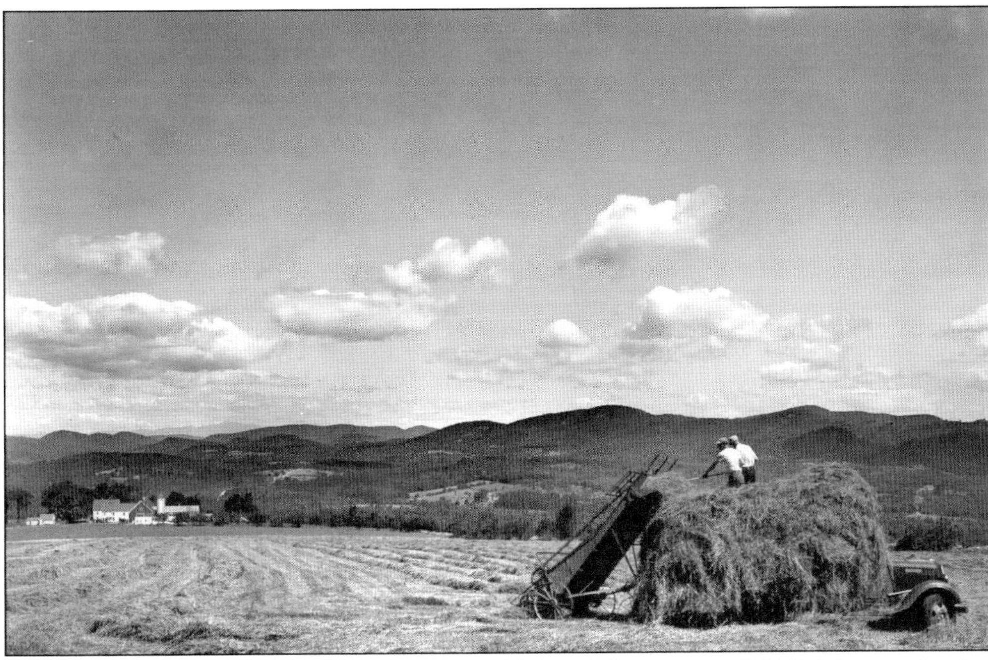

Robert Pike and his hired hand are haying at Highland Farm around 1943. They are loading hay into a modified truck. Note the hay loader. As the truck moved forward over the haymows, the hay would be raked up and into the wagon. The men used pitchforks to balance the load on the truck.

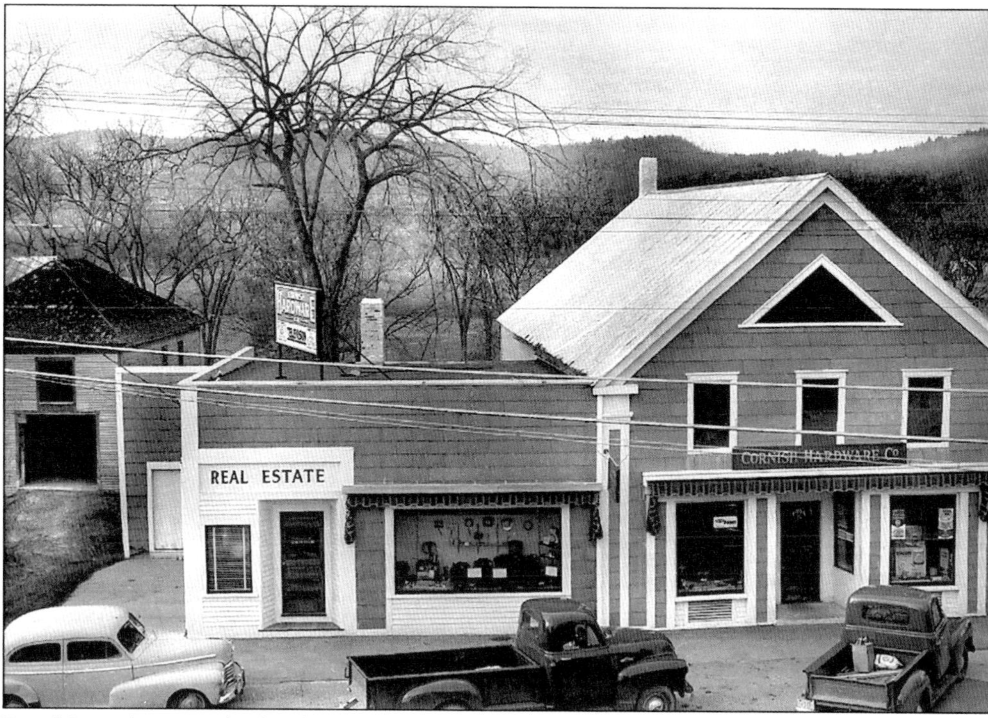

Royal Lincoln started a hardware store in 1810 and it was run by a secession of owners until 1996, when the Ray family moved the business to its current location on Maple Street, thus making it the oldest hardware store in the state. It is shown here in this c. 1940 photograph.

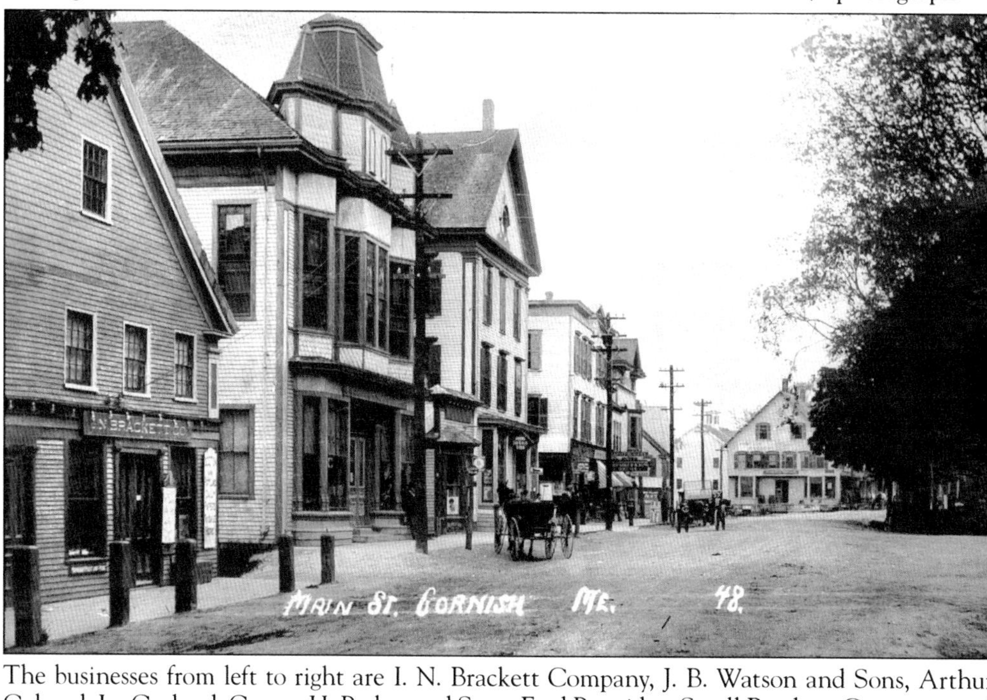

The businesses from left to right are I. N. Brackett Company, J. B. Watson and Sons, Arthur Colcord, Ira Garland, George H. Parker and Sons, Fred Partridge, Small Brothers Company, and Pendexter's. Main Street is seen here around 1920.

This is Cecil Bannister in his World War I army uniform. His father, Fred, was a minister who came from England to serve the Cornish church. Fred's wife, two daughters, and sons were going to come over after him on the Titanic, but their furniture did not arrive in Liverpool in time so they had to take a later ship.

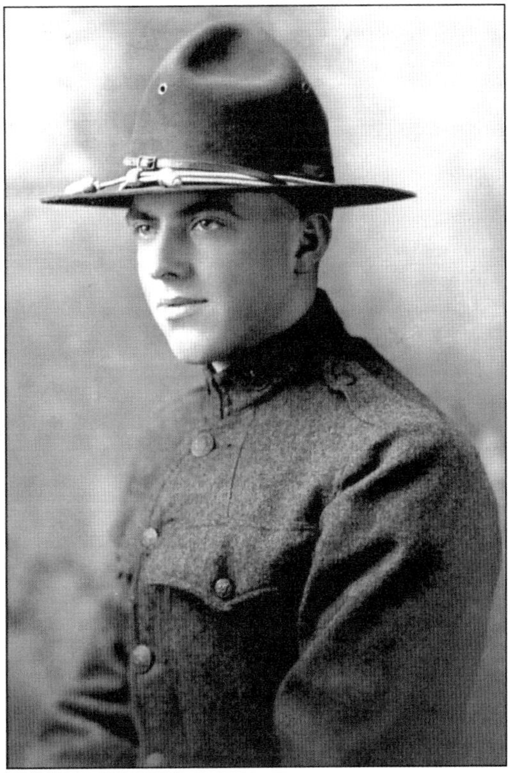

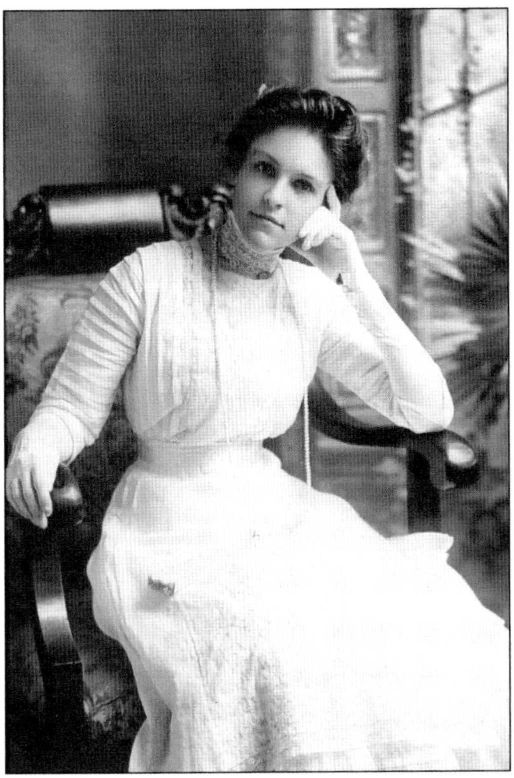

Addie Blake Small collected much information about Cornish's history in many small notebooks. She was born in 1891 and died in 1967. This picture was taken in 1920.

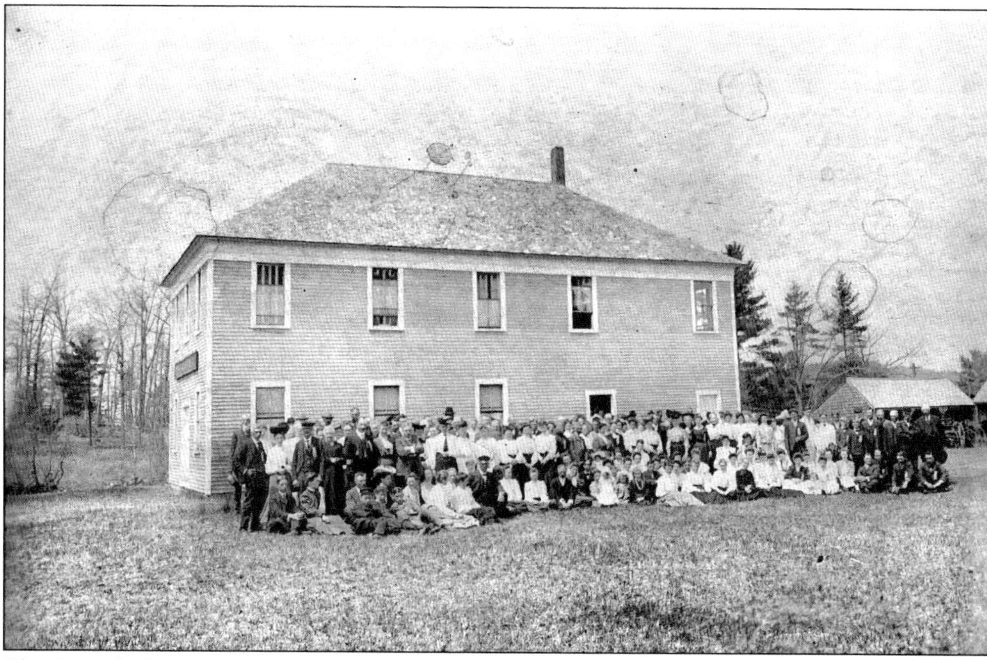

The Cornish Grange was organized May 7, 1875. The hall was built in 1896 and cost $1,200. Grange meetings were to discuss problems concerning farmers, as well as to provide social events. Note the carriage shed beside the Grange. The building burned in July 1992. It is shown around 1910.

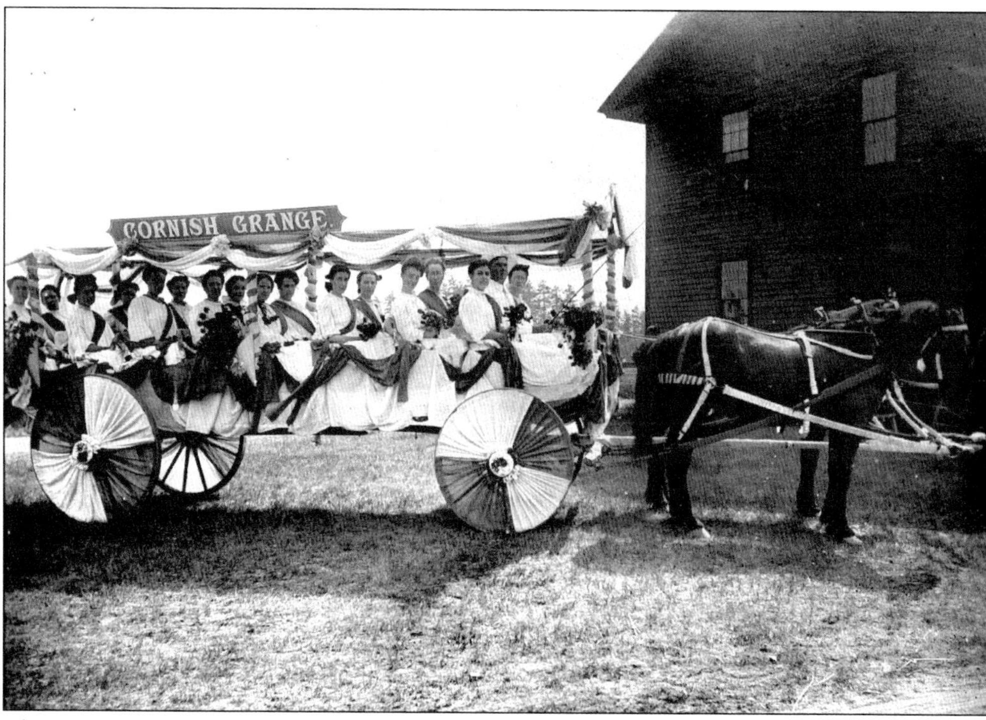

This photograph of the decorated wagon of the Cornish Grange was taken at the fairgrounds in front of the old Exhibition Building.

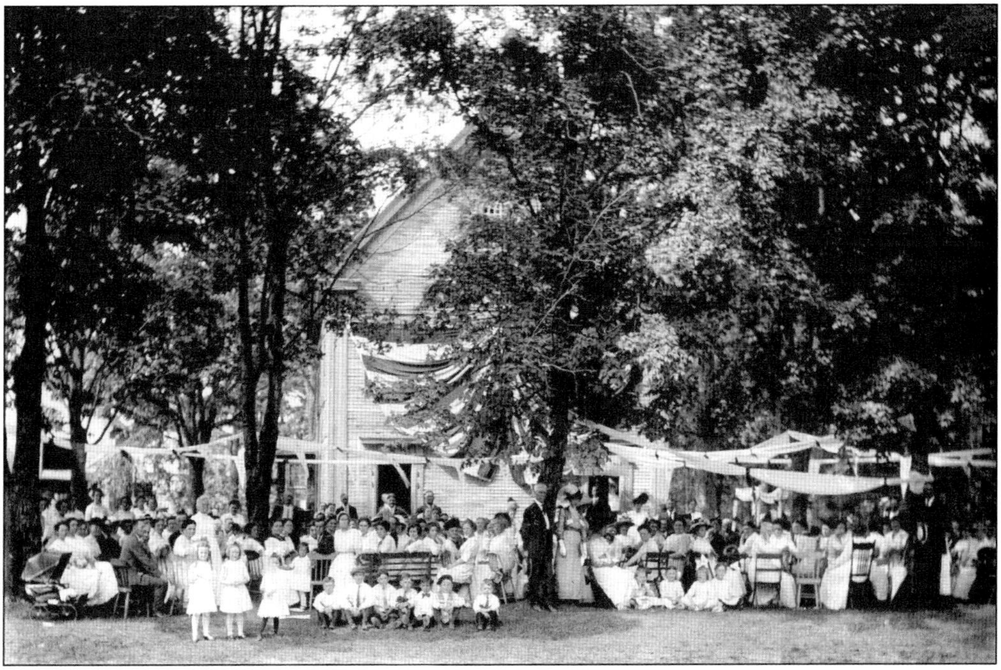

The Cornish School Association was formed in 1911. Membership is open to past teachers and pupils. They met annually at the Rose Schoolhouse until 1923, when the land was deeded to the town for the construction of the town hall. The association still continues to meet annually.

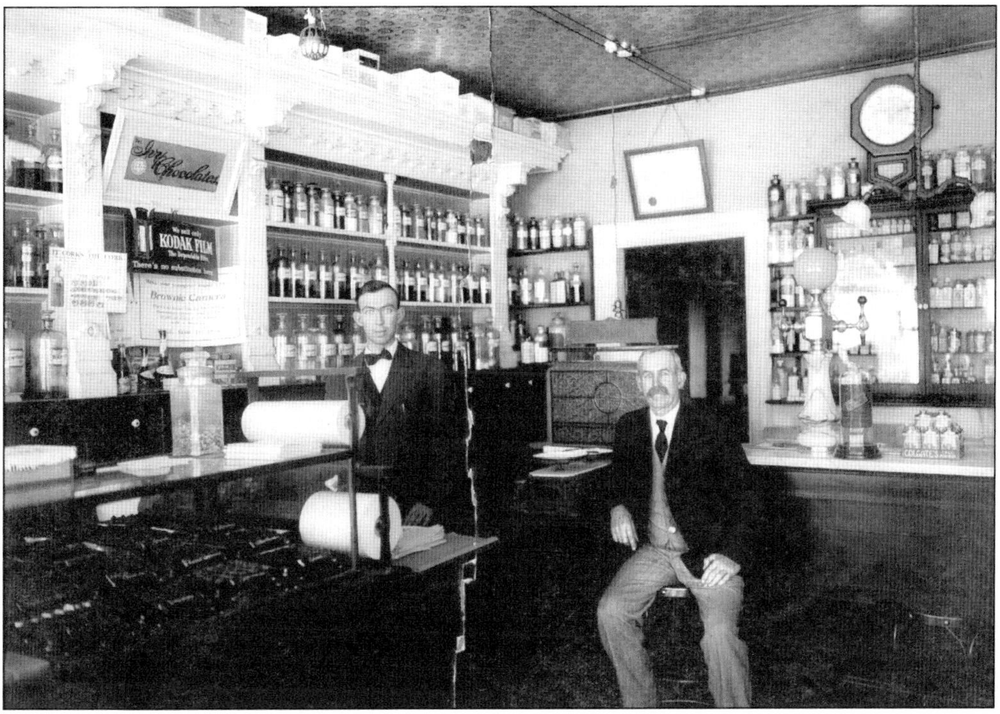

Here is a view of the 1916 interior of G. H. Parker and Son Apothecary with George Henry Parker and Elmer Winthrop Parker. The store was in the Central Block.

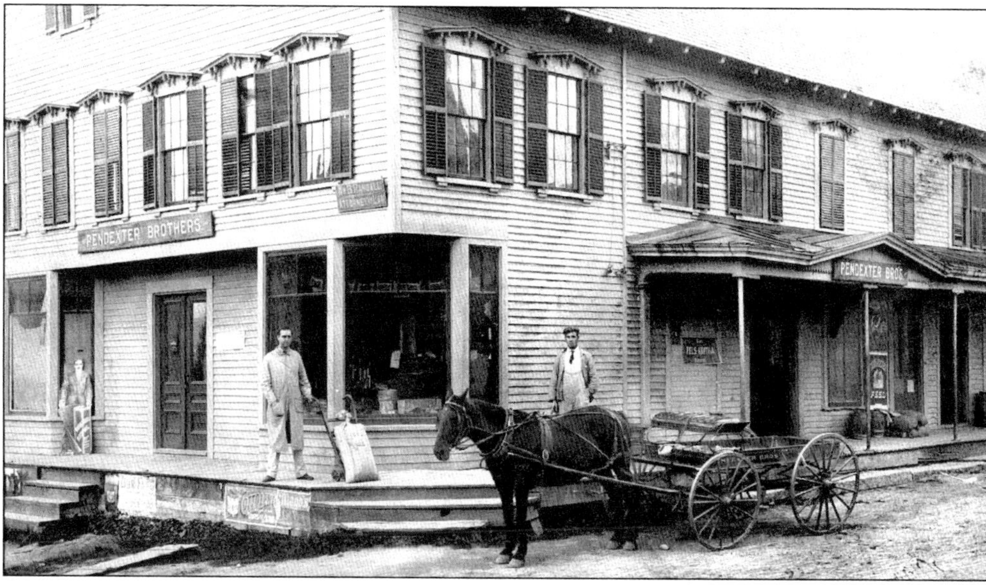

Nathan and Royal Sanborn originally built Pendexter's Store for a shoe factory. Jacob Pendexter bought the building in 1905. In 1920, the building was torn down and the land sold to Samuel Sawyer, who agreed to give the land outright to the Cornish Welfare Corporation providing that it would be developed into a proper place to be used as a theater and other purposes beneficial to the corporation. This never came to fruition.

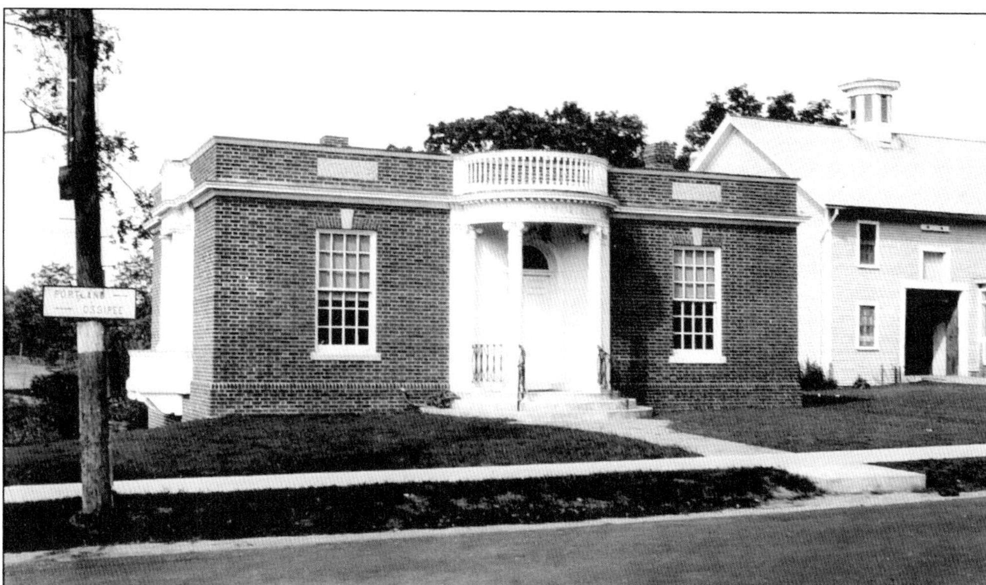

The Bonney Memorial Library stands on the site of Pendexter's Store. The Cornish Library Association, formed in 1867, used space in the upstairs of the Small Brothers Store. They were raising money for a building when Dr. Calvin Bonney donated the funds to memorialize his parents. The building was dedicated on June 27, 1929.

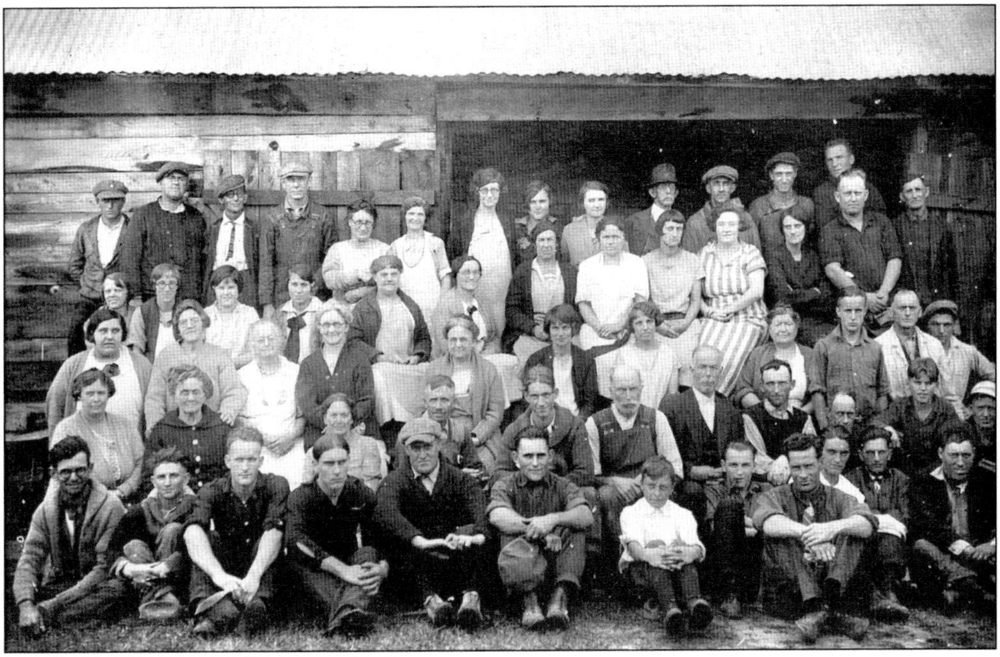

In the Corn Shop, the ears went by on a belt and the huskers were on a high plate. There were six cutters, a cook, and they canned and labeled the corn for the IGA, First National, and the A&P. The man in the felt hat (middle of the doorway, back row) is Joe Perkins who always wore a suit and tie, even in the hayfield. He is shown here in the 1930s.

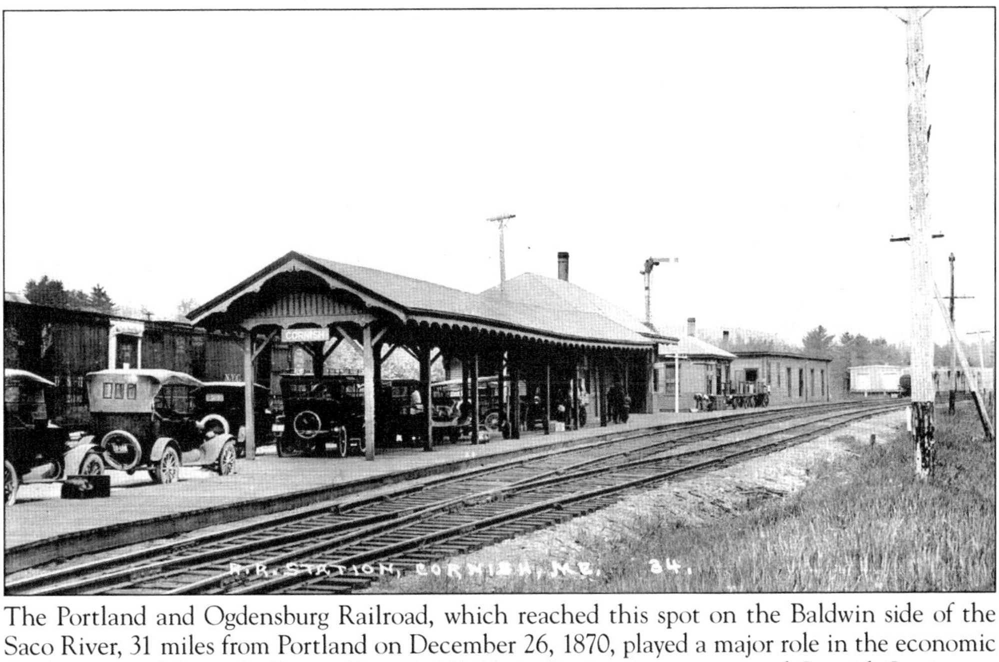

The Portland and Ogdensburg Railroad, which reached this spot on the Baldwin side of the Saco River, 31 miles from Portland on December 26, 1870, played a major role in the economic development of Cornish. Originally called Baldwin Station, it was renamed Cornish Station on December 11, 1888, the same year the railroad was renamed Maine Central Mountain Division. Cornish Station was closed on February 14, 1962, but the sidings were used to deliver oil and grain for many years afterward.

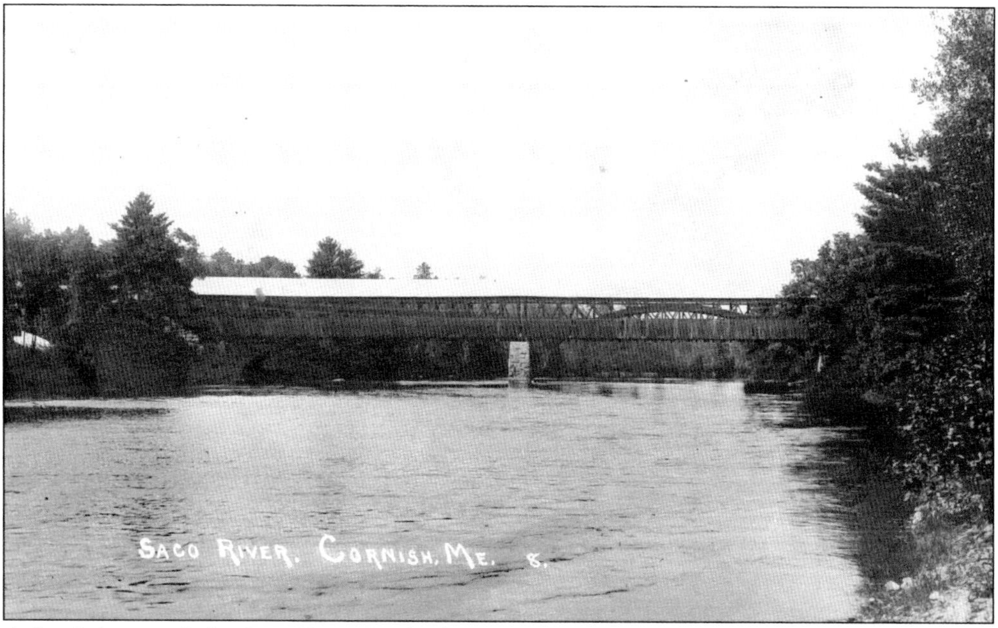

A flood destroyed the Saco River Bridge between neighboring Baldwin, Maine, and Cornish in 1898.

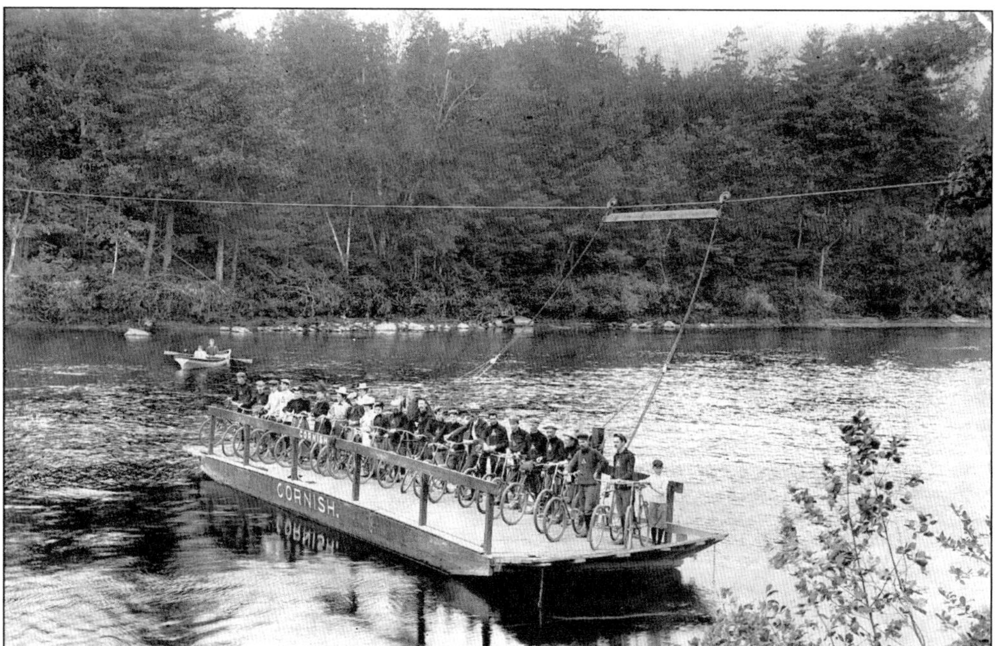

Leroy Pike, on the Saco River between Cornish and Baldwin, operated the Cornish Ferry, after floodwaters destroyed the bridge. It was a necessity for hauling goods and people from Cornish Station in Baldwin.

Two

LIMERICK

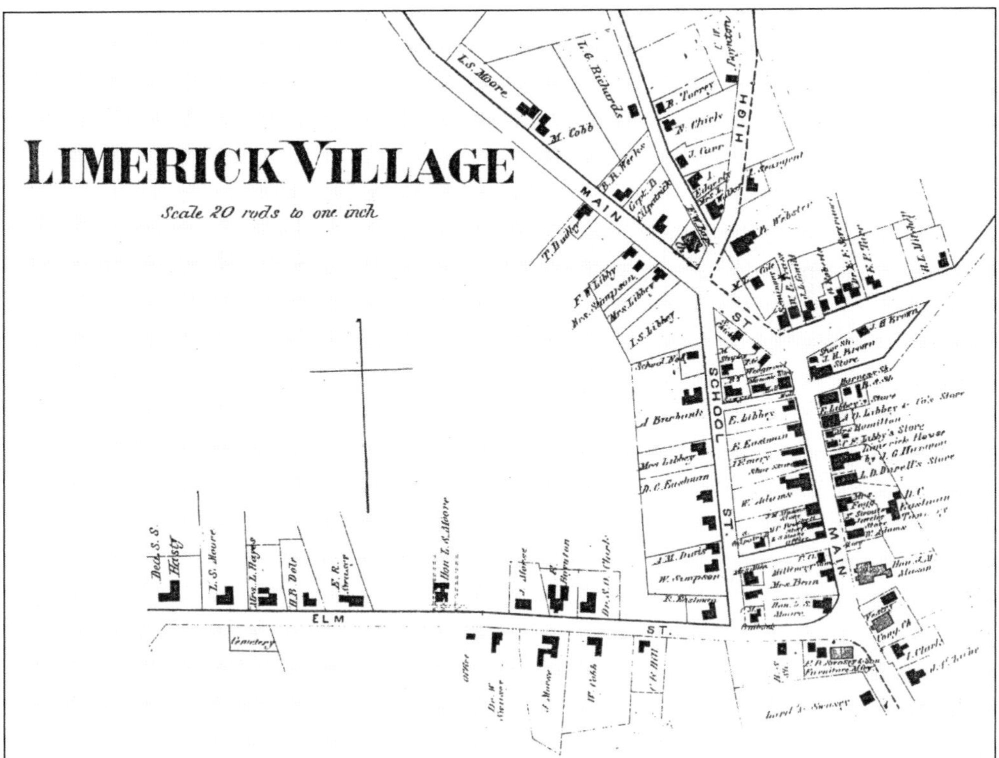

On April 10, 1786, the pioneer families of Limerick petitioned the Massachusetts General Court for town incorporation. One of the reasons listed for their action was "the difficulty and impracticability of establishing and supporting the gospel and schools of learning among us" without a proper town government. The plantation of Limerick became the town of Limerick on March 6, 1787, when the Act of Incorporation was passed.

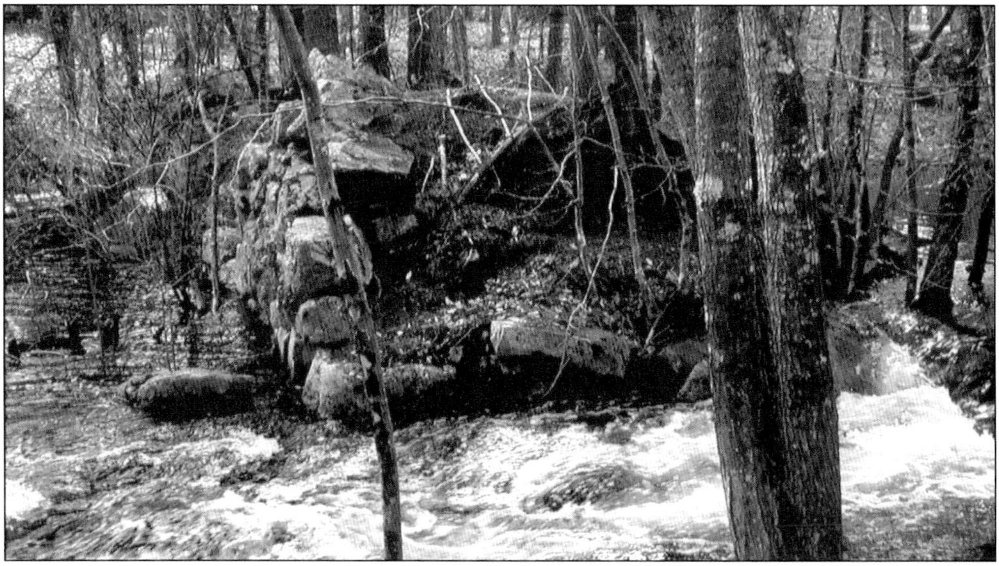

Shelter and food were the top priorities of our earliest settlers. Isaiah Foster, given land to settle in Limerick, built a shelter in 1772. In 1777, Foster and two new settlers, Thomas and Joseph Gilpatrick, constructed the first sawmill in town on Brown's Brook. The remnants of the Foster Privilege are pictured above. The sawmill was located on the west side of the brook and produced the first boards for building in Limerick. On the east side of the brook, a gristmill was built for grinding corn. The Little Ossipee River powered the Stimpson gristmill. It appears on a 1795 map. The Stimpson Mill, long a landmark, was lost in a spring freshet in the 20th century.

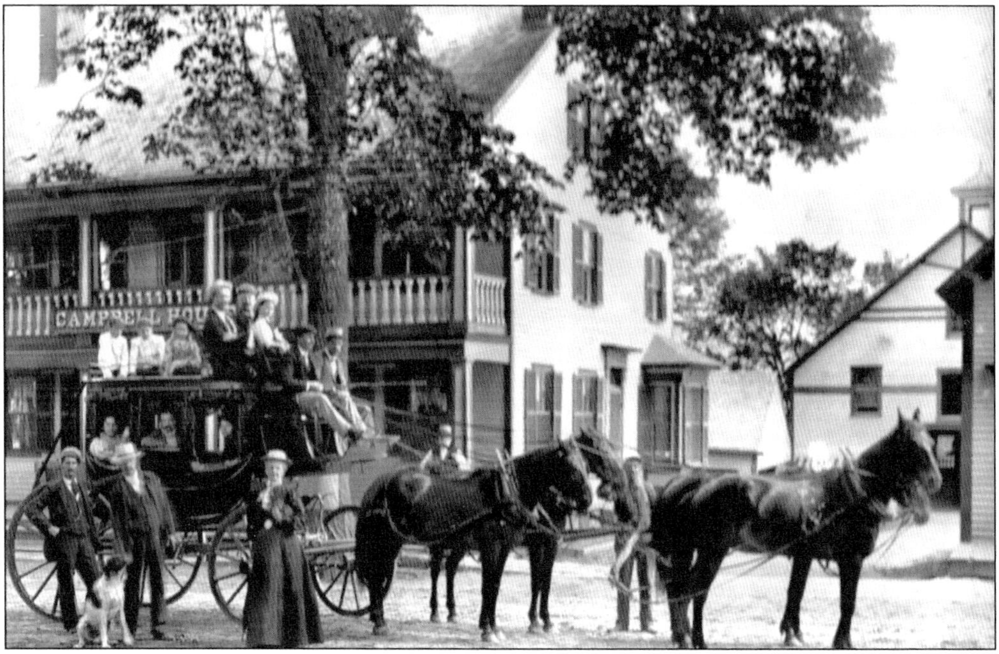

Stagecoach trips ran through Limerick as early as 1826 carrying passengers and mail. This four-horse coach is in front of the hotel on Main Street. When J. C. Ricker drove in 1877, the stage would leave Limerick every morning at 6:15 a.m. (except Sunday) and connect with the trains in Waterboro. It would return to Limerick at 6:00 p.m.

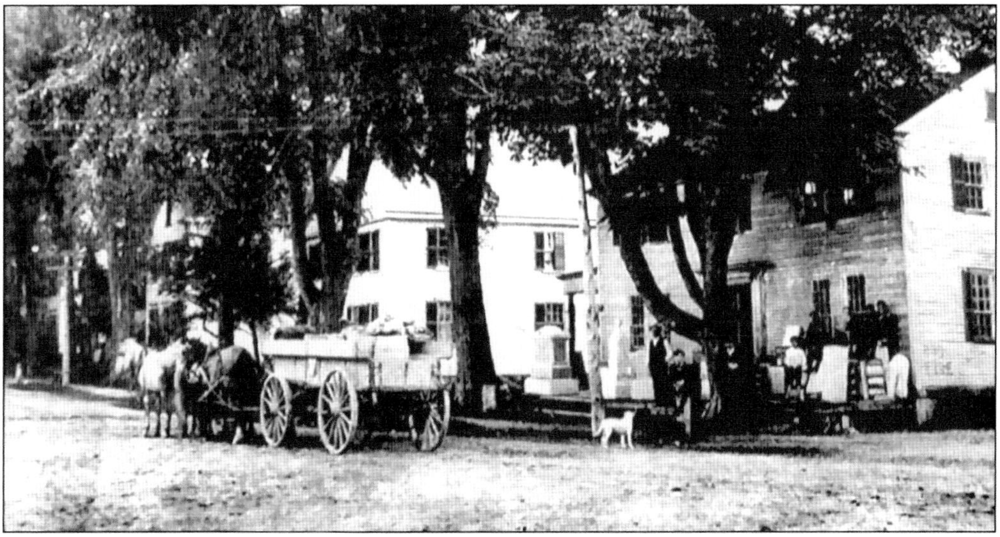

A company of brethren of the Freewill Baptist Church first issued the *Morning Star* newspaper in Limerick, Maine on May 11, 1826. The first building pictured on the right on Main Street was used as the printing office according to Lamprey's *History of Limerick*. Elders J. Buzzell and S. Burbank were the editors, and William Burr the printer. "The deeds of darkness among the churches, the nation, and in the world, are being discovered and brought to light by it (*Morning Star*)." Reportedly, Burr "hated evil in all its forms with intensity, and fought it with determination." For years, the *Morning Star* published articles against slavery with Burr at its helm. He lived to see the end of slavery in this country.

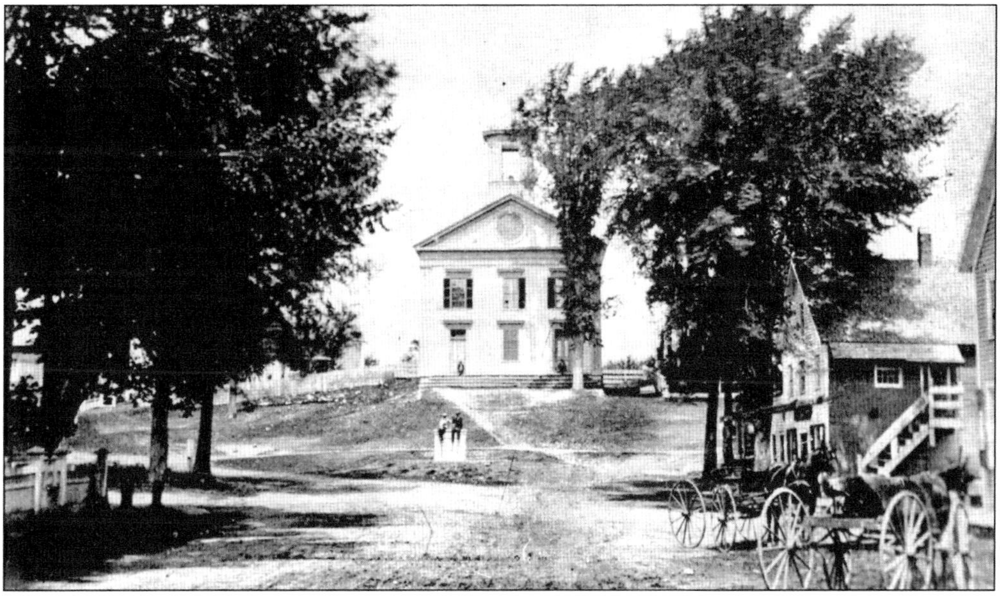

The Limerick Academy was established in 1808 and financed through private donations, including one from a Bostonian named Paul Revere. Pictured here is the second academy as it looked in 1870 before it burned. A third academy was built in 1881 and stands today. Students attended, not only from Limerick, but also from other surrounding towns. Latin, Greek, and English were all taught there. Presently the building is under the stewardship of the membership of the Limerick Historical Society.

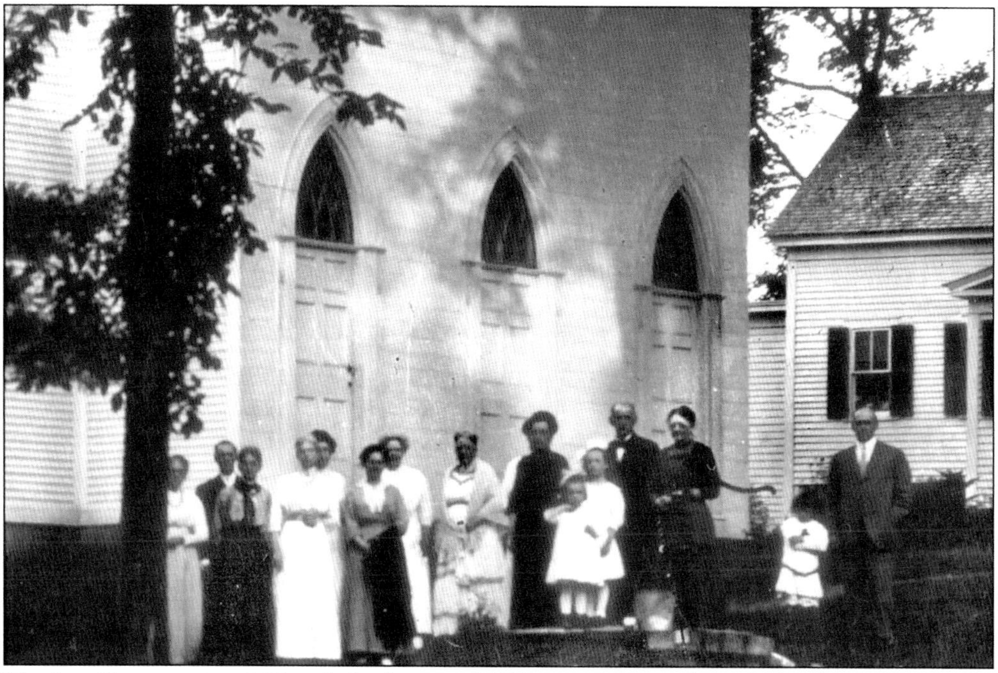

The first Congregational Church, built around 1793, stood about where the bank on Main Street is today. At a 1795 town meeting, it was decided to offer Rev. Edmund Eastman, a Dartmouth graduate, the position of pastor. He accepted and became the first settled minister in Limerick. Reverend Eastman was instrumental in the establishment of the upper village and the Limerick Academy. The structure that we see today was built in 1833 during the pastorate of Rev. Charles Freeman. The Hayes and Dole families appear in this photograph.

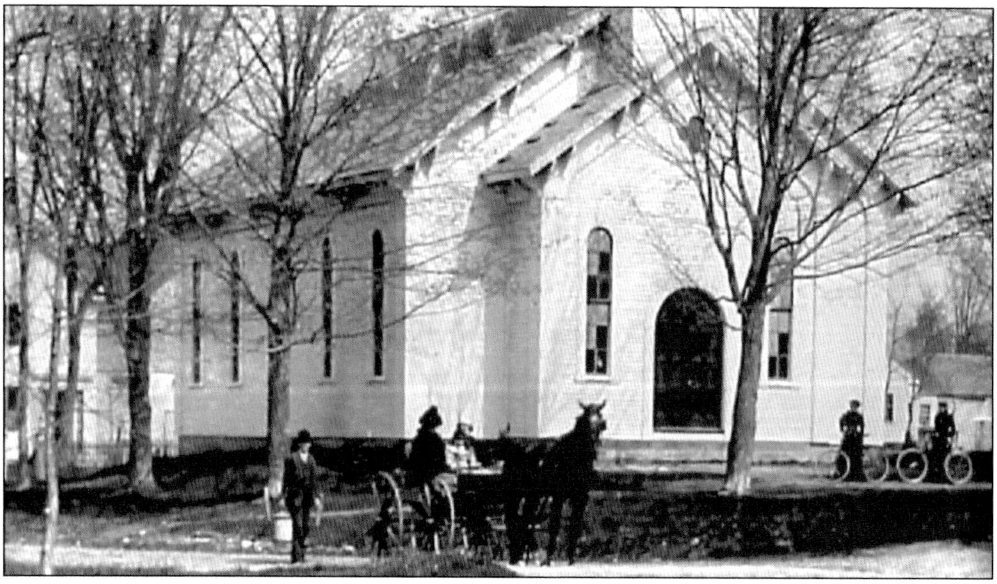

The Freewill Baptist church was organized in 1822 under the leadership of Rev. Elias Libby. In 1837, a meetinghouse was constructed. The church building was raised and renovations began in 1924. Earlier church members wrote themselves into America's history books when they established the second religious newspaper in the country, the *Morning Star*, in 1826.

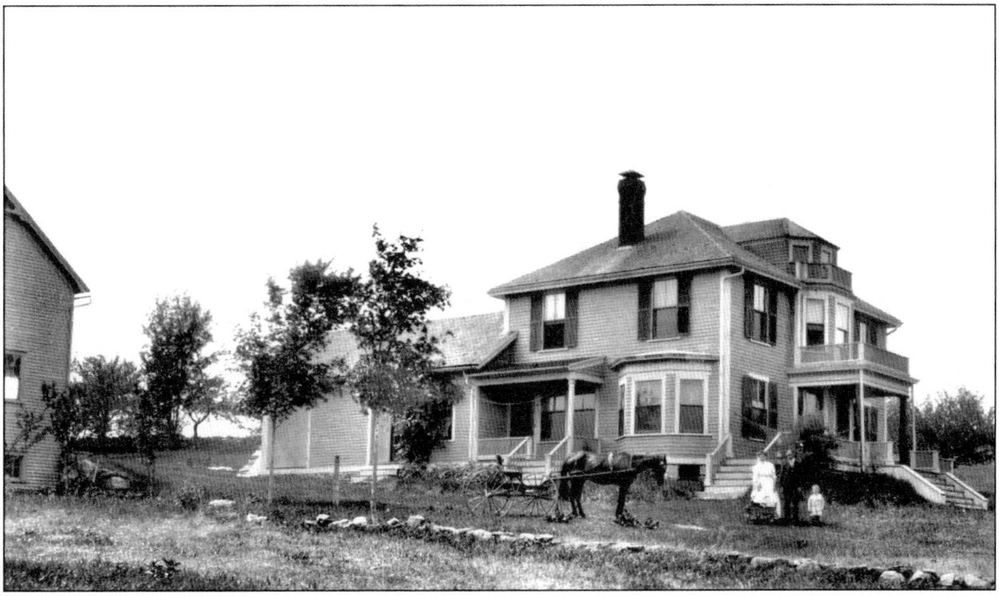

This home is located at the southern entrance to Limerick on the Sokokis Trail. For years it was also the office of Dr. Dana Rowe, an osteopathic physician. Dr. Rowe started his practice here in 1946. Limerick's rural country doctors treated more than just the body. They became community advisors, caretakers, and friends. Doctor's names like Carpenter, Tibbetts, Swasey, Clarke, Fogg, Severance, and Paine appear in years of town records serving in many roles, as they cared for the spirit and well being of their neighbors.

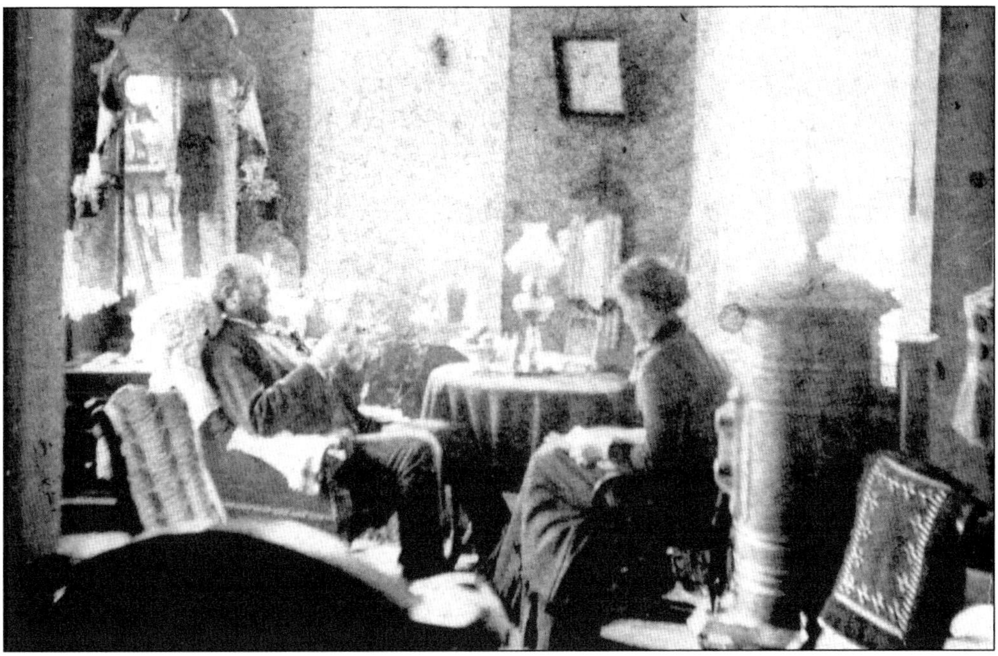

This image affords us a rare, inside view of a Limerick parlor. Henry and May Eastman are relaxing in their parlor on School Street. These living spaces often included the parlor stove, chairs covered in velvet, marble topped tables, and ornate clocks and mirrors. Kerosene lamps were often used for lighting.

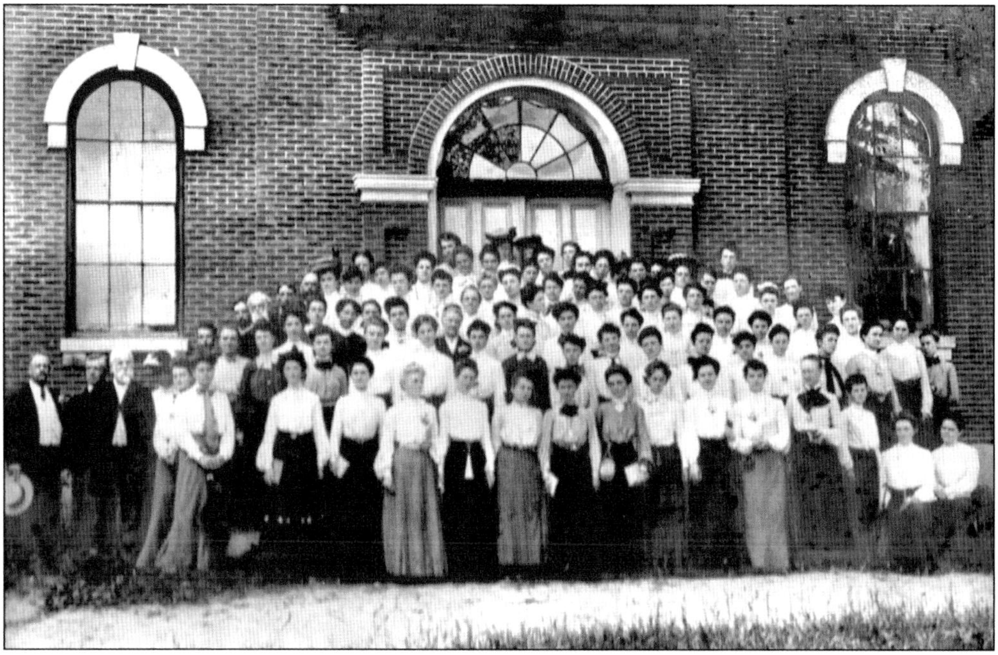

Limerick Academy students pose in front of the Limerick Town Hall. Students attended school in the Limerick Town Hall and the Congregational Church on Main Street between 1870 and 1880. In 1881, a new academy was ready. Around 1904 the students raised the funds for a new school bell. The bell, not installed at the present time, is in the academy today on Locust Hill.

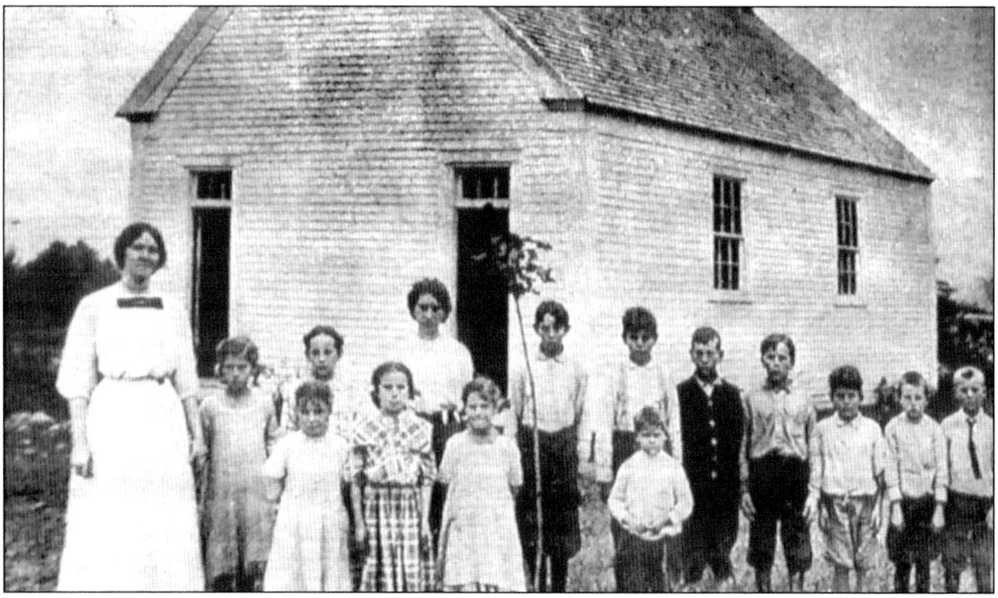

Taterborough School was one of a dozen one-room schoolhouses in Limerick (officially the Pierce School District 5). This *c.* 1912 photograph appears to have been taken on the occasion of a spring tree planting. The teacher Edith Pierce (née Usher) is with her students. From left to right, they are (first row) Doris Lepage, Julia Pierce, Nettie Foss, and John Woodsome; (second row) Alice Woodsome, Jenia Pierce, Sarah Lapage, Floristan Pierce, Waldo Haley, Elwood Pierce, George Lapage, Morris Tufts, Will Pender, and Charles Lapage.

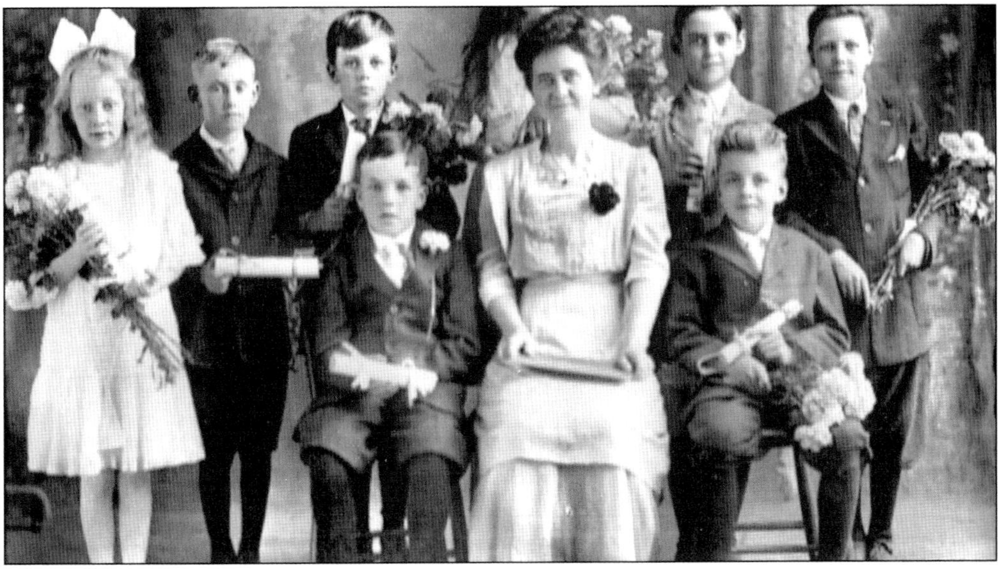

Rose Moulton taught the children of Limerick for almost 40 years. She started teaching in Limerick district one-room schoolhouses in 1903, teaching at the Brick Schoolhouse, transporting children, and performing janitorial duties. For a number of years she was at the Limerick Mills School and then transferred to Longfellow Primary on School Street. She retired in the 1940s while teaching at the consolidated school on Washington Street, where she started as the first grade teacher in 1925. She appears here with a graduating class. The little girl with long blond hair is Thelma Smith (née Wallace).

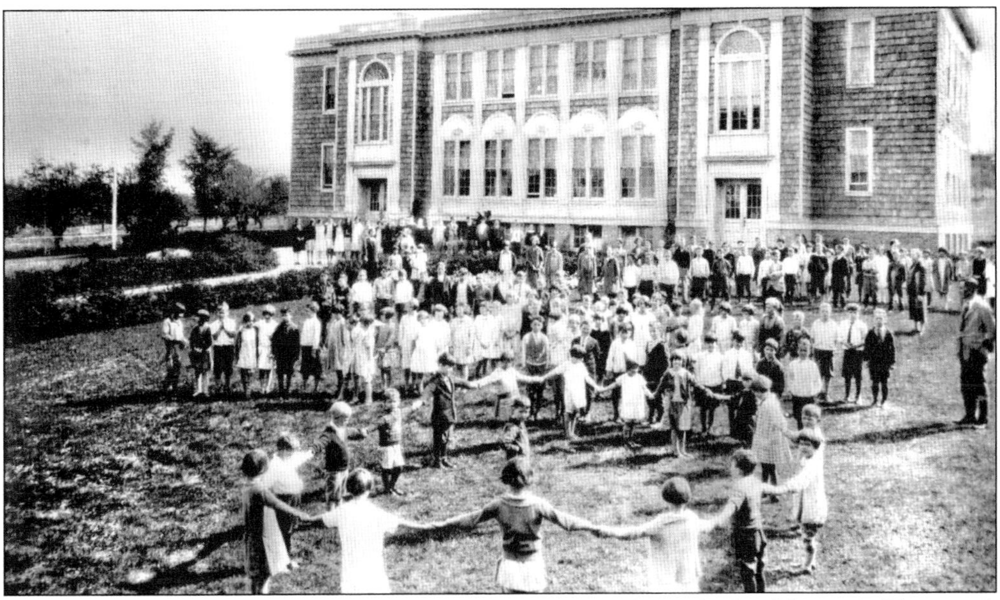

Limerick school officials were lobbying strongly for a consolidated school by 1910. The town's scattered one-room schools were in constant need of repair, teachers changed frequently, attendance was erratic, and schools were constantly opening and closing as district populations shifted. Although conveyance of the students was an issue, all was overcome by 1925 when a new consolidated school building opened its doors. Industrialist and school board member Charles Moulton gave generously towards the new school, as did Limerick taxpayers.

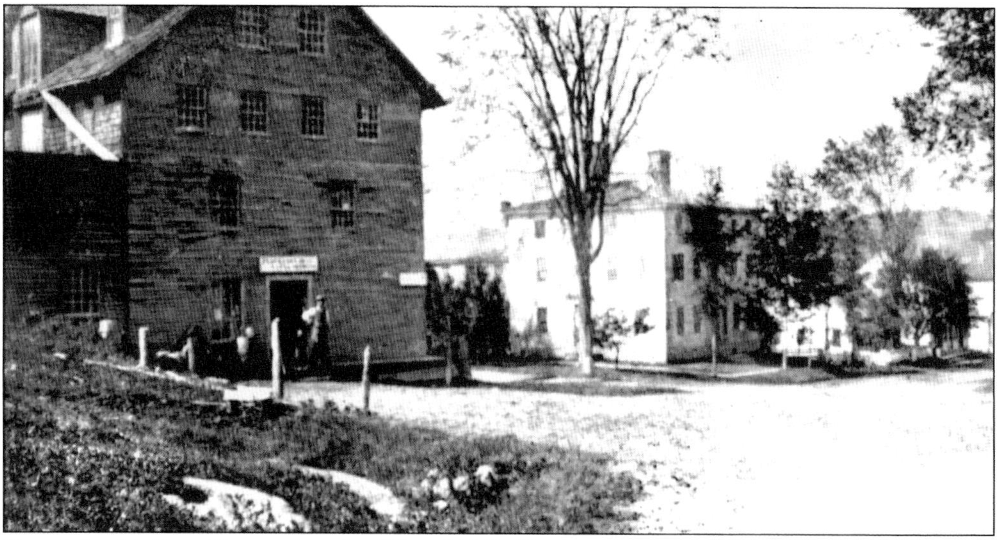

Gen. John McDonald served in the War of 1812. He received his title from serving in both the Massachusetts and Maine militia, being appointed an ensign in 1802. In 1812, when the war broke out with England, he was a lieutenant colonel, and the following year was made a brigadier general, serving in the defense of the coast throughout the war. In 1822, he was promoted to the rank of major general. He was a deacon of the Congregational Church and one of the founders of the Limerick Academy. A story is told that General McDonald trained Maine militia in the house on the right located on Main Street. The third floor ballroom accommodated marching practice. The building on the left is the F. R. Swasey and Sons furniture factory.

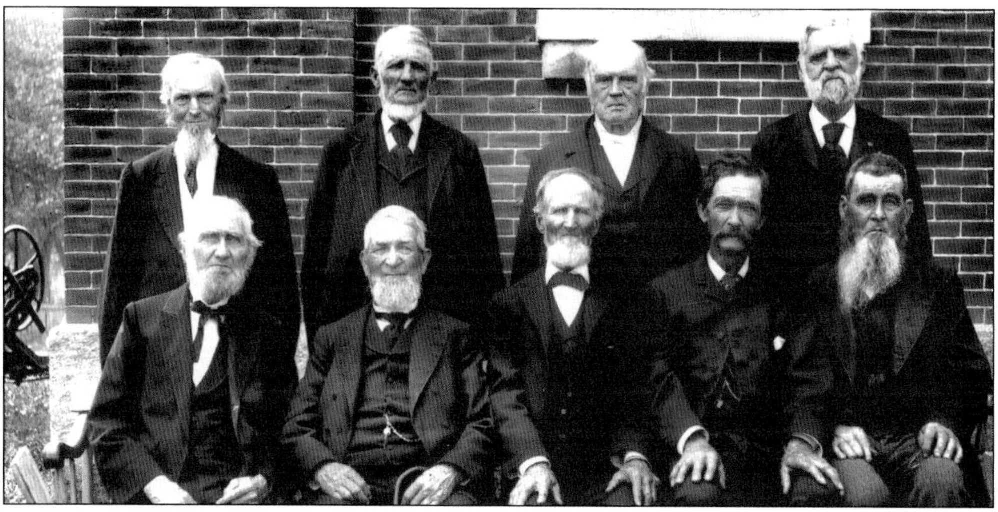

On October 18, 1886, sixteen of the surviving members of the State of Maine Militia met for a reunion at the town hall. In 1836, these Limerick men had formed an artillery company, training with a cannon borrowed from Limington. During its existence it was "the pride of the community and surrounding county for the character and standing of the members as men, for the excellence of its military discipline and the richness of its uniforms." Participating that day, from left to right, were Capt. Joseph G. Harmon, Lt. Nahum Morrill, Lt. James Perkins, Luther Dole, Ira Clark, Joseph Boothby, Edmund Libby, Isaac Emery, Mark L. Burnham, Charles H. Morris, James H. Fogg, Philip Gilpatric, Moses Philpot, Andrew P. Philpot, and Benjamin I. Hayes.

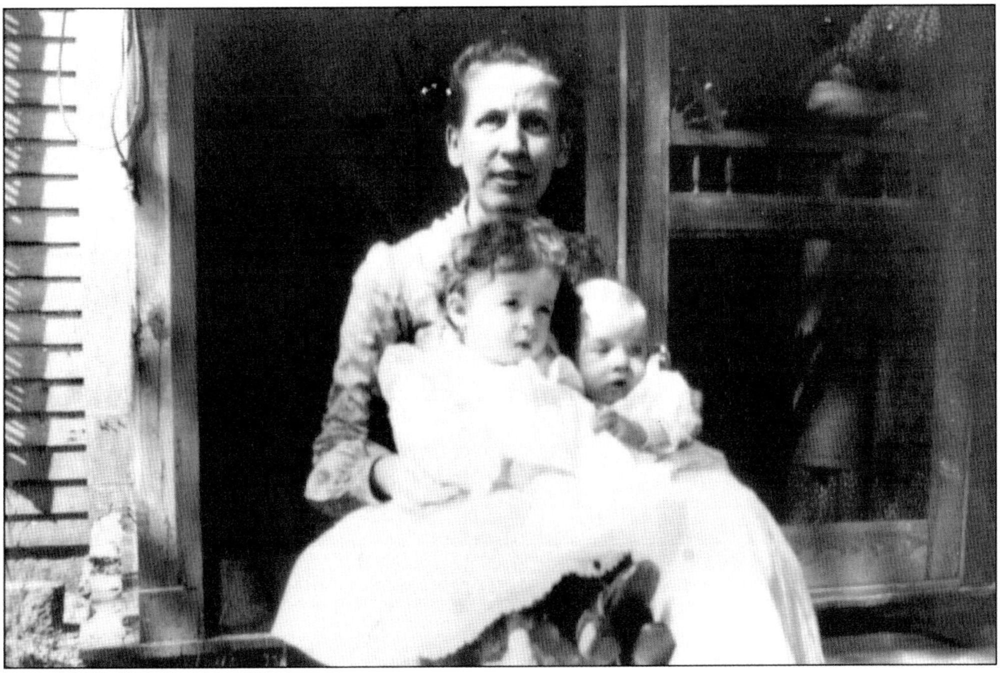

Edwin Cobb and his wife Minnie raised their children, Eva and Harold shown here, on Elm Street. But Edwin Cobb traveled a long road before he could enjoy the peace of family and Limerick. On May 10, 1864, at the battle of Spotsylvania, Cobb, a member of Company D, 5th Maine Infantry, was wounded, losing an arm. The 5th Maine Infantry was one of 12 regiments selected to charge the right center of the enemy's line. In the charge that they led, 11 out of 17 line officers of the regiment were killed or wounded, and half of the men were shot down in less than two minutes while crossing a field not more than 10 rods wide. He fought at many battles including Bull Run and Gettysburg.

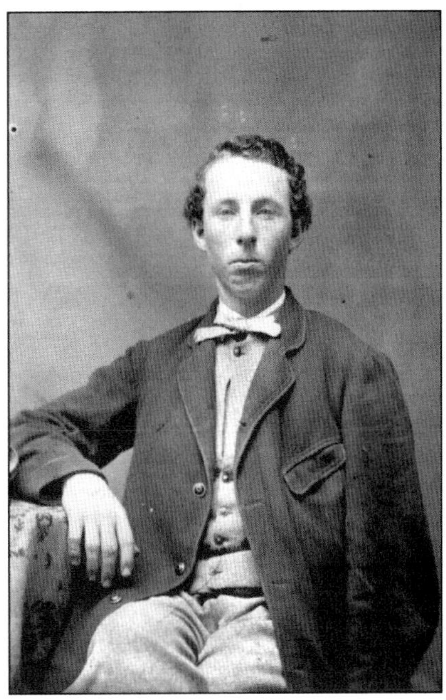

In March of 1865, Edwin Cobb was working in Washington, D.C., where he had a position as watchman at the Treasury Building. He would work from 6:00 p.m. until midnight one night and the next from midnight until 6:00 a.m. One fateful April day he had the evening to himself until midnight. He decided to go to Ford's Theater as it was expected to be a grand night. He was sitting in the fifth row back from the orchestra when Lincoln was shot. He saw Booth drop to the stage and disappear in the wings. A few days later, Colonel Cobb was in the company of soldiers that accompanied Lincoln's body to Springfield. This photograph is c. 1865.

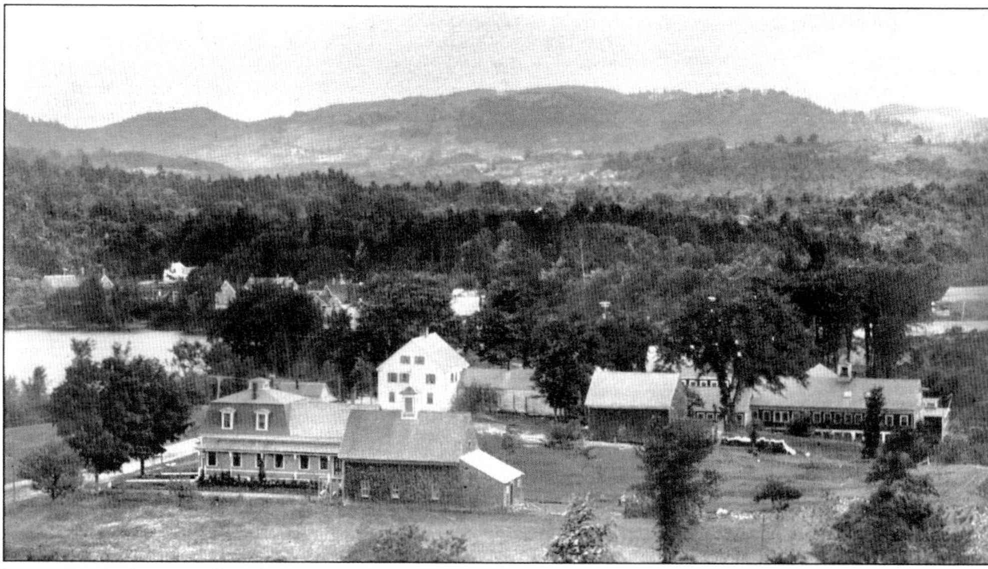

In 1852, Joshua Holland moved to Limerick and established his Woolen Blanket Mills. He purchased the rights to Brown's Brook and developed Holland's Ponds, now Sokokis Lake. He employed 125 people. The wage of his help was one dollar a day. Employees worked six days a week from 6:00 a.m. to 6:00 p.m. with one hour for lunch. A 6:00 a.m. bell called the workers in the morning and a 6:00 p.m. bell dismissed them. A 9:00 p.m. bell signaled them to return home if they were out. When one of Holland's workers was ill he would visit them, call the doctor, and pay all the doctor's bills for them. Holland lived to be 84 years old.

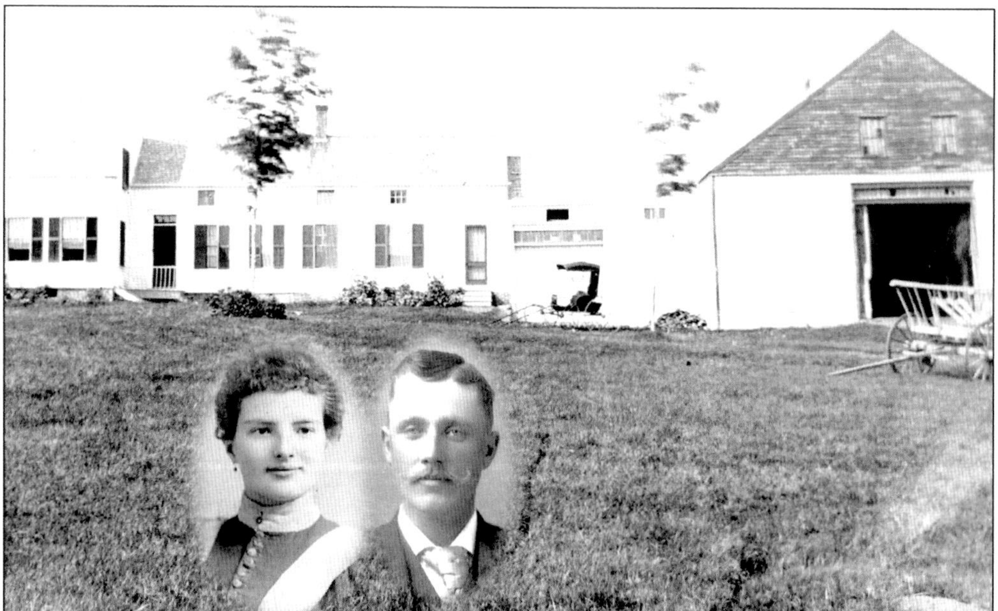

Joseph Libby followed his father to Limerick from Kittery in the late 1780s. In 1794, he and Sarah Staples declared their intention to marry to the Limerick town clerk. In 1797, he purchased 200 acres of wild land in Limerick Range G3 and G4. For the next 200 years, the descendants of Joseph and Sarah would farm and live out their lives on this land. Pictured is the Libby farm, then owned by Harrison and India Libby (inset). The farm was lost to fire around 1920.

The Cobb family worked a farm located on Sawyer's Mountain from the late 1700s. One day the farm was located in Limington; the next in Limerick. Residents of the area had petitioned to be annexed from Limington and in 1870 their wish was granted. It has been estimated that some 2,000 acres was added to the town of Limerick by this action. In this photograph, Ralph Cobb is hunting on Sawyer's Mountain. Note the lack of trees, clear to the mountain's top. Cobb was master of Freedom Lodge in 1926, and served as a selectman from 1936 through 1938.

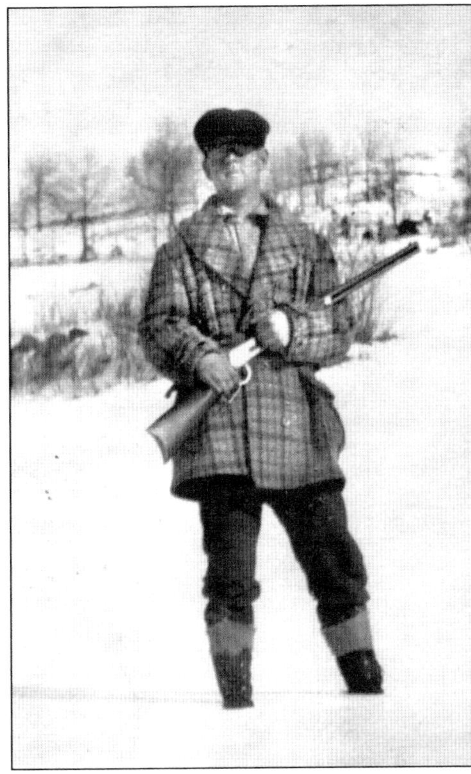

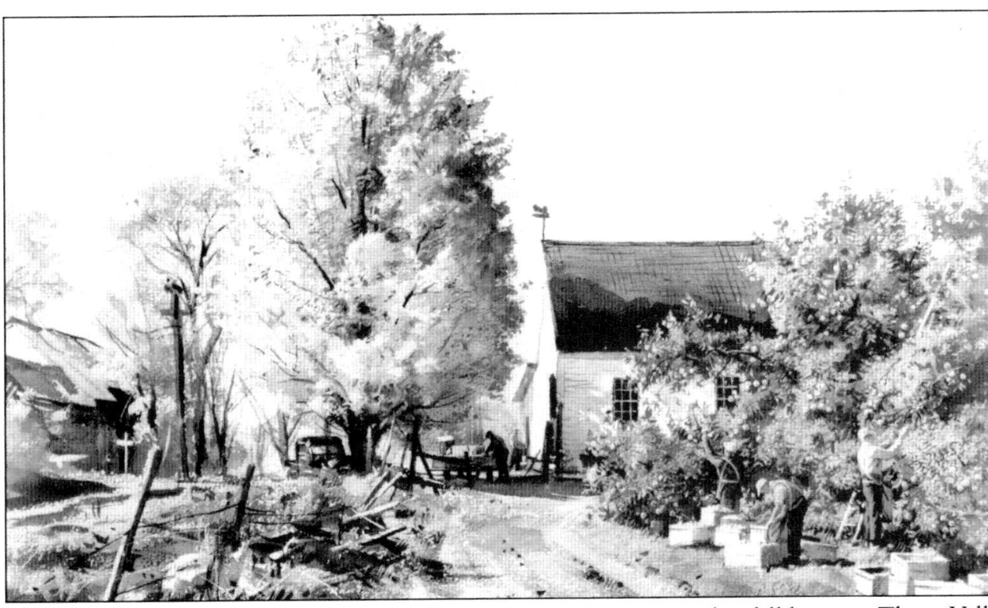

Apple orchards grace the landscape of Ossipee Valley. Overseeing this fall harvest, Three Hills Farm foreman Ralph Cobb is packing apples under the tree and is being assisted by a young man named Donald Libby. Henry Roosevelt (Franklin's nephew) lived on the farm. Residents of Emery Corner Road still remember the day the black limousine raced up the road carrying Eleanor for a visit. Apples, pumpkins, and blueberries are still grown and sold at Emery Corner by the Libby family.

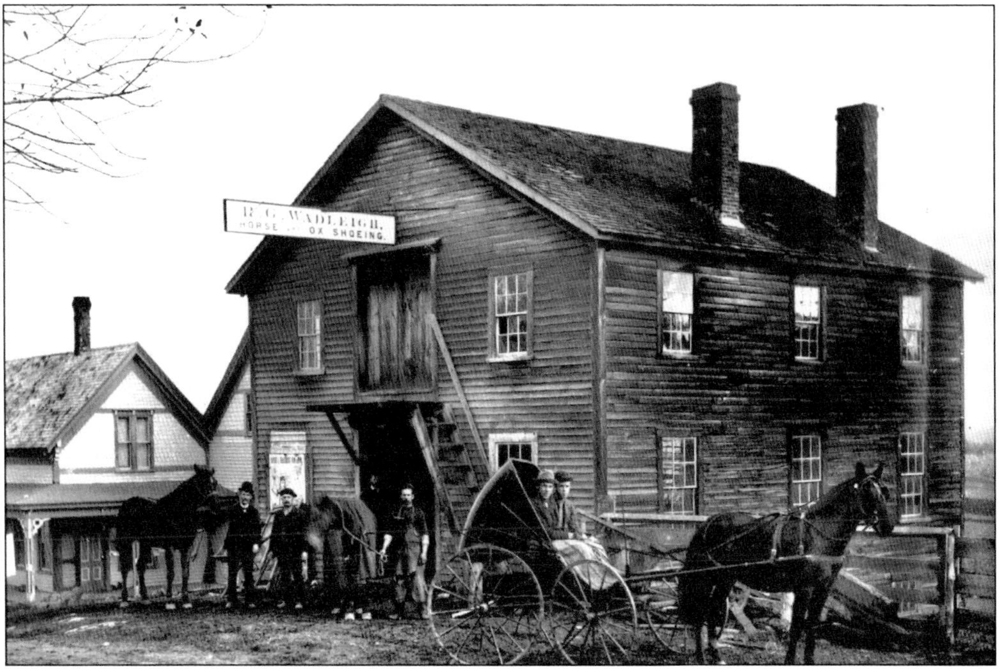

In 1919, the village smithy was Roscoe G. Wadleigh. His business, a horseshoeing and general smithing business, was located on Washington Street. When he was a child he lived in Canada where his father was a blacksmith. Wadleigh moved to Limerick around 1884. For years the second story of this business was also used as a carriage shop. Two runners, built on to the right side of the building, brought them down from the second floor when they were road ready.

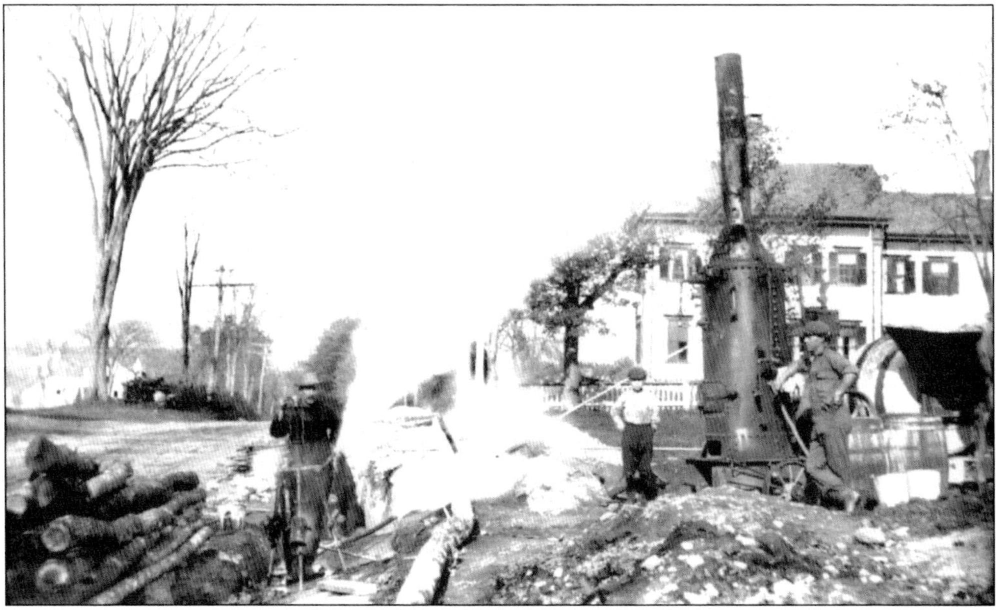

These men are hard at work on Washington Street fashioning a trench with a steam-powered jackhammer for the new water lines laid around 1916. The favored machine of the day for such work was a portable drilling machine. A team of horses hauled the wheel-mounted machine until tractors became available. In addition to the drilling, blasting was employed.

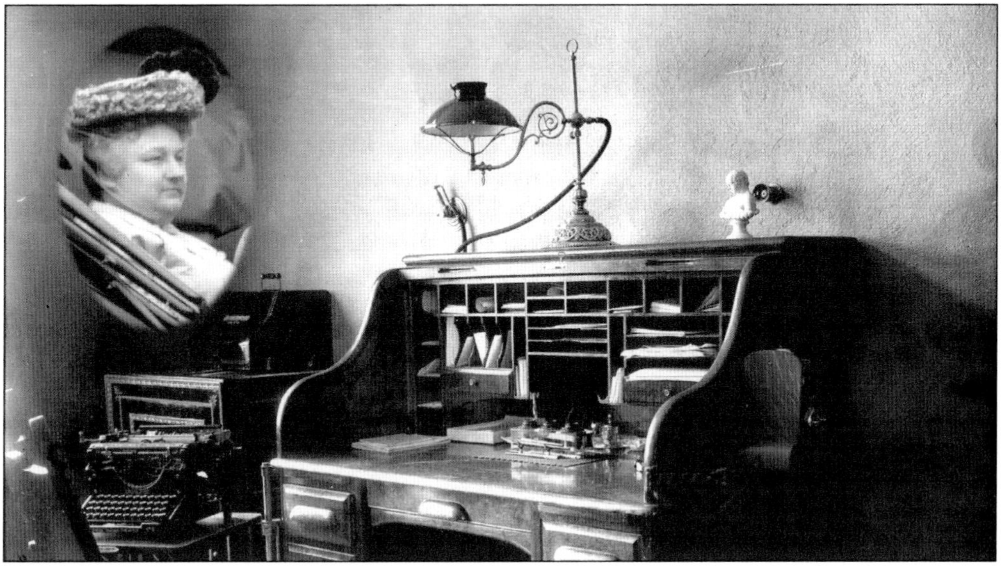

In 1903, the building housing the Limerick National Bank was completely renovated and dedicated solely for banking purposes. It was equipped with state-of-the-art equipment and elegantly furnished. The bank was founded in 1882 by Jeremiah M. Mason and served the entire Ossipee Valley. In 1892, the bank's board of directors voted to offer interest-bearing savings accounts. This idea was adopted by Portland, Maine, banks and quickly spread across the United States banking industry. In January 1897, Frances Estelle Mason (inset) was named president, becoming the first woman bank president of a national bank in the state of Maine. The family sold the bank in February of 1929.

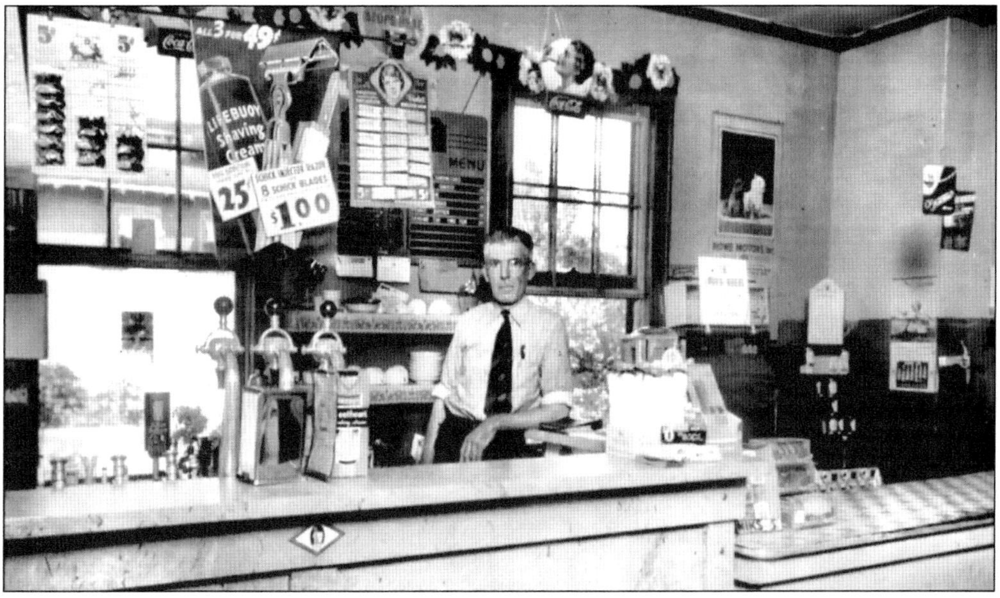

Arthur H. Carpenter's soda fountain served as a meeting place on Main Street for some 12 years. Carpenter kept shop, was a postmaster, fire chief, and at one time, a tax collector. At 90 years of age, he became the holder of the Boston Post Cane on March 9, 1975. Since 1909, Limerick selectmen have presented the ebony cane to the oldest citizen of the community

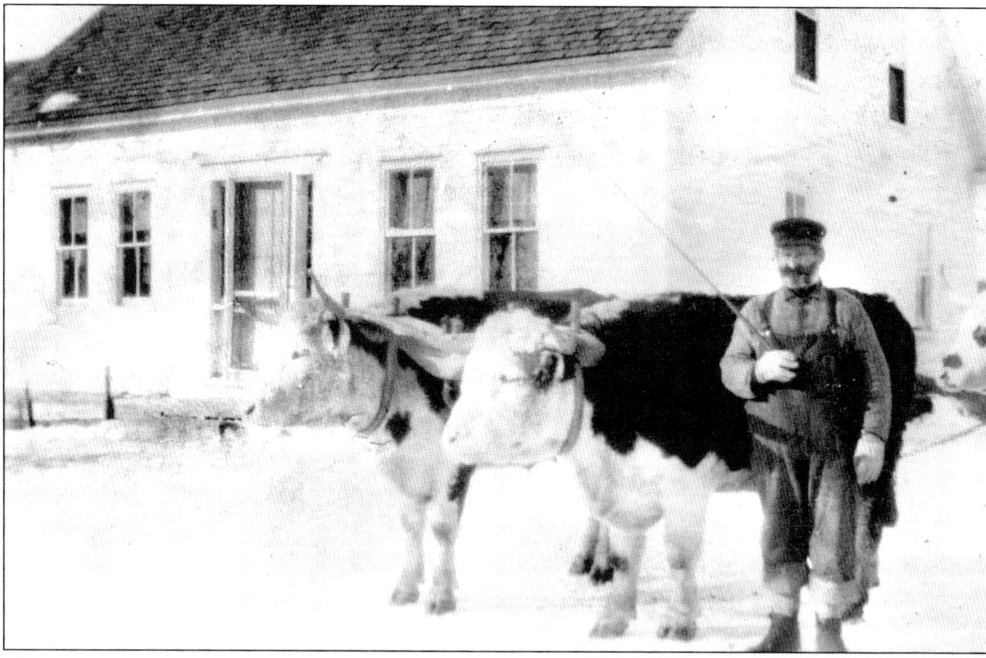

Sherman Lord conducts his team of oxen to the barn on his farm on Stover Lane in 1918. Sherman and his wife, Sarah inherited the farm from the Stover family. Their daughter, Mary Abby, was born on the farm in 1887, the farm was passed down to her, and she and her husband raised their family there.

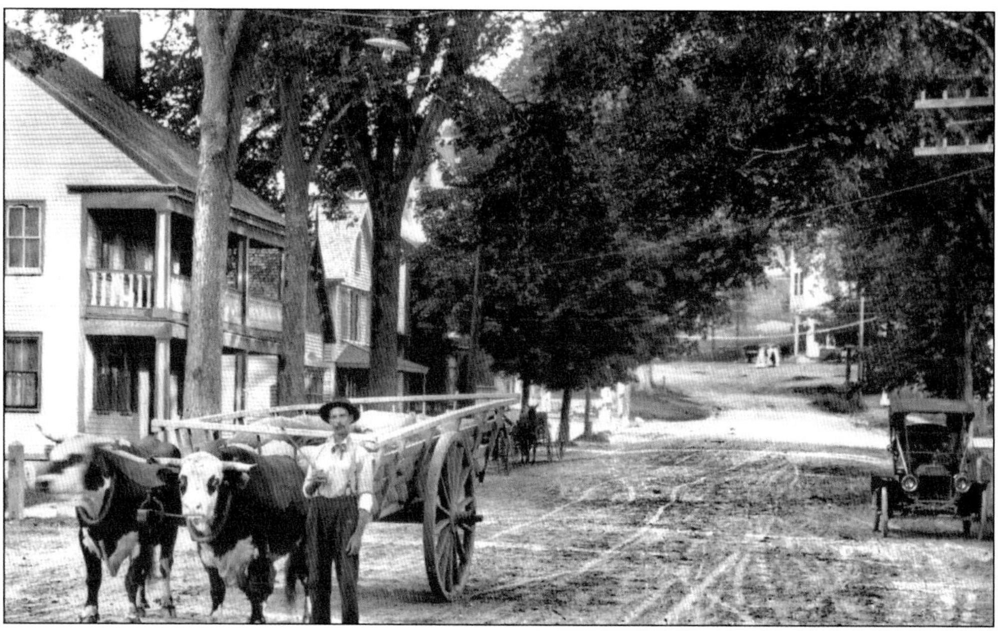

John Brown Wales (born in 1866) is taking a stroll down Main Street Limerick with Philpot's team of oxen. Oxen were often used for plowing and heavy hauling. They were slow but resolute and provided a steady strength. The Wales family were early settlers of Cornish. As this picture shows, a new source of power was close at hand with the advent of the Model T. This car belonged to Dr. Herman Tibbetts.

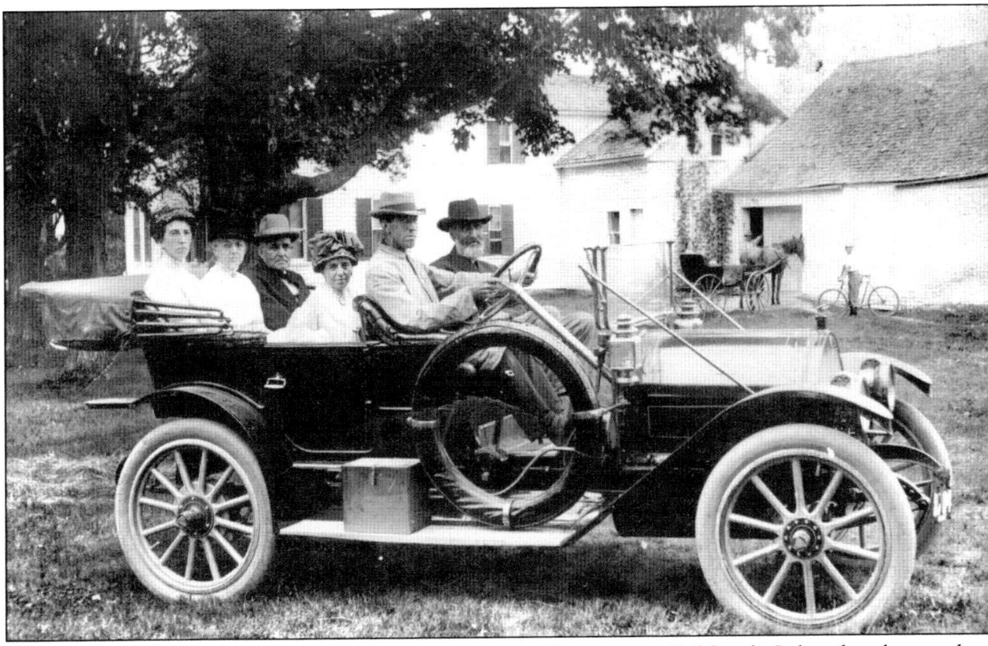

Arthur Hayes and his wife Hannah enjoy their brand new 1911 Oakland. Other family members out for a spin are Mr. and Mrs. Hayes Sr., Myra Hayes, and a relative from out west. Arthur Hayes was a York County Commissioner.

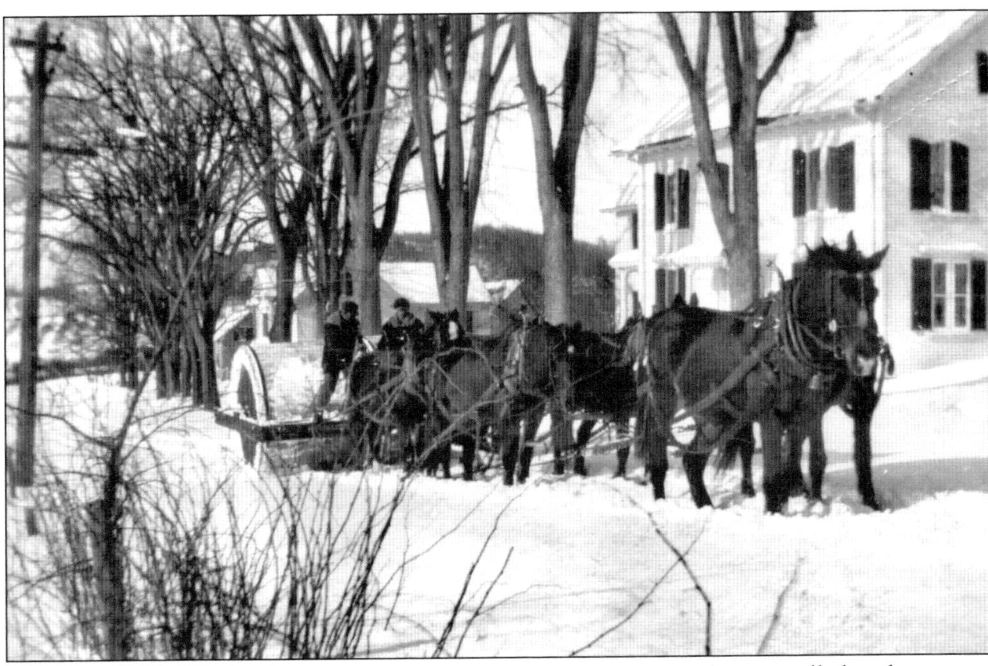

Before the appearance of the gas-powered plow, snow-covered roads were rolled with teams of horses or oxen. Here on Elm Street, the snow is being packed in February 1917 so that sleighs can glide over it easily. The house in the background is Louisa and Amelia Swasey's.

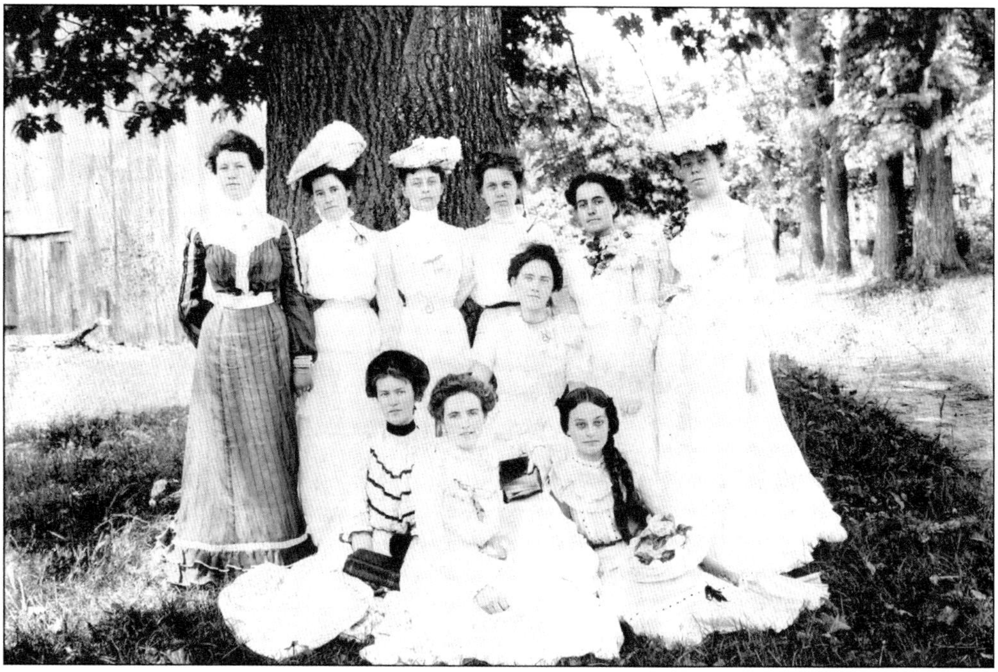

These fashionable Limerick ladies sport their high-collar blouses, bell skirts and elegant occasion hats. Wearing white at this time was a symbol of wealth, as it visually told onlookers that the wearer could afford to pay someone to launder their clothes (or perhaps their indulgent mother was doing the laundering). Pictured here, from left to right, is (sitting) Etta Sawyer, Mildred Brown, and Theo Townsend; (standing) Eva Carpenter, Maud Plaisted, Grace Nason (teacher), Bess Libby, Vera Boothby, Alice Boody, Rose Moulton (teacher).

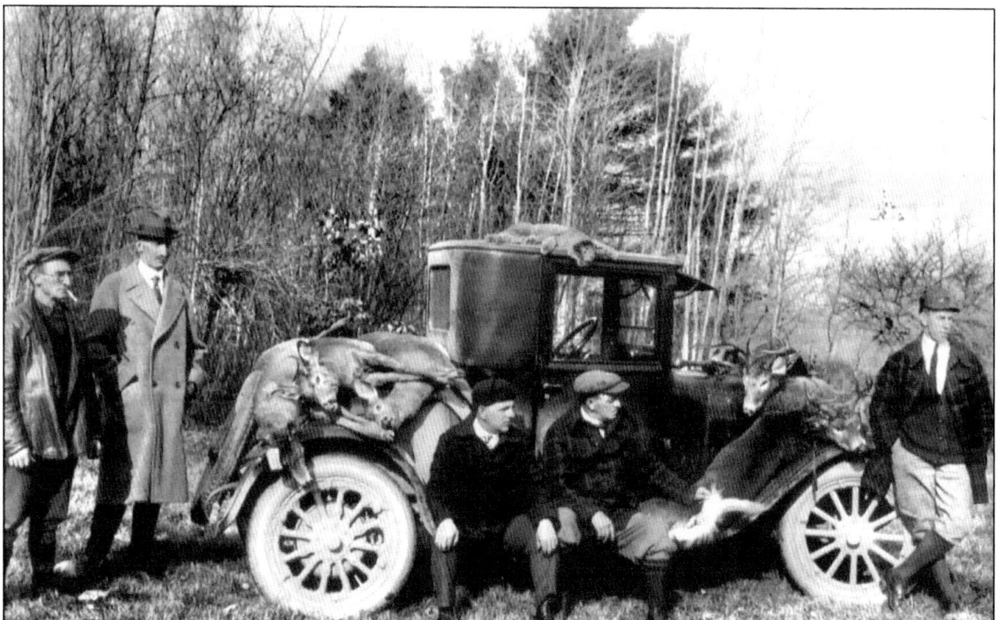

A November pastime, long enjoyed in Limerick, has been the annual deer hunt. These Limerick sportsmen appear to be very well dressed for the event.

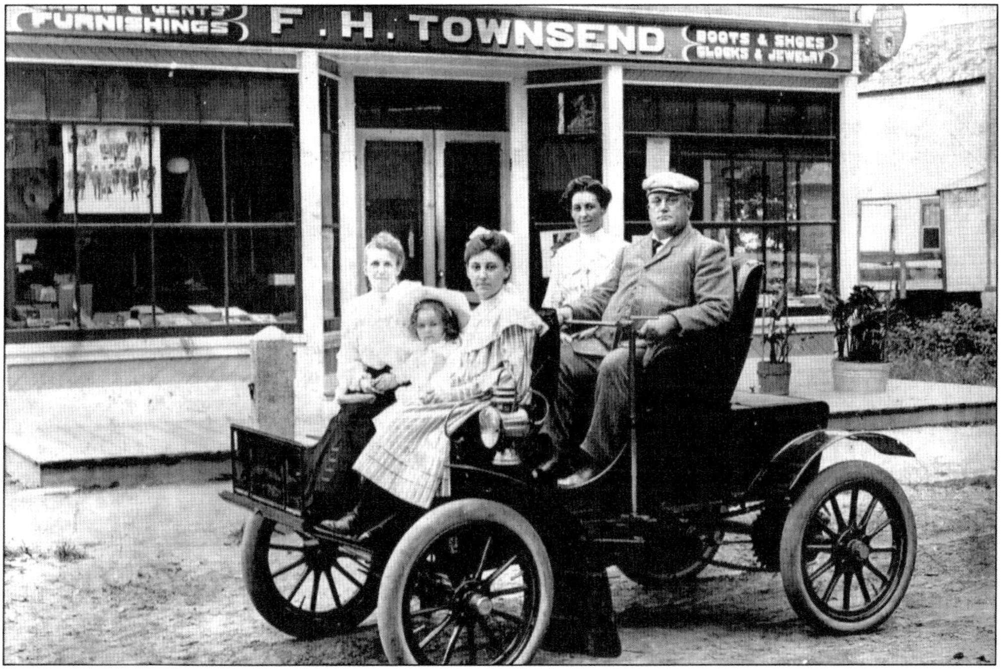

Fred and Dora Townsend take a ride in their chain-driven Knox car in 1904. Accompanying them are daughters Berniece Dow Townsend (then 15 years old) and Mattie B. Mason. The little girl is Olga M. Moulton. The Townsend's ran a dry goods store on Main Street. (Photograph courtesy of Jane Lougee Bryant.)

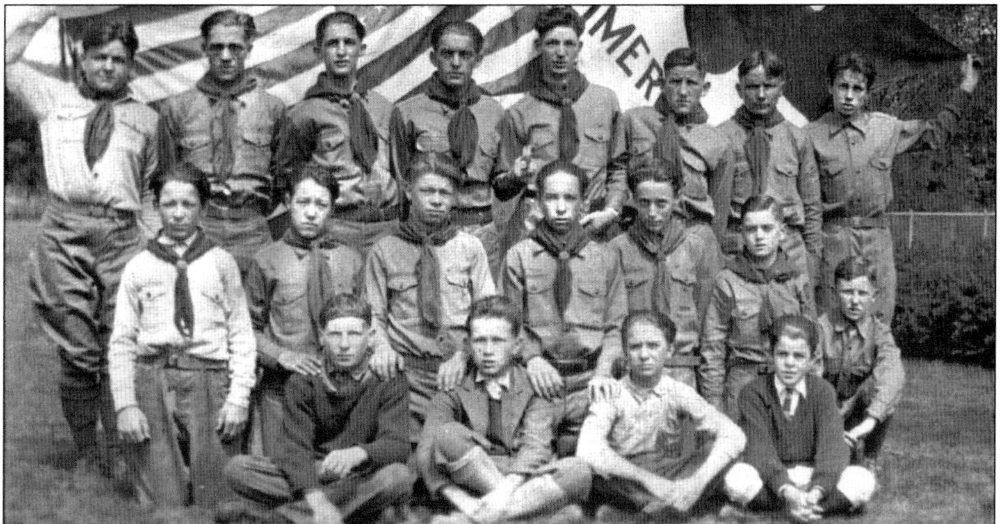

Hollis Orcutt, principal of the Limerick Academy, organized the first Boy Scout Troop in Limerick. They met for the first time at a private home on the evening of April 29, 1918. Twelve boys were present. Limerick Boy Scout Troop 8 proudly displayed the colors in 1930. From left to right, they are (first row) Sylvester Carroll, Waldo Allen, Herman Lepage, and George Jones; (second row) Glen Gilpatrick, Stanley Haskell, Albert Whiteley, Oscar Gilpatrick, David Morrill, Arnold Dall, and Herbert Goodman; (third row) Henry Martel, George Leland, Elmer Nason, Herbert Nason, Bradley Perkins, George Goodman, Laurence Smith, and Rudolph Sadler.

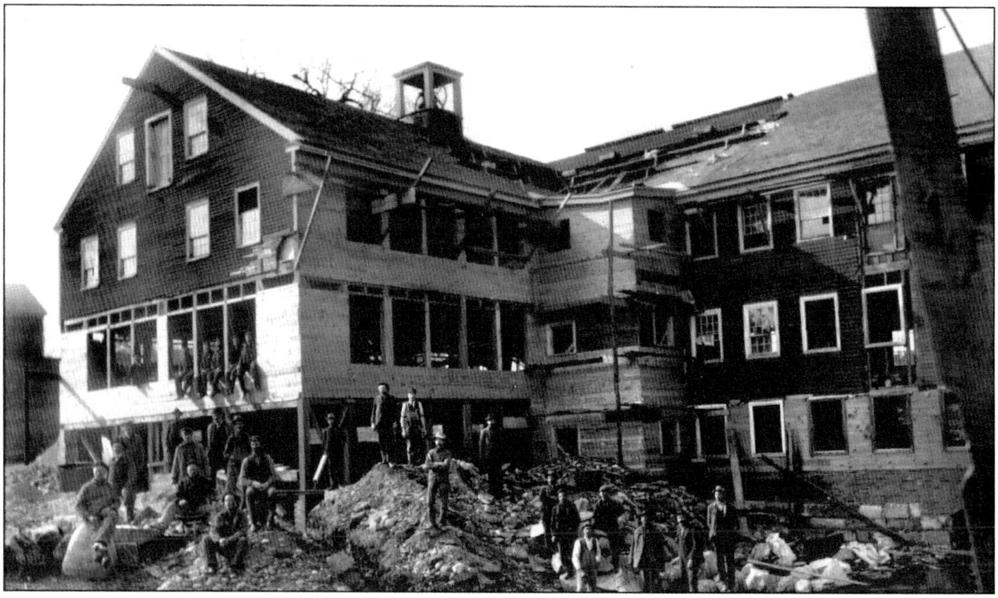

When the mills were purchased in 1899, the buildings were falling down and the machinery was old and obsolete. The mill stood idle until Robert Halford was hired as superintendent in 1905. A major renovation was undertaken and the building was equipped for production. Charles Moulton, Limerick industrialist, and his associates worked together to build a prosperous woolen industry. At peak production, 38,000 spindles were spinning worsted and mohair. The yarn was sold to the Sanford Mills that wove it into plush. The automobile industry in Detroit became the great consumer.

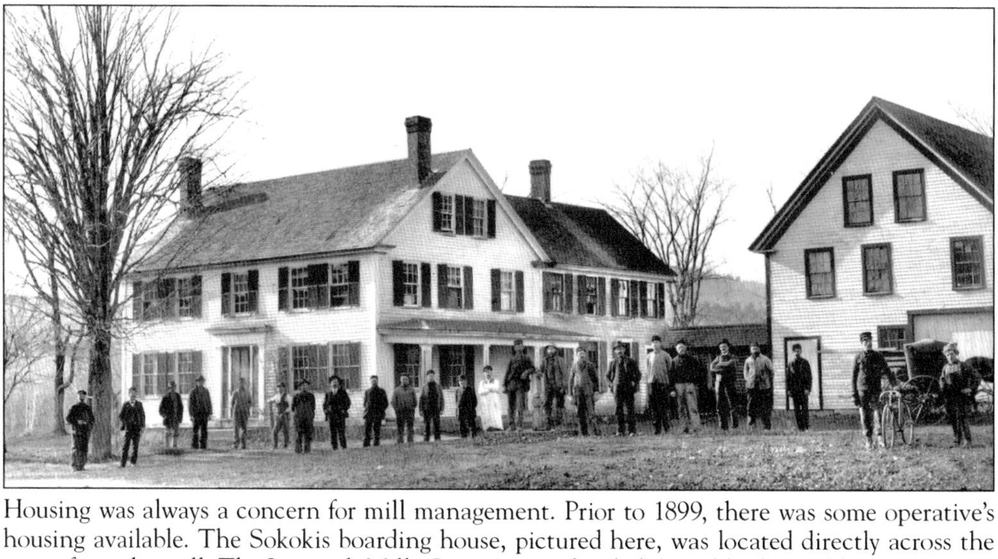

Housing was always a concern for mill management. Prior to 1899, there was some operative's housing available. The Sokokis boarding house, pictured here, was located directly across the street from the mill. The Limerick Mills Corporation decided to tackle the problem of housing mill employees, hired architect Charles Boynton and renovated the old tenements and put a plan in place to build more housing. By 1920, clean, modern houses with cement cellars, electric lights, and running water had been built. Fire hydrants had been installed for fire protection. The houses were rented for $4.50 a week and a garage for 50¢. A new village had appeared and the mill was booming.

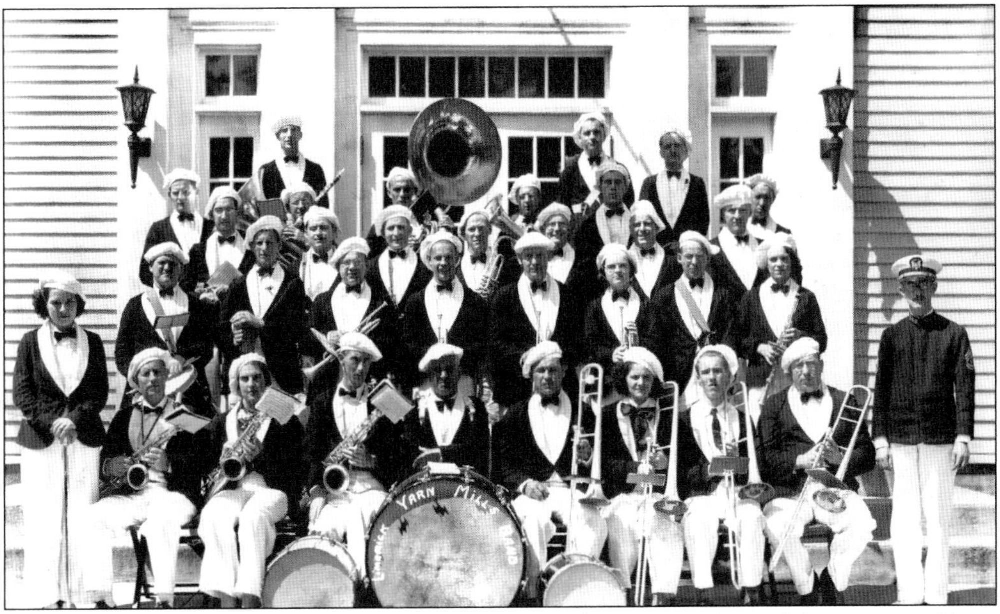

The Limerick Mills Band stops for a formal photograph in 1937. Many of those pictured here would see service during World War II. But the years preceding that war were filled with work, music, and romance. Two trombone players, Walter Lanoue and Mabel Legere, are pictured in the front row. "That summer we simply joined the band to learn how to play the trombone and we ended up falling in love." Walter and Mabel married in 1938.

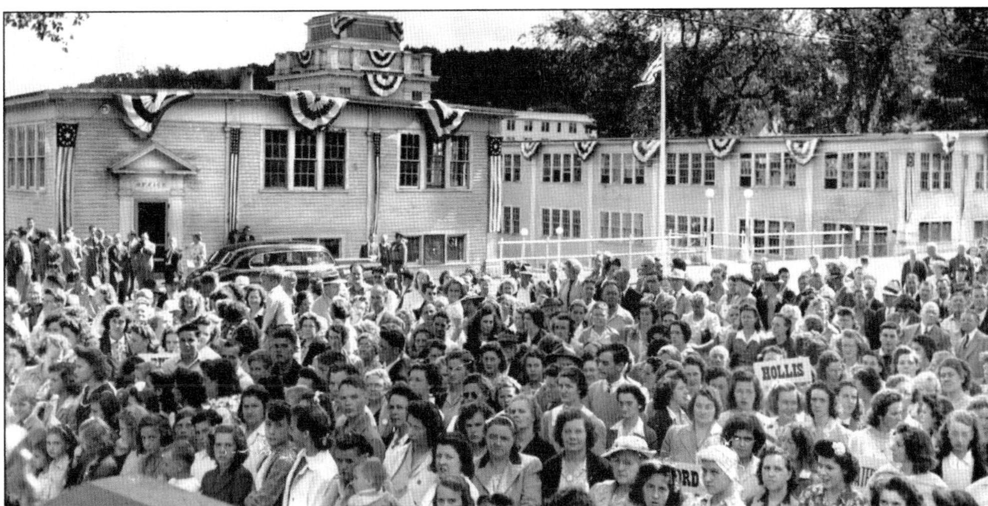

In 1935, the Jordan group purchased the Limerick Mills. The sale was unique as it included the mills, 53 tenement homes, a hotel, and even a theater. Spindles "whirled throughout World War II making yarns for army uniforms, neckties, socks, and flying suits." On a spectacular August day in 1944, the employees of the Limerick Yarn Mills were awarded the Army-Navy "E" Award "for skill, industry, and devotion on the production front of the greatest war in history." The people were told "you are carrying on a sustained drive in the battle of production that is making itself felt on the battlegrounds in Europe, all over the blue Pacific and all roads that lead to Berlin and Tokyo." The Limerick Mills employed 450 people from all over the Ossipee Valley and beyond.

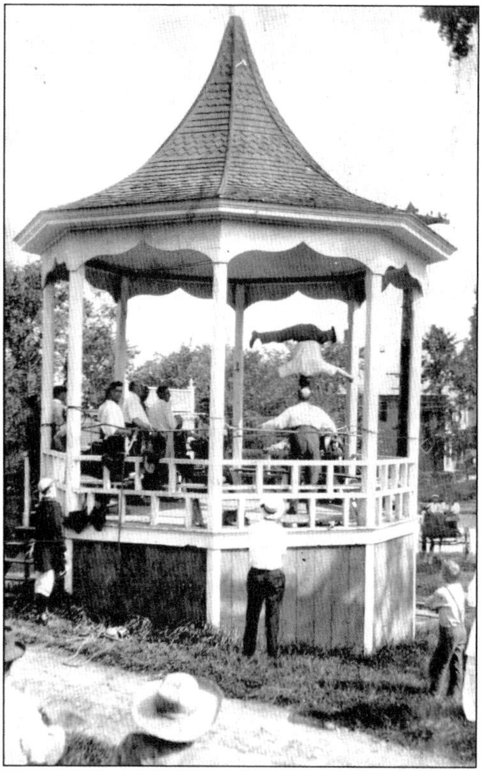

The Limerick Bandstand was built in 1882. The Limerick Cornet Band had been organized in 1881 under the direction of Charles Welch of Limington. The band learned some simple and well-known pieces under Welch's tutelage. The town bandstand was central to outdoor entertainment, providing a place for music and special events. Here, Lester Gilpatrick and Charles Hacker entertain townsfolk. They had previously performed internationally with the Barnum and Bailey and Ringling Brothers circuses.

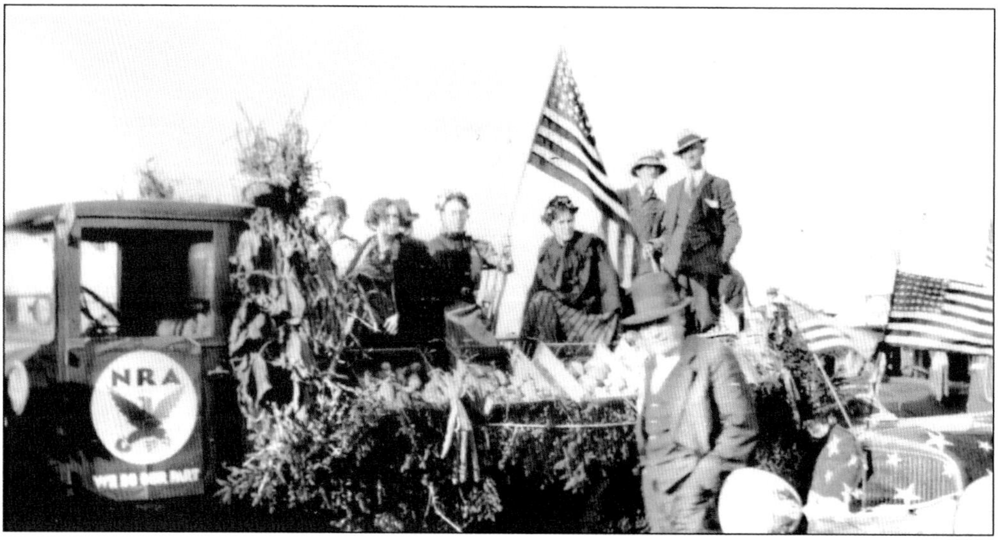

Roosevelt's 1933 National Recovery Act was welcomed in grand style at Limerick by all of the Ossipee Valley towns on October 19. Announced as "the greatest celebration ever . . . in the history of the town," the parade led through the factory village to Main Street. Businesses were decorated to signify their support of the act. In Limerick this act meant that the standard 54-hour work week and child labor had come to an end and many would receive a pay raise. The Limerick Grange float proudly displayed the Blue Eagle announcing "We Do Our Part." Pictured, from left to right, are Alice Plaisted, Mollie Libby, Katherine Kallock, Gladys Bisbee, Charles Kallock, Leon Bisbee, and Ed Haskell.

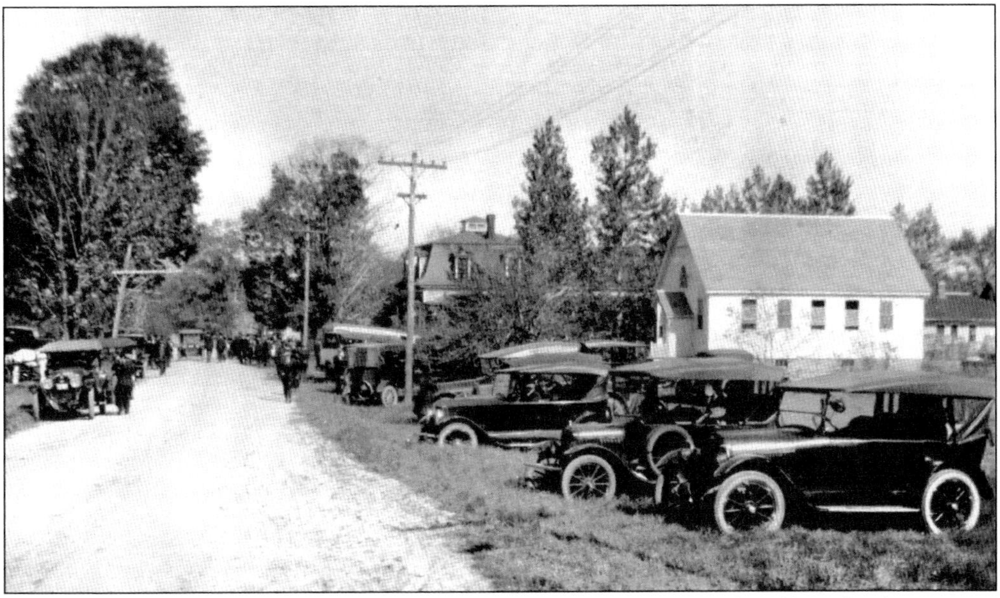

The "Sokokis Village" area was home to many Canadian immigrants lured here by the promise of work at the mills. Even though they were supplied with jobs, houses, and leisure activities, the workforce was unhappy because they did not have a church. Weddings were being held in the shipping room of the mill and services were in the front parlors. They expressed this concern to superintendent Whittaker, some threatening to leave unless they had a place of worship. Eventually, Whittaker's home would be sold to the Catholic Diocese for a rectory and the land next door would be donated by Lincoln Watson and Cora Watson (née Holland) for a church. The church was dedicated in October 1921.

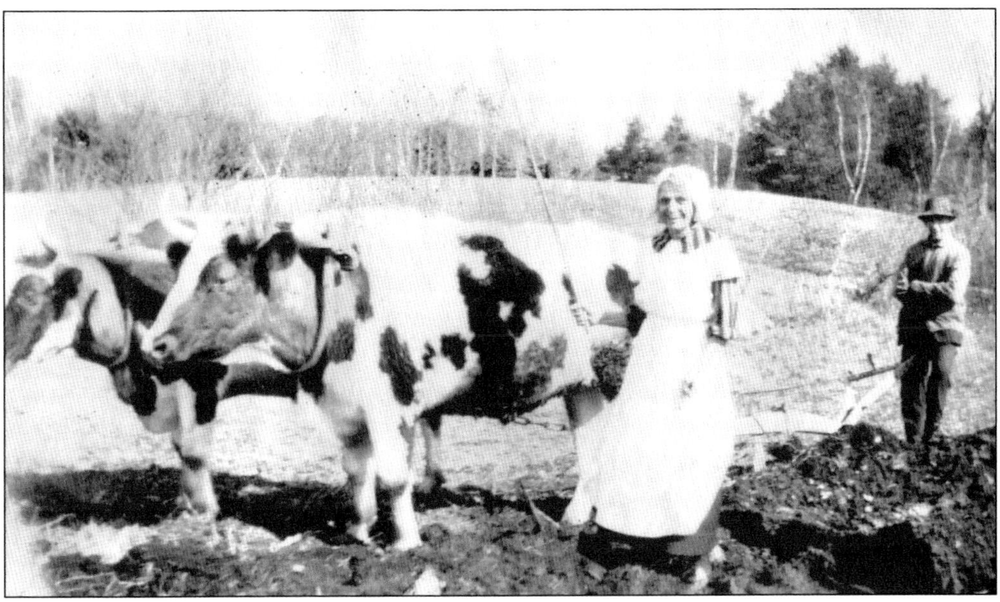

Even the ladies got into the act with the planting. "Auntie Binns" is helping Wilbur Whiteley with the spring plowing on the Whiteley farm bordered by Pickerel Pond. She came to town just for a visit and enjoyed Limerick so much she decided not to return to her native England. The Whiteley family adopted this foreigner as one of their own.

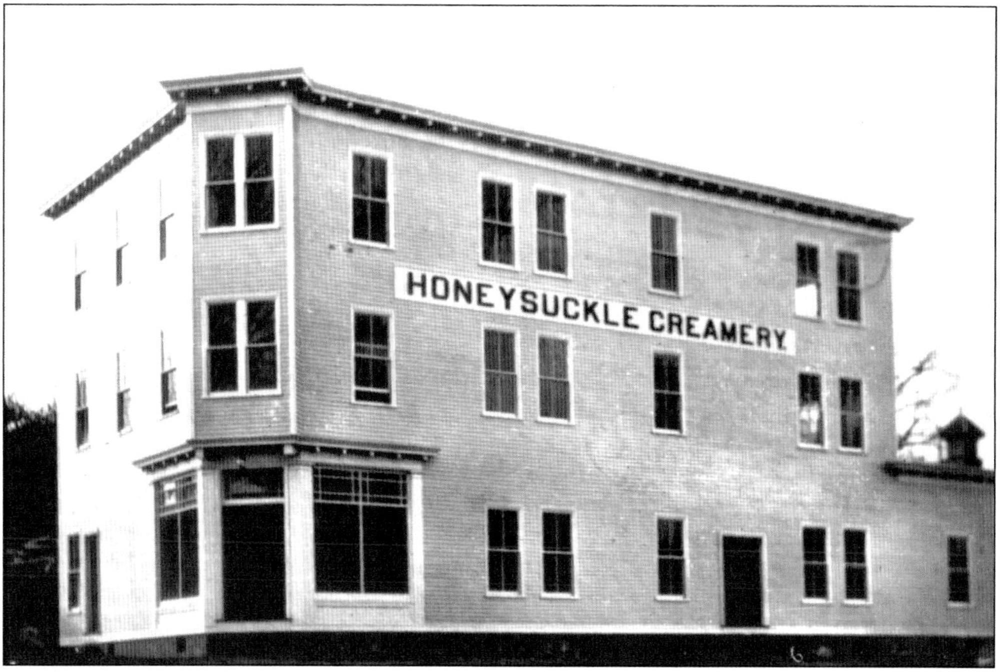

Frank S. Harper built Honeysuckle Creamery in 1904. The creamery stood where Tibbetts Memorial Park is now located. A pioneer in the creamery butter business in York County, one of his products was widely known under the name of Willowdale. Butter was presented in pound cakes, and marked into quarter squares for the convenience of families. Later the creamery became a pasteurized creamery, accepting raw product from local farmers, making a large quantity of butter, and selling it widely.

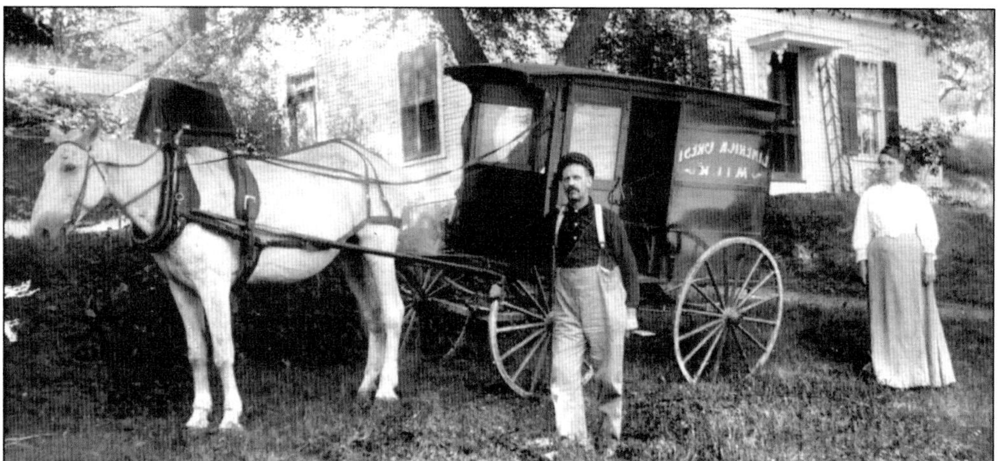

The Crescent Creamery, established in 1909, furnished dairy farms in the Ossipee Valley, a ready market and quick return in cash. The pasteurized creamery employed six collectors who covered a route of farms throughout the valley and into New Hampshire. Cream was brought back to Limerick and tested for butterfat. The price paid was dependent on the fat content. The product was then shipped to wholesale markets in 10-gallon cans. Pictured here is a creamery employee delivering milk on Cannon Hill. Limerick residents enjoyed home delivery of milk until the 1960s, when Elmhurst Farms in Parsonsfield discontinued services.

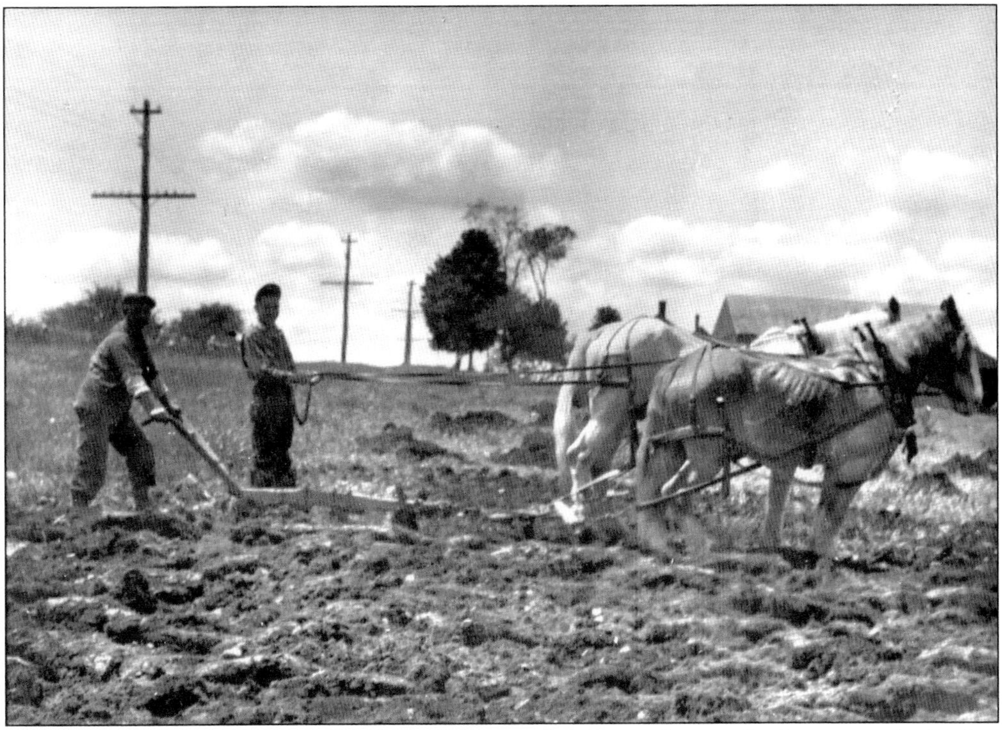

Walter E. Ricker is manning the plow while David I. Hayes directs the horses on the Ricker Farm on the E Range Road in the late 1930s. Walter enjoyed his garden, cows, and chickens. The farm at one time was Swett's Tavern.

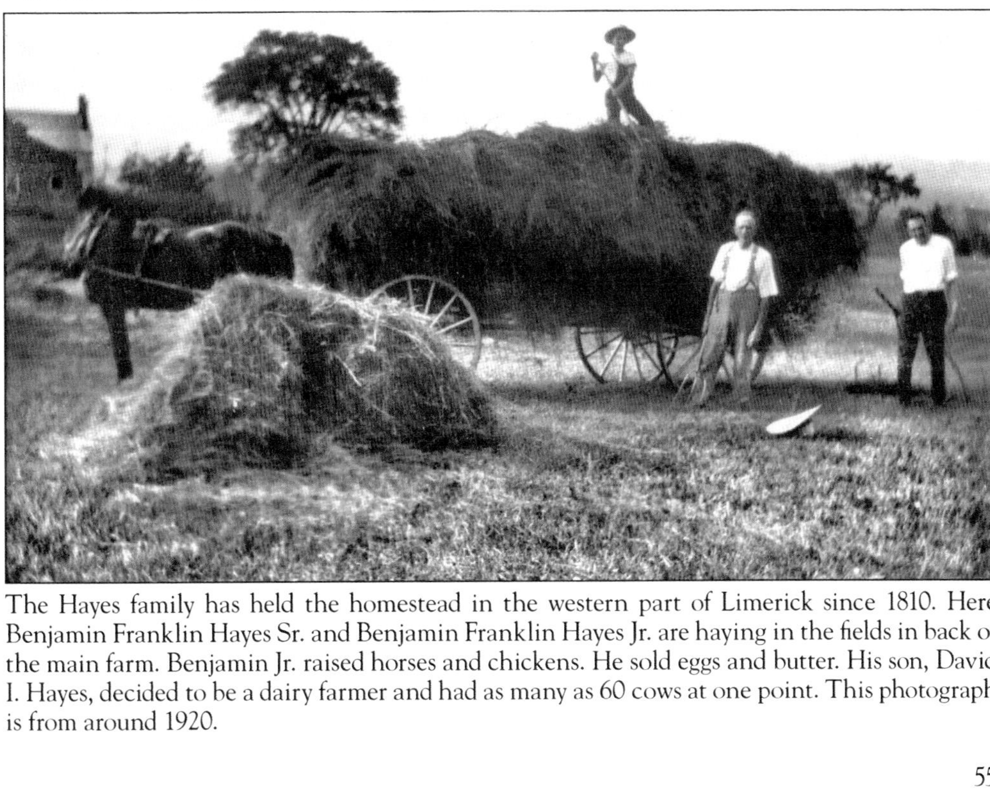

The Hayes family has held the homestead in the western part of Limerick since 1810. Here Benjamin Franklin Hayes Sr. and Benjamin Franklin Hayes Jr. are haying in the fields in back of the main farm. Benjamin Jr. raised horses and chickens. He sold eggs and butter. His son, David I. Hayes, decided to be a dairy farmer and had as many as 60 cows at one point. This photograph is from around 1920.

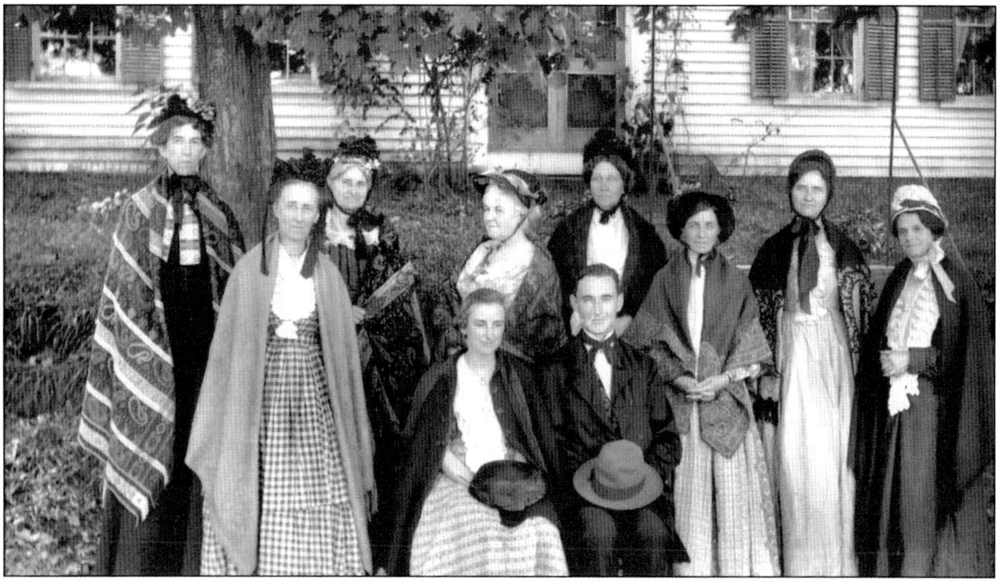

Limerick Thespians recreated Kate Douglas Wiggin's Christmas romance *The Old Peabody Pew* at the Baptist Meetinghouse in 1920. Posing for a photograph in front of church caretaker George Carpenter's house are, from left to right, (sitting) Ethel Brown King and Arthur Fogg Lougee; (standing) Myra Hayes, Allie Libby, Cora Cram, Alice Boynton, Carrie Hoyt, Hannah Hayes, Rose Moulton, Gracie Packard. The Calvin Baptist Society Meetinghouse, pictured below, was originally built in 1796.

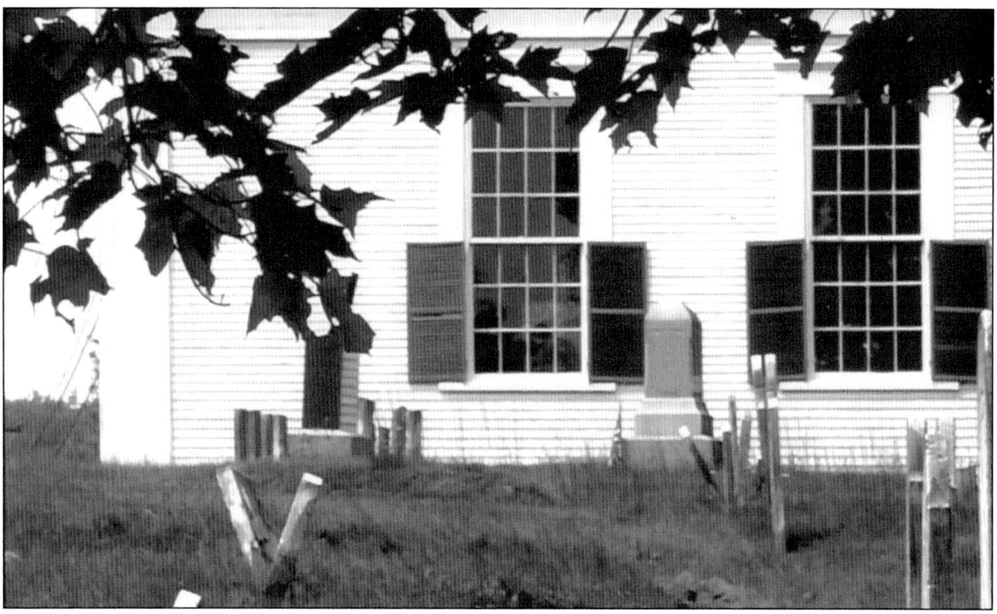

"As you have sat there on open-windowed Sundays, looking across purple clover-fields to blue distant mountains, watching the palm-leaf fans swaying to and fro in the warm stillness before sermon time, did not the place seem full of memories . . . ? You heard the hum of droning bees and followed the airy wings of butterflies fluttering over the gravestones in the old churchyard, and underneath almost every moss-grown tablet some humble romance lies buried and all but forgotten." Kate Douglas Wiggin.

Three

LIMINGTON

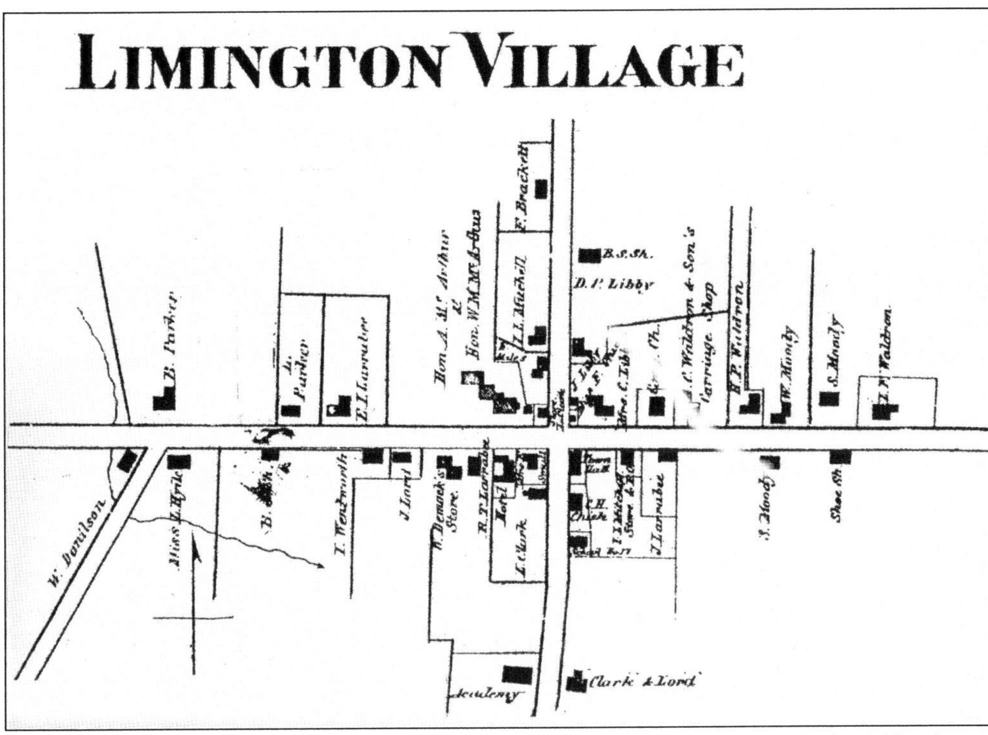

In 1774, the Ossipee Proprietors met and voted that 75 lots of 100 acres each should be drawn. On June 8, 1791, the settlers petitioned the Commonwealth of Massachusetts: "From the Inhabitants of the Plantation called Ossipee in the County of York: "That your partitioners have made great exertion to clear and subdue this stubborn soil. They begin to wish and hope for some of the privileges enjoyed by people in the towns from whence they removed. That while they are labouring for a temporal they may not forget an eternal inheritance and their families sink into a state of savage ignorance and barbarity." The town was incorporated in 1792.

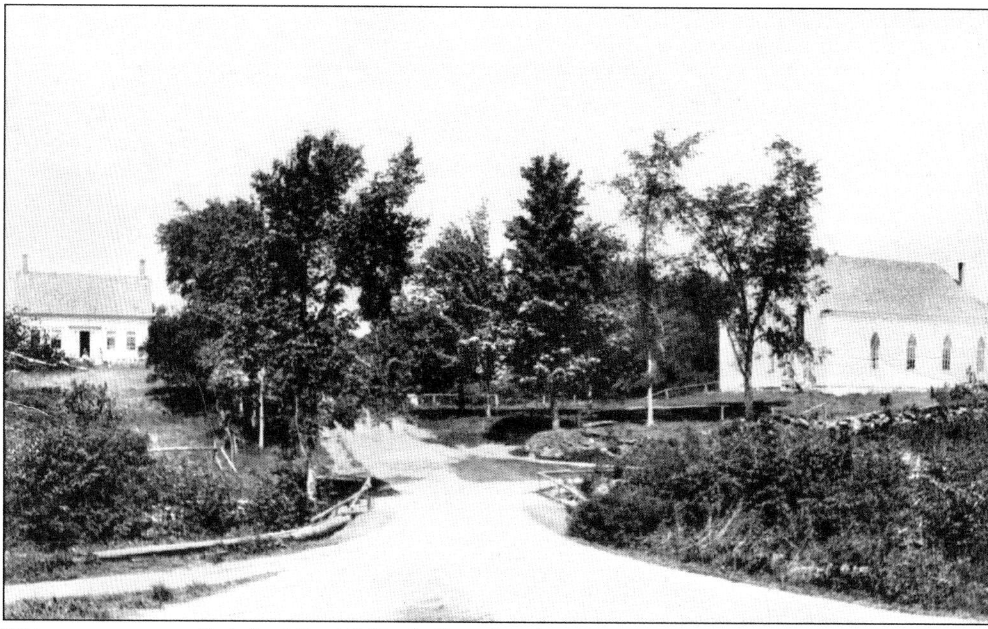

This corner was called the "Crick" (Barbel) in South Limington. You see the Moody Road with South Limington Baptist Church on the right and the Parsonage where Julia Gammon lived on the left. The church burned in 1959 on a Sunday morning before services. The wood furnace in the basement caught the building on fire.

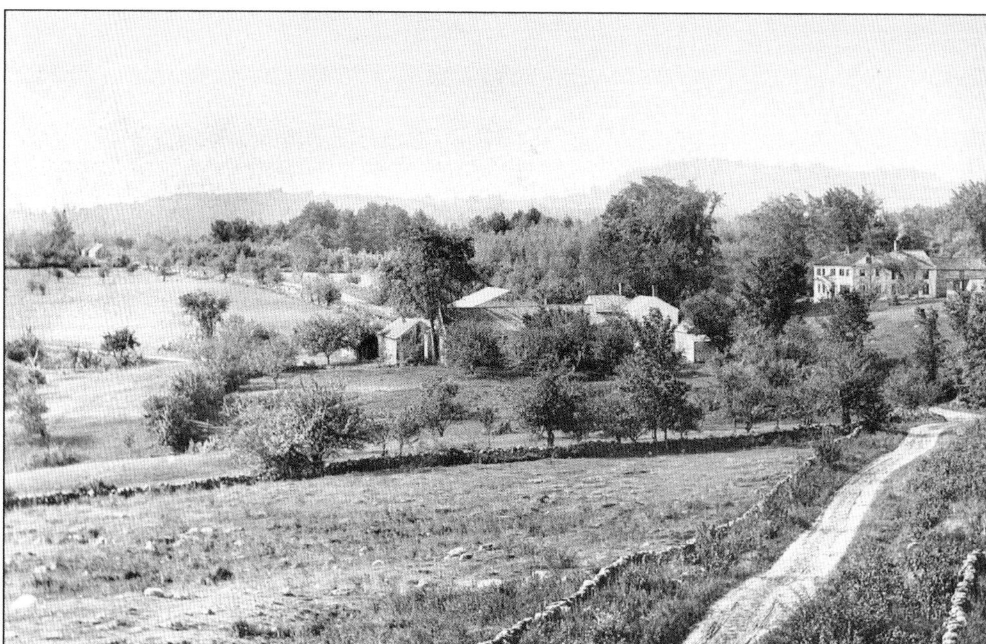

This view of the Boothby Road faces south and shows the farm of Harry and Ethel Maxim. The farm has since burned.

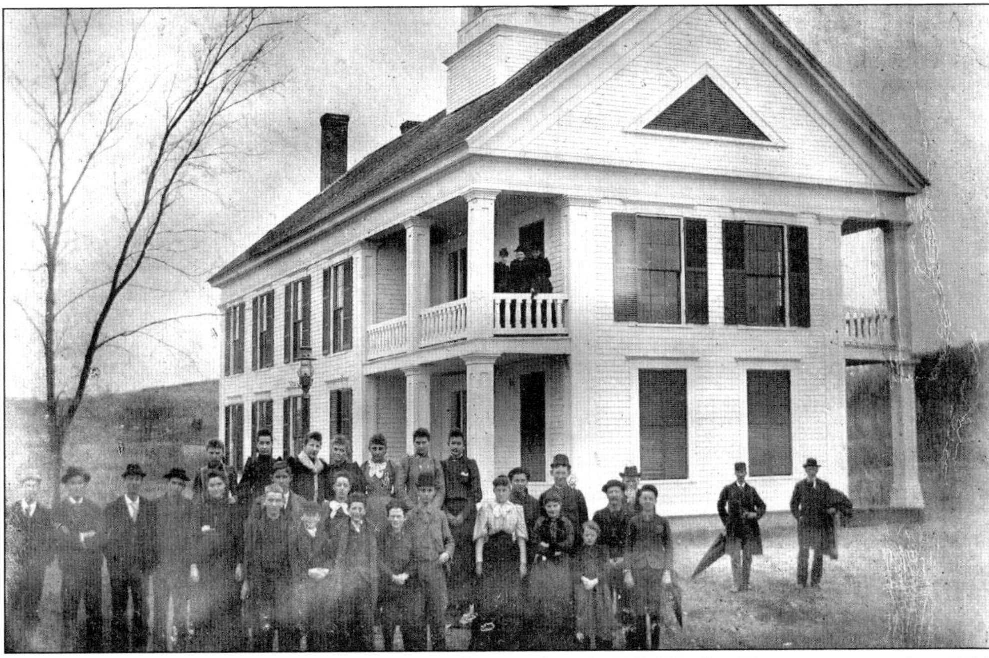

This photograph of Limington Academy students is dated 1895. The building was erected in 1854. The hill behind the school shows the land was no longer forest. Today the Limington Academy Trustees still own the building and the Maine School Administrative District (MSAD) No. 6 rents space for H. B. Emery Jr. Elementary classes.

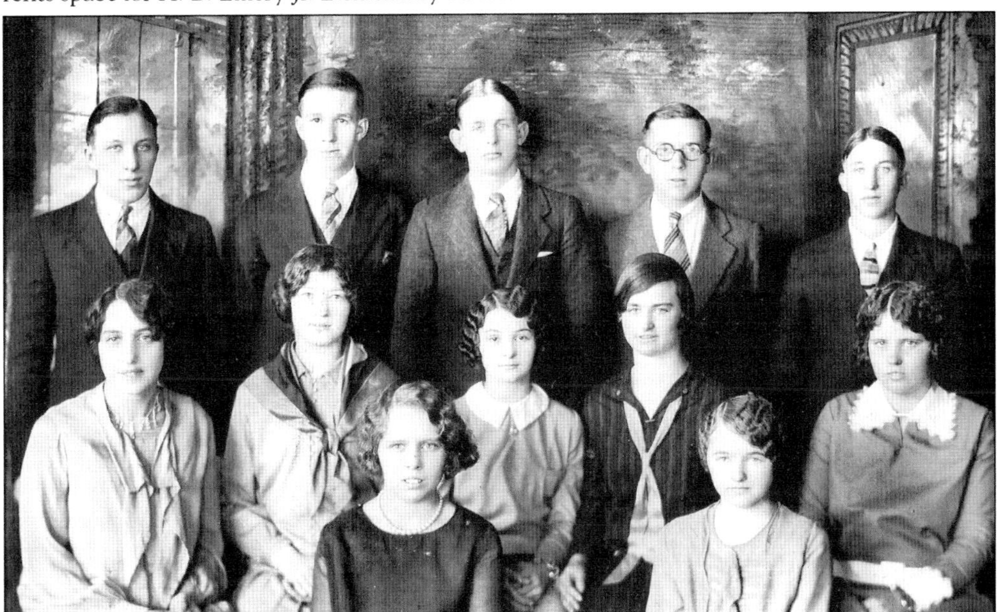

Limington Academy students posed for their class picture in 1928. From left to right, they are (first row) Elinor Blake (née Edgecomb) and Elsie Thorne (née Boothby); (second row) Doris Varnum (née Batchelder), Helen Merrifield, Katherine Chick (née Pulsifer), Elsie Moulton, and Dorothy Usher; (third row) Elmer Meserve, Arthur Libby, Don Taylor, Kenneth Weeman, and Maurice Gammon. Abner Braley was not present for this photograph.

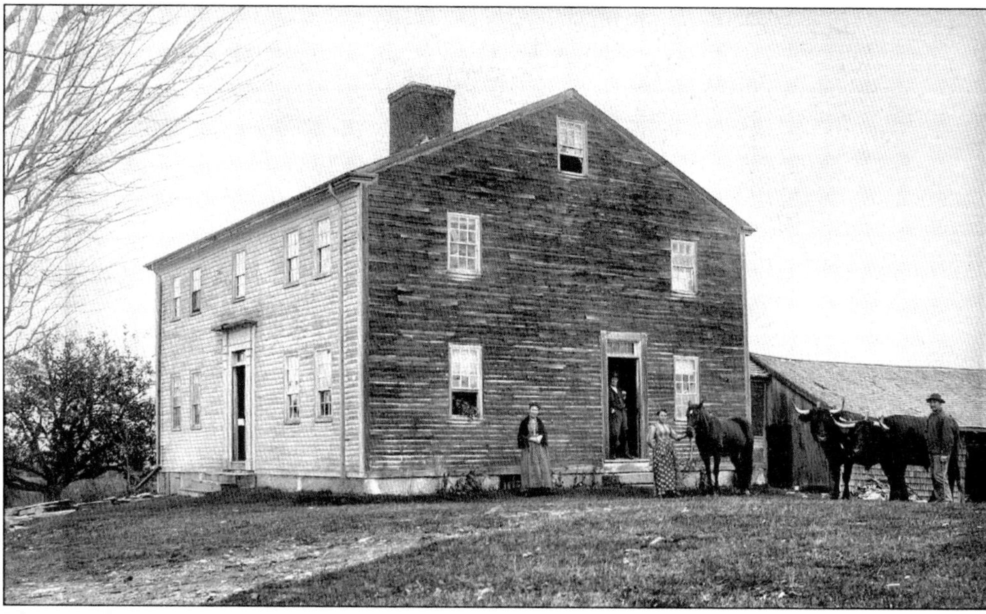

The Dearborn farmhouse on the Boothby Road was built in the 1830s by Asa Boothby who is buried on the property. A farmer by the name of Jacobs left his farm and 100 acres to George H. Dearborn in 1899. George later married Sara Boothby, a widow and the next door neighbor. Both farms came together to total 200 acres and are still in the Dearborn family.

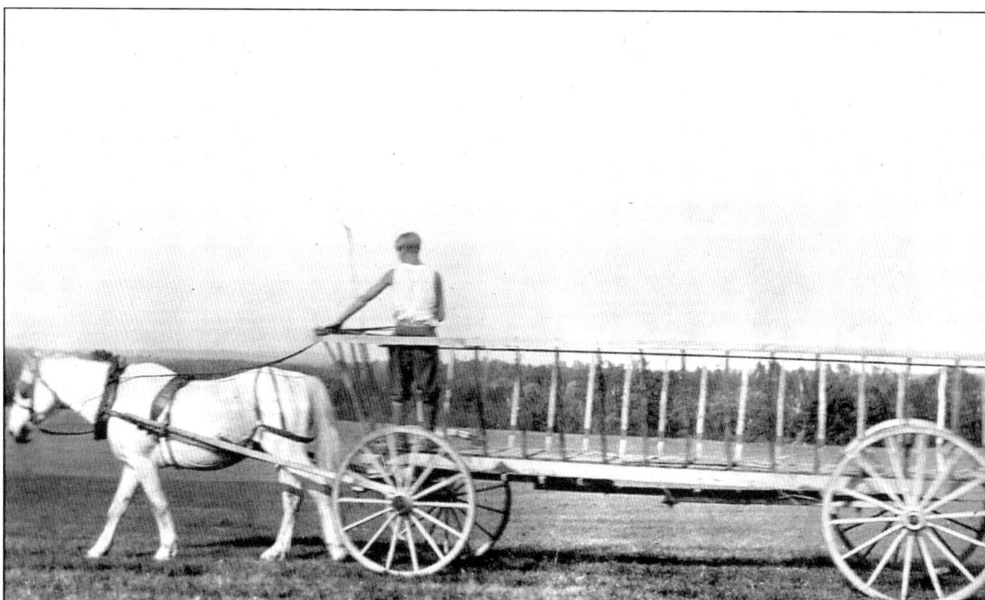

Rob Dearborn is driving the hay wagon built by his brother George B. Dearborn. Through World War II, horses were used when possible instead of tractors because of gas rationing. Most local farmers used the horses they still had to work on the farm and in the woods.

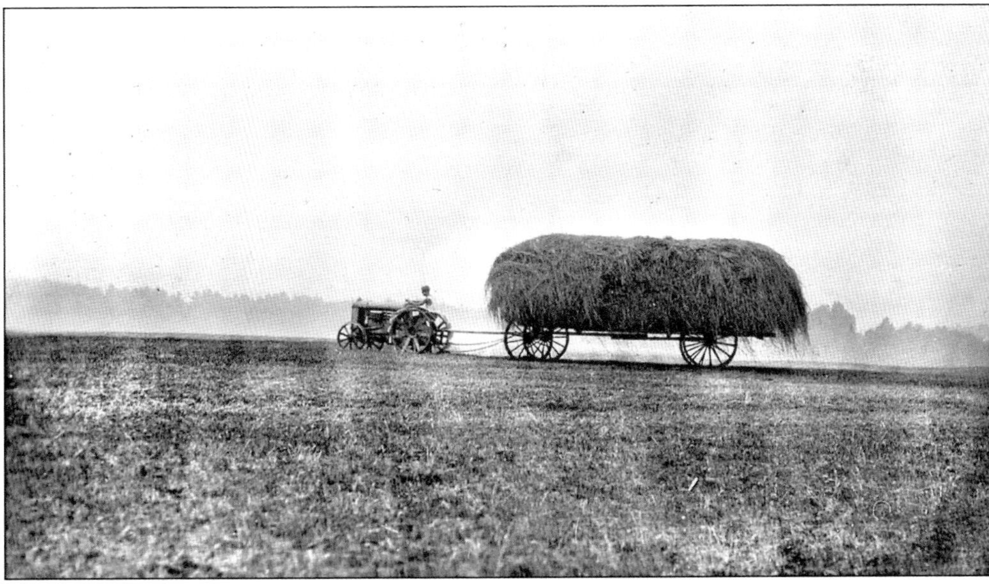

Rob Dearborn, younger son of George H. Dearborn, is shown pulling a nice load of hay using a Fordson tractor in the 1920s. Rob was a driver in the spring log drives down the Saco River and kept cows at his farm.

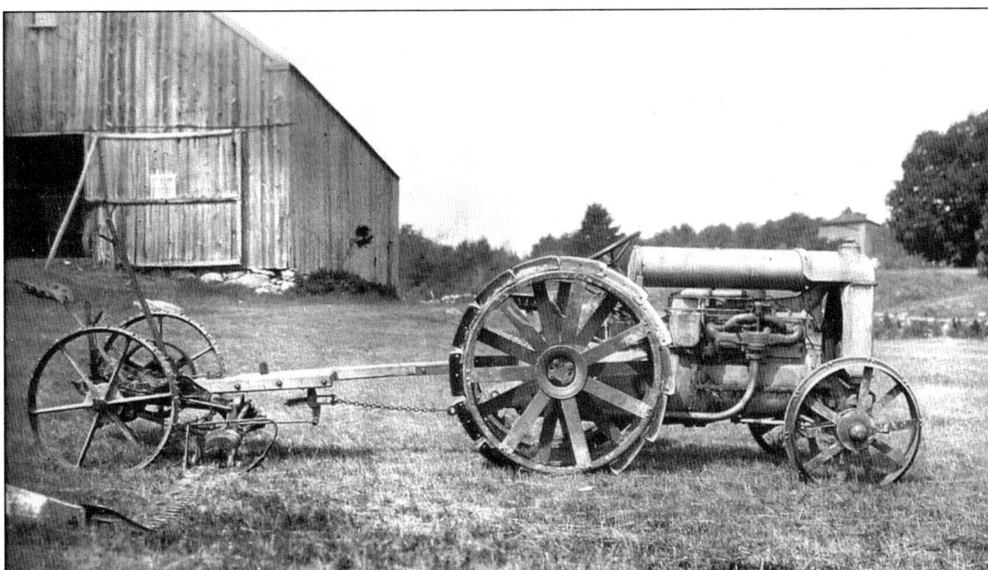

The Fordson tractor that replaced the horse in the field is parked in front of the barn on the Dearborn Farm. It was started with a hand crank and then it kicked like a mule.

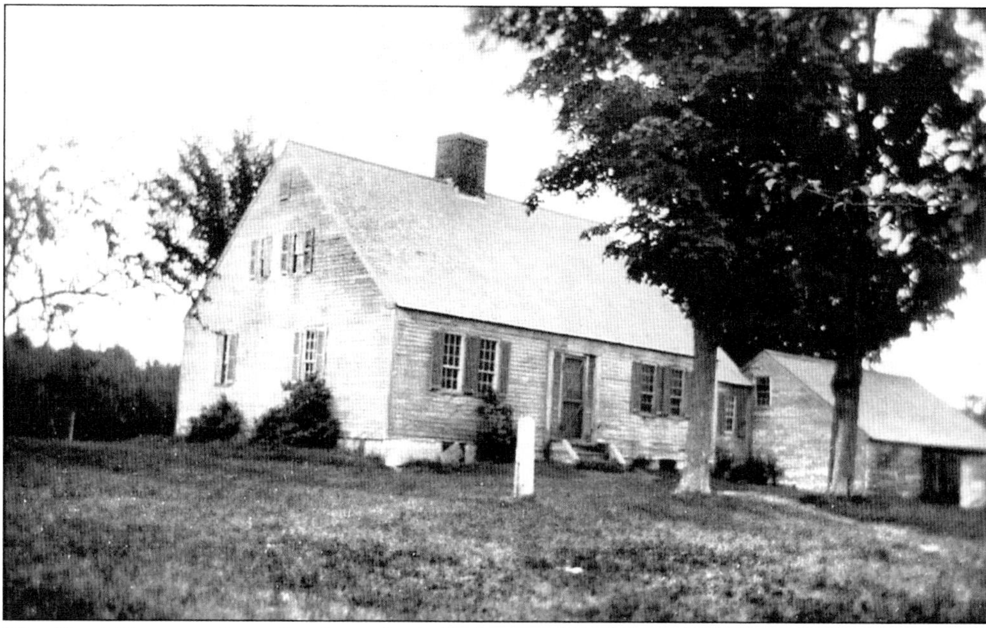

The Hurd Place on Cape Road was built by Issac Hurd in the early 1800s. Issac, his son Issac Jr., and grandson Andrew Jackson (Jack) Hurd lived there until he died. His widow Annie then sold the house to John Frank McKenney in 1897. The house burned in 1942 and Delmont Estes built on the site.

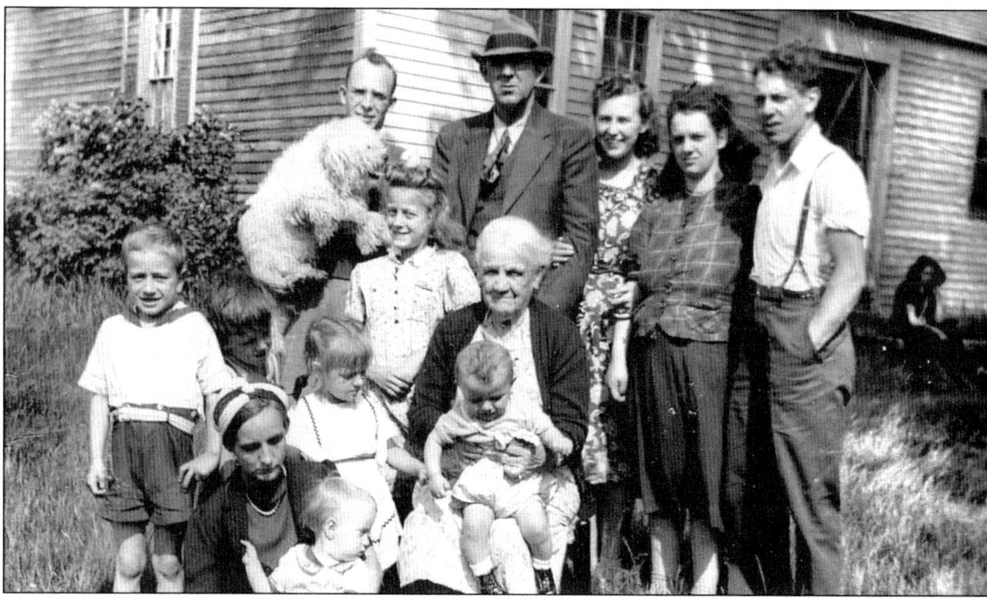

"Gram" Artie S. P. McKenney, age 83, is holding Everett and Mildred McKenney's first-born son. Sitting on the ground, Mona Braley, age 26, is holding her son Roger William (Billy) who is 16 months old. Behind her, Mona's four other children, from left to right, David Reynolds, 7; Harold Keith, 5; Janice Elaine, 3; Bernice Madelyn, 10. Standing behind Gram is Emery Johnson McKenny, 53. Johnson is standing between his son Reginald, 24, and his daughter Margaret, 18. On the right is Emery's son Everett and his wife, Mildred, both age 22. Gram's house, which is in the background, burned five months later, in October 1942.

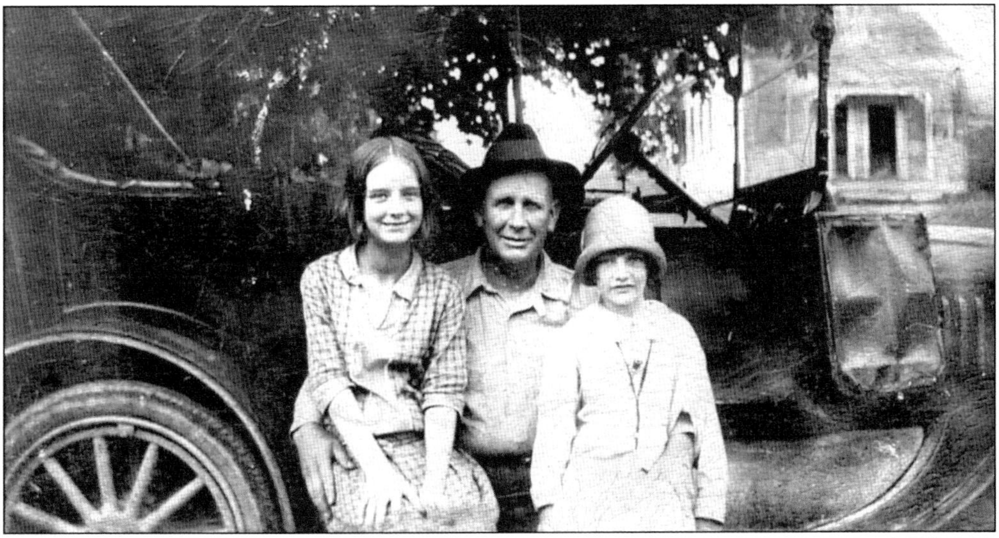

In 1927, from left to right, Mona Belle McKenney, William H. McKenney, and Ellen E. Hendrickson are sitting on the running board of a 1923 Ford. The Bean School can be seen in the background. Edith Hendrickson, Ellen's mother, was keeping house for the McKenney's after Mona's mother, Myrta, had died.

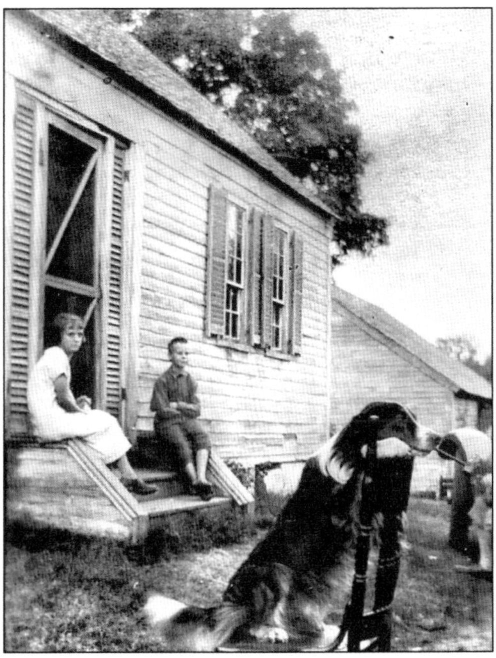

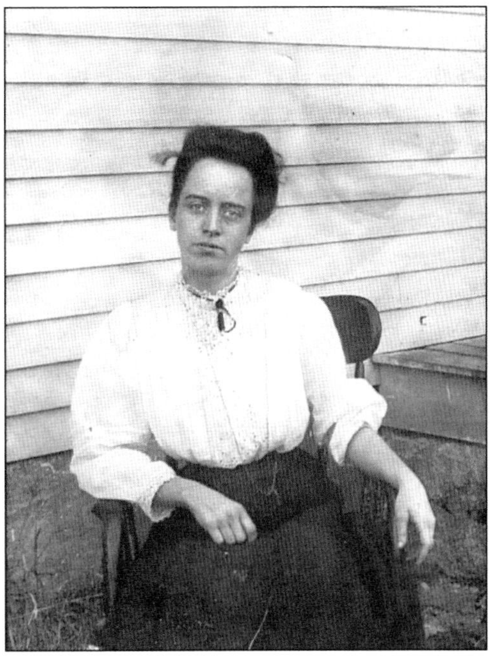

When Fred Cleveland McKenney enjoyed his after dinner pipe, Teddy, the family dog, would have his own corncob pipe. Mona McKenney and her cousin Norman McKenney are on the front steps of the house. Myrta Libby McKenney, at age 25, taught at the Franklin School in Franklin Square, North Limington. Myrta died September 28, 1917, at age 34. The cause of death was certified as meningitis, but was probably polio.

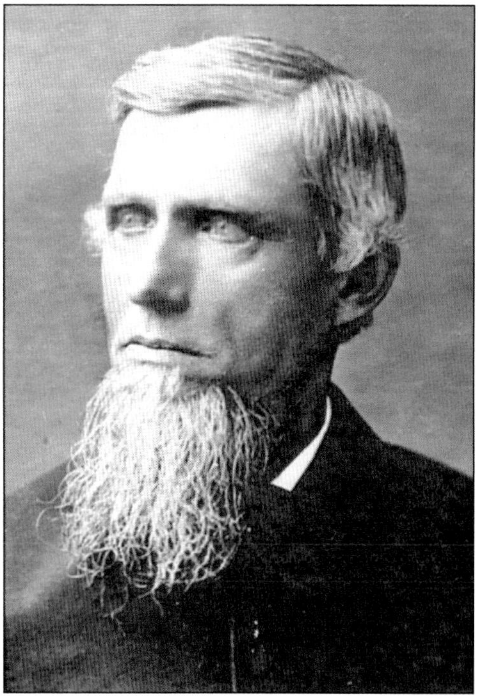

Citizens of the town pledged to build an academy and a board of trustees was elected in 1848. William G. Lord, who had graduated from Colby College, was called back to Limington to be principal. Lord was principal of the academy from 1851 to 1894. His residence was across the road from the academy and is still in the Lord family. Attendance at the academy was more than 100 at a time when neighboring towns had no high schools.

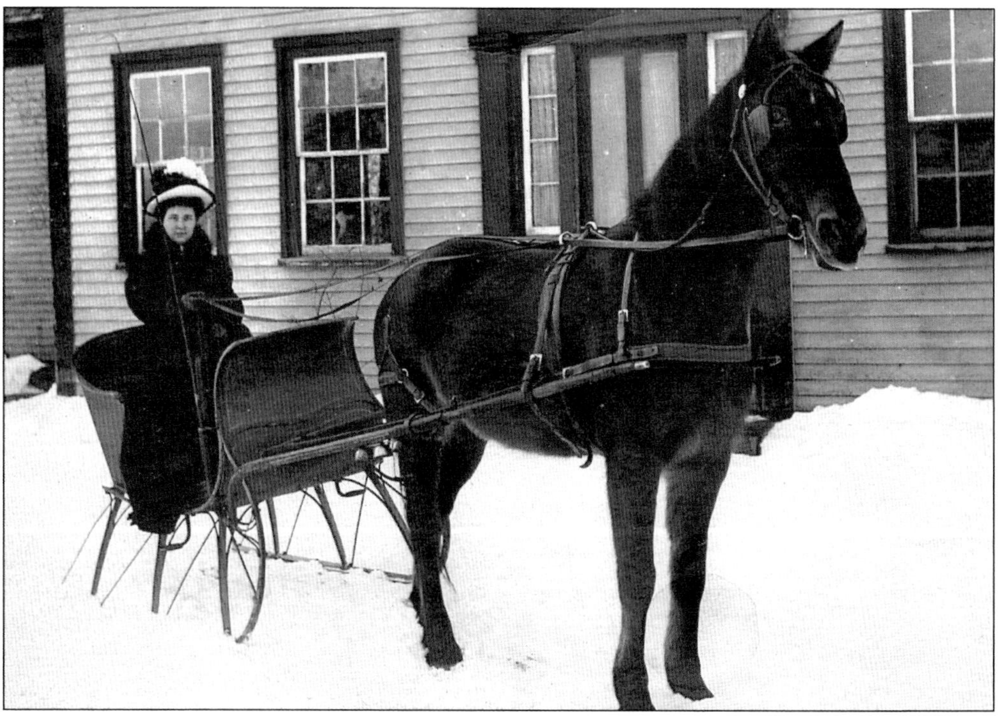

Ethel Small Maxim lived in South Limington across from the store after she married Harry Maxim. Harry and Ethel's surviving children were Herbie, Louise, and Katherine (later Dearborn Hilton). A son Francis had drowned in the Little Ossipee River in 1932. A daughter had died at an early age of whooping cough.

Josiah Elden Chase had the Octagon built in 1864 and 1865. The eight-sided house was modeled after a hatbox at Julia Chase's request. Josiah was a whaling captain and left 300 acres to his son, Charles.

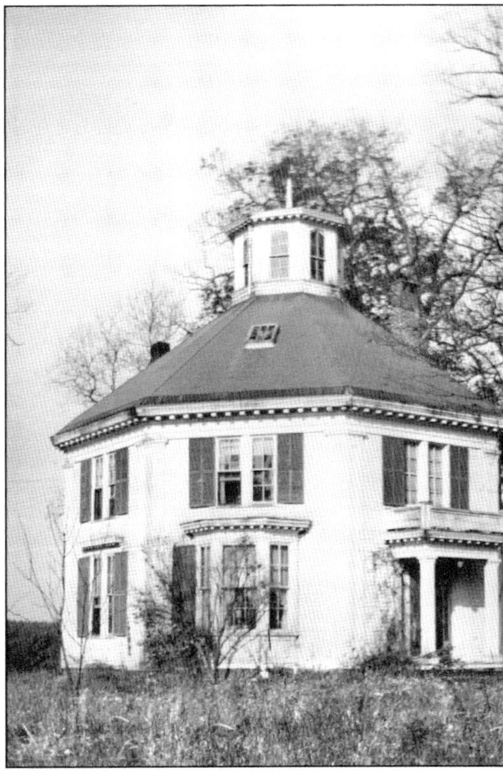

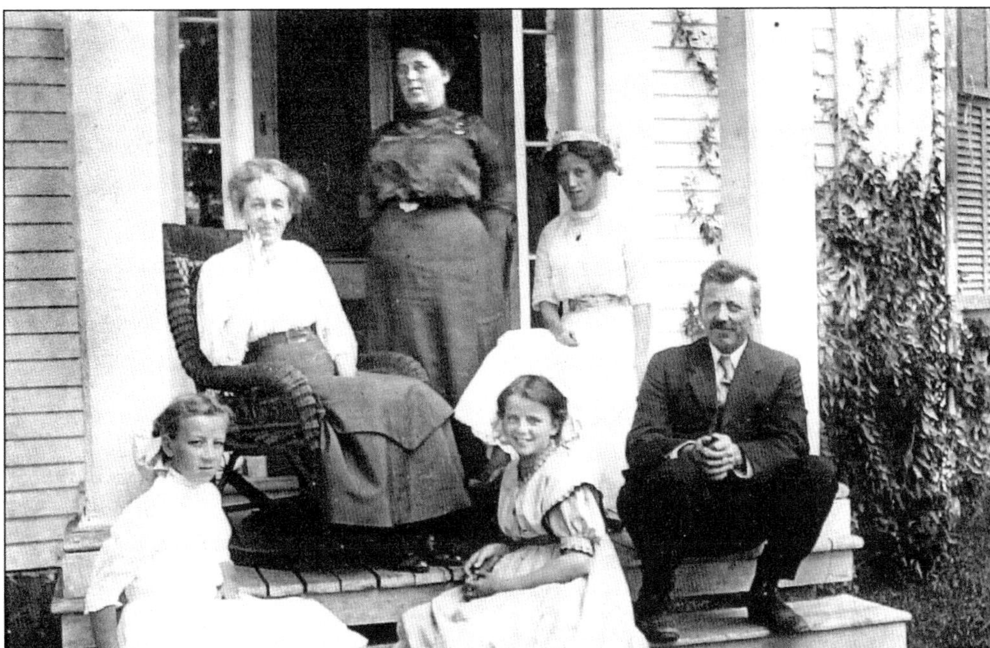

The Charles Chase family was photographed around 1908 at the front door of the octagon. From left to right are (first row) Nancy Doris Chase, Julia Catherine Chase, Charles Nichols Chase; (second row) Fannie Chase (née Meserve), Bessie Florence Chase, May Baker Chase.

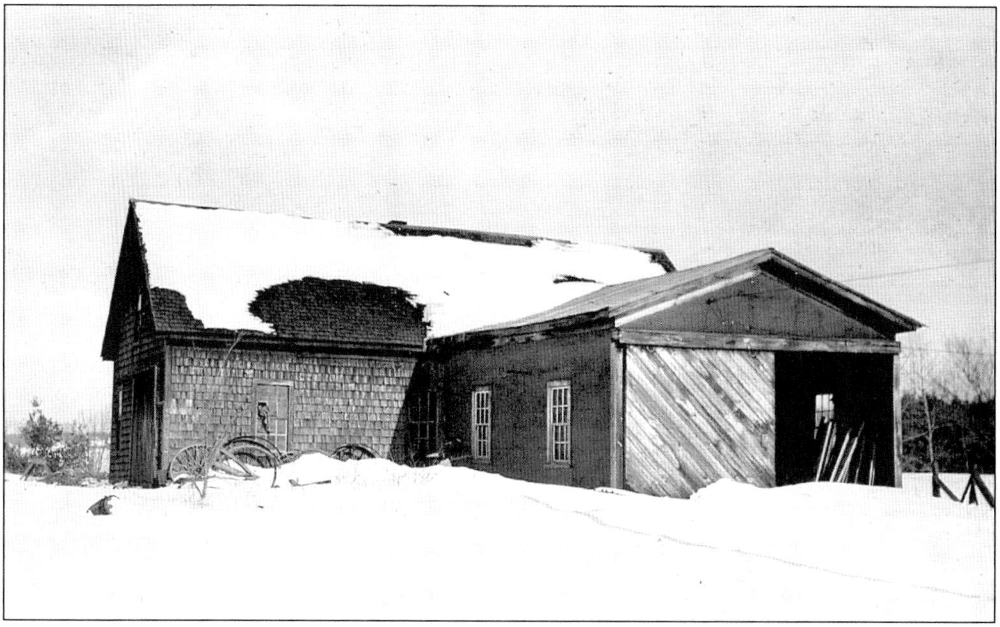

Chase's blacksmith shop is shown here in 1925. Charles Chase began blacksmithing around 1888 and was repairing snow rollers as late as 1910. The building was on the left side of the driveway to Octagon House and has since collapsed.

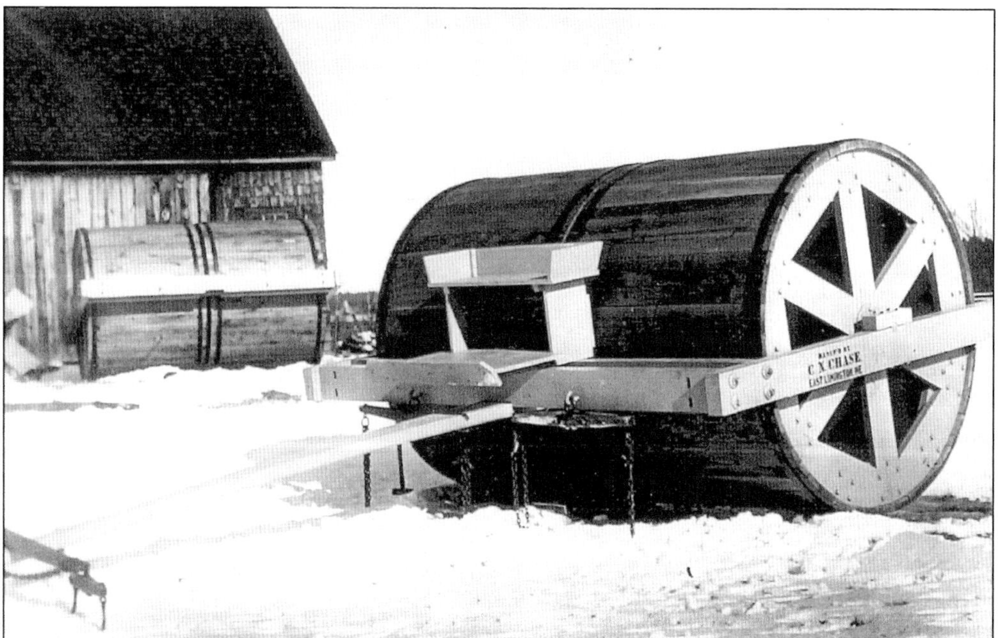

This roller is marked "Manufactured by C. N. Chase, East Limington, ME." It was one of the many snow rollers built at Chase's mill. In one year alone, they shipped over 100 by rail from Steep Falls. They were purchased by other Maine towns for winter road maintenance.

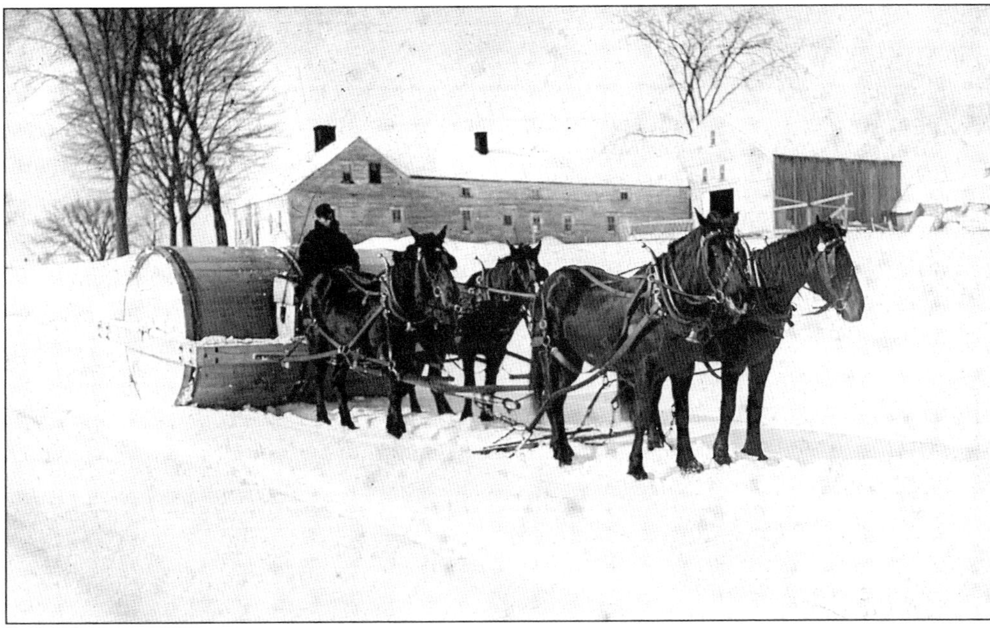

George Dearborn is driving his roller past Riverview Farm on the Ossipee Trail (Route 25).

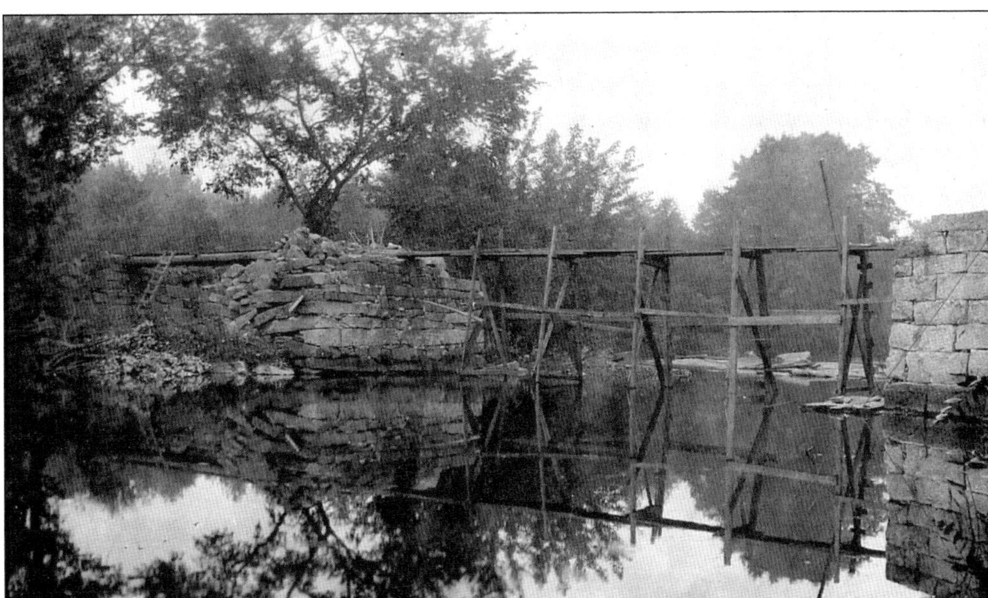

The East Limington bridge over the Little Ossipee River was undergoing repairs after being washed out in a flood during a heavy march snowstorm. A steel bridge eventually replaced the hemlock bridge over the river in 1935 and is still there today.

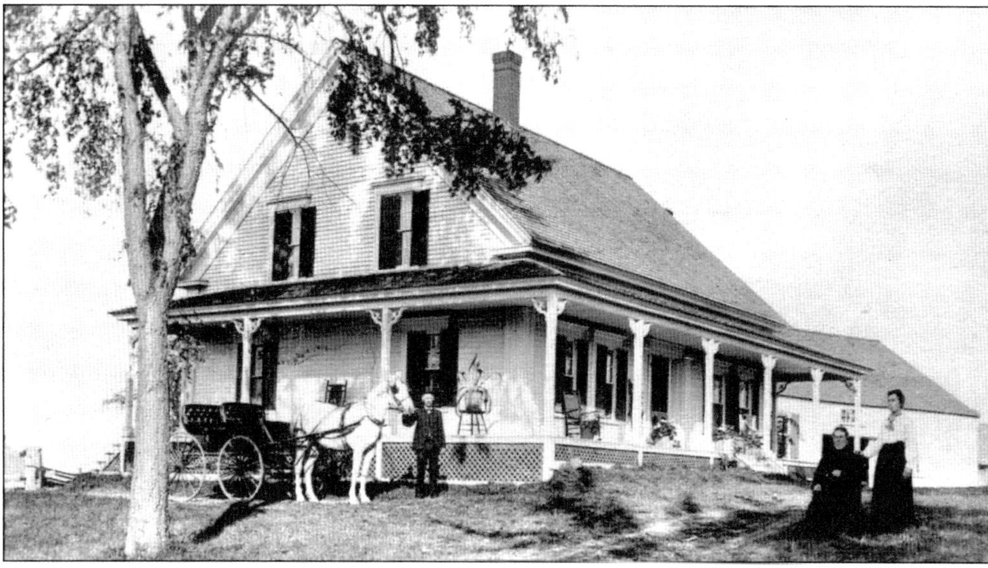

This house is located on the North Road, but the porch is no longer there. At one time it was referred to as the Maj. J. Meserve House. This became the vacation training camp and was used as a businessman's retreat.

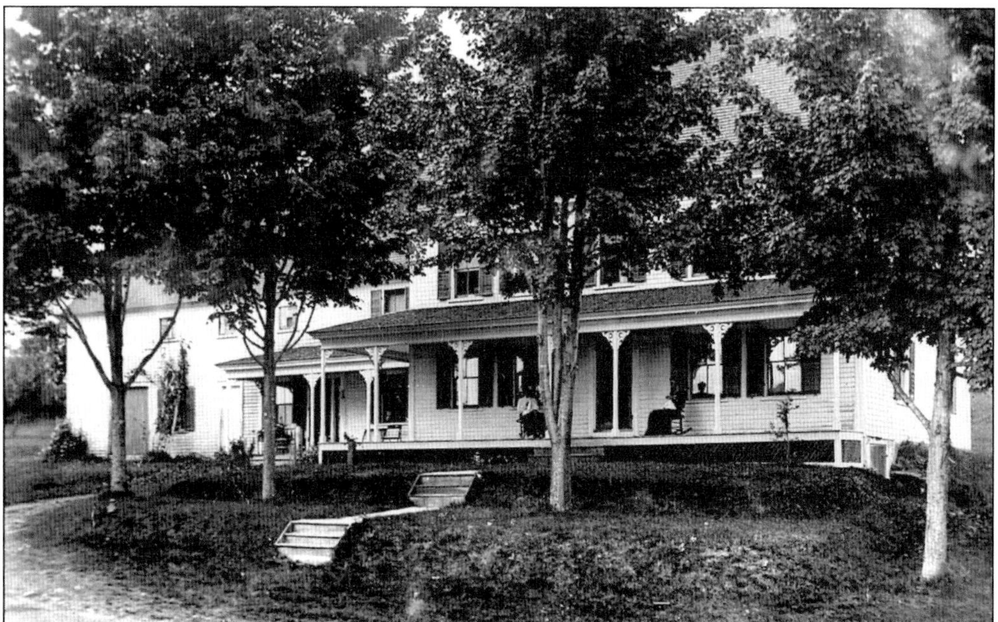

The wing and porch are gone today from this house, which was built in the early 1800s and located on Norton Road. The earliest owner was Charles Fogg (1763–1839) who was a Revolutionary War soldier and resided in Limington for 27 years. He left for Brownfield in 1816. Cephas Norton left the house to his children, Eugene and Lizzie Norton Storer. Eugene and Lizzie supposedly did not speak to one another for many years, but communicated through the cat when necessary: i.e. "The cat says . . . " The house remained empty for 20 years after Ned and Efthalia Childs moved in 1955. It is now owned by Peter and Linda Childs.

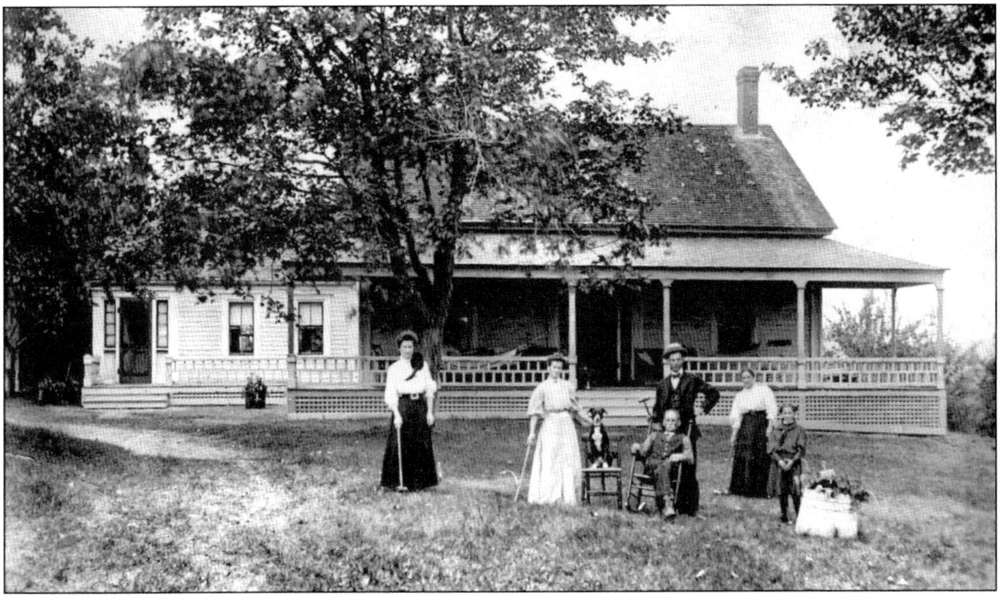

On the top of Peter's Hill (after Brackett's Orchards), this house was known as Peter's place. The house remains, but the porch is gone. Elisha Strout (1746–1811) was a Revolutionary War soldier who had come from Gorham in 1792 to settle. His descendant, Edith Strout, married Joe Peters. She had taught at the Rapid School on the Beaver Berry Road in South Limington. The school had the distinction of being the only school in town with a fireplace (built in 1897). She was town clerk for many years and was known to be a staunch Democrat.

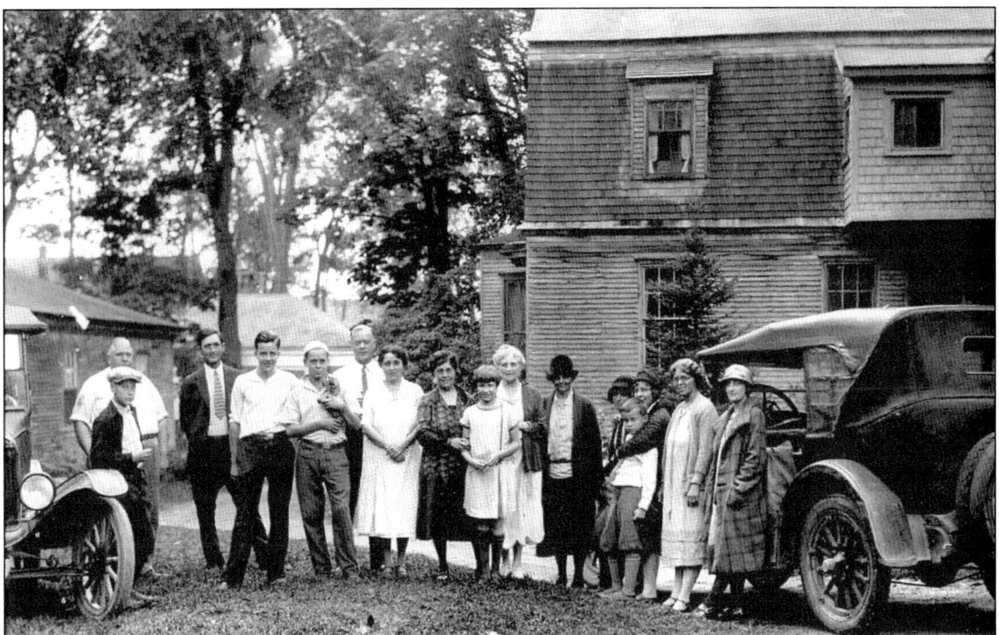

There was quite a gathering at the McArthur House around 1926. The folks included here are, from left to right, Richard Gordon Botkin, S. Perkins, Norvel Botkin, Frank Barry, Richard Yennie, Frank Barry, Princie Barry, Katherine (Katie) Perkins, Martha Barry, Isabel McArthur, Edith Peters, Barbara Peters, Isabel Yennie, David Barry, Anna Yennie, and Zetta G. Botkin.

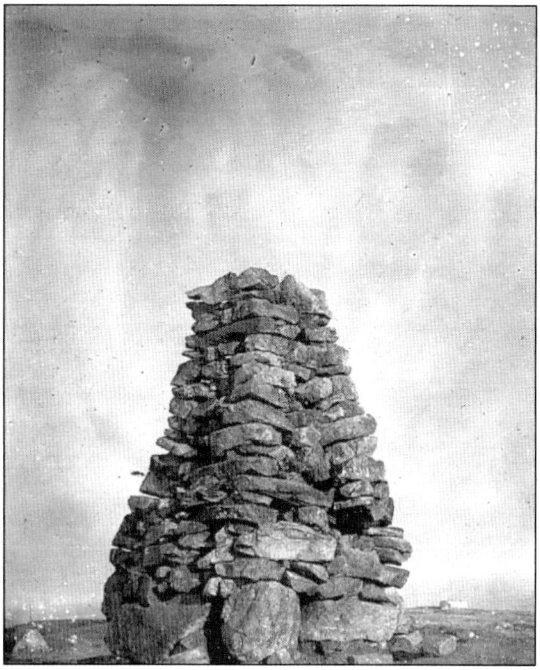

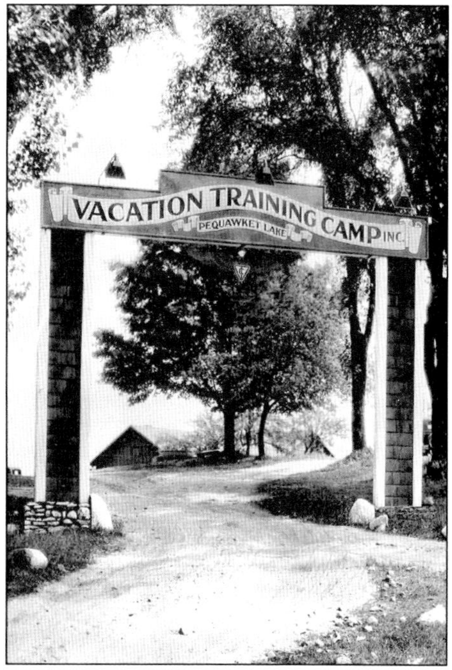

In 1884, the U.S. Geological Survey placed this stone tower 15 feet high upon Sawyer's Mountain. It was built by Autien Sawyer, great-grandson of William Sawyer for whom the mountain was named. Eventually the tower was struck by lightening and now only scattered stones remain of this landmark. This was the entrance to the Vacation Training Camp Incorporated, at Pequawket Lake, in Limington, Maine. It was located at the end of the North Road before the intersection with Hanscom School Road. It is remembered by few of today's residents. It is believed that it was attended by businessmen as a retreat.

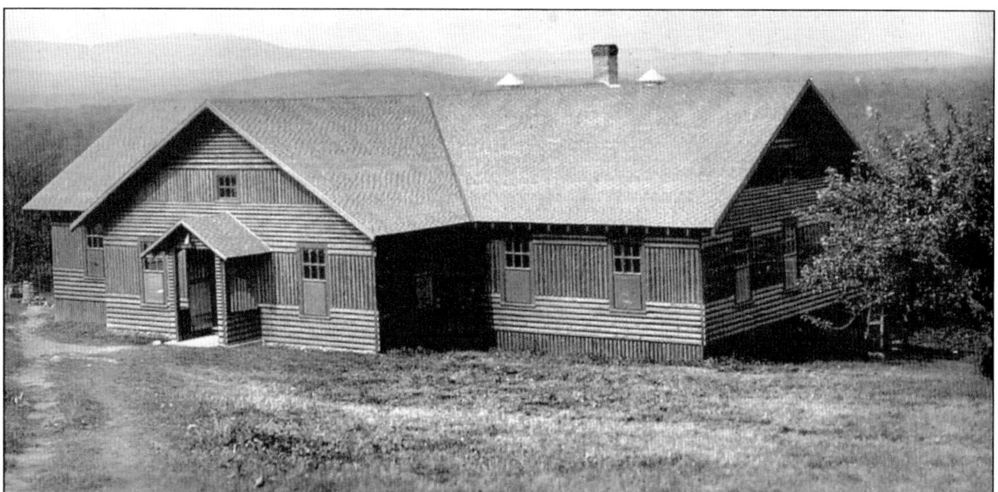

This mess hall must have been the largest building at the camp. The siding is typical of that manufactured at Hubbard's mill in East Limington. The mill produced this log siding for portable camps that would be used on woodland job sites. It was told that this camp project kept the mill busy for quite a while. The mill workers not only worked the materials but completed the construction.

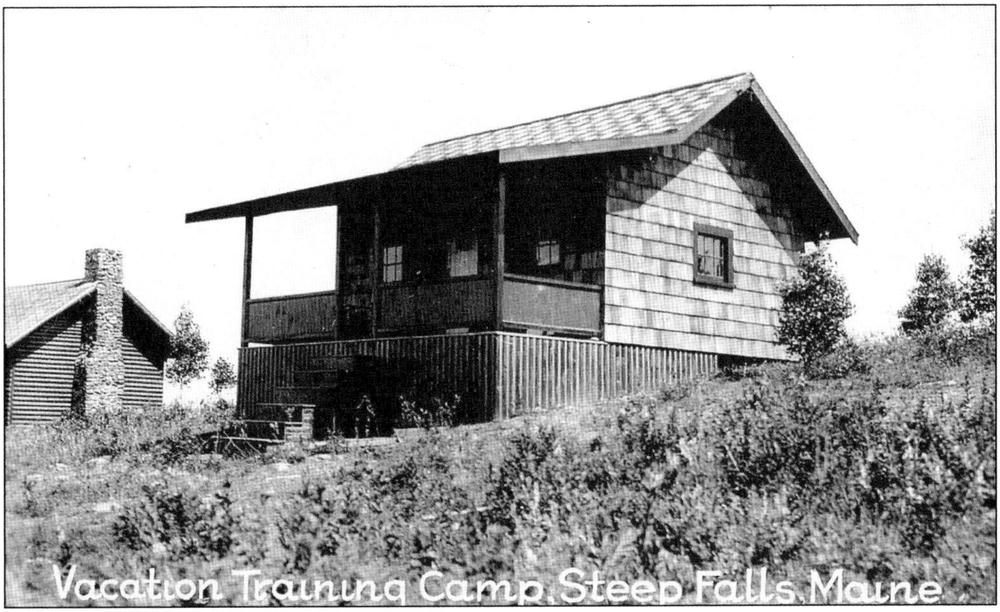

This cottage at the camp is very much in the open and would have had a good view of the surrounding countryside. Today the area is overgrown around the remaining abandoned camps.

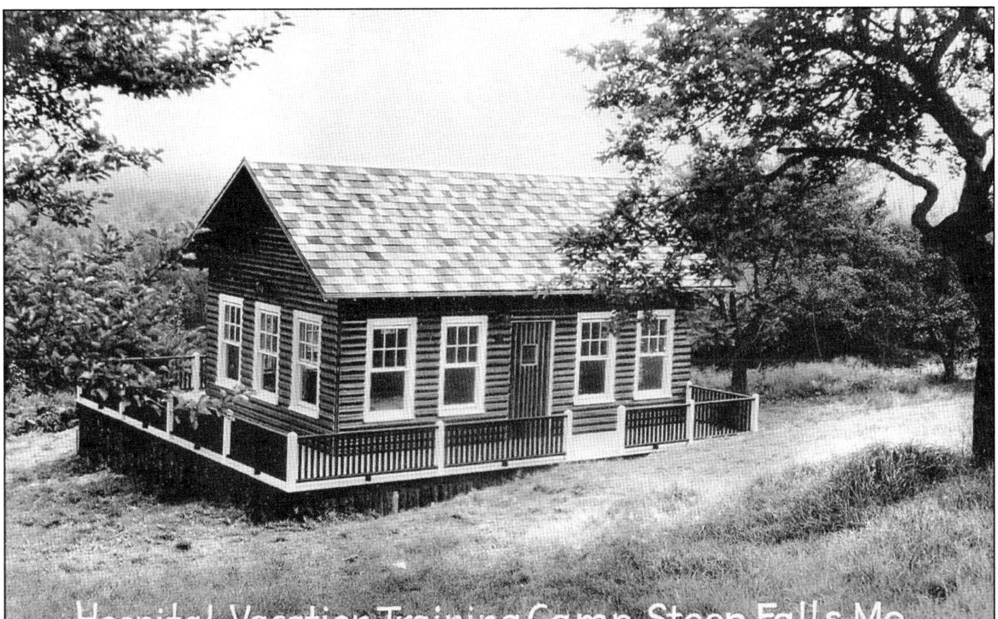

This postcard shows the wonderful detailed workmanship that went into the construction of these buildings. The mail in those days came through the Steep Falls post office as noted on the picture.

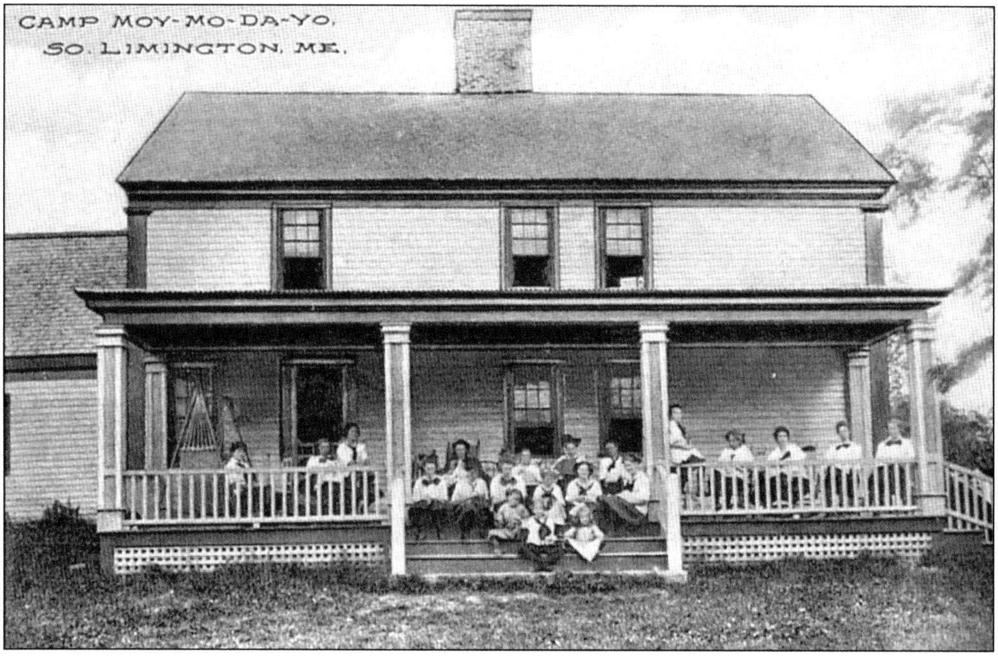

Camp Moy-Mo-Da-Yo, a summer camp for girls, was founded in 1907 by two retired maiden school teachers, Elizabeth Moody (1863–1919) and Helen Mayo. The old Randall place on Moody Road was used as the first building. That building burned in January of 1918, and the women moved to Pequawket Lake.

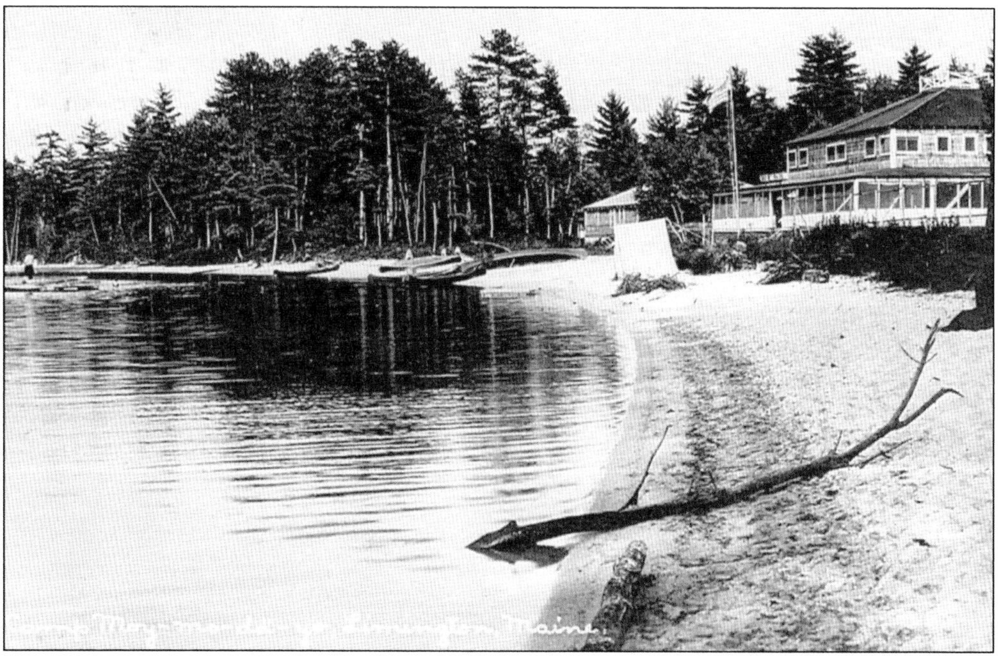

Camp Moy-Mo-Da-Yo relocated to Pequawket Lake (also known as Horne Pond) on 50 acres of tall pine trees edged by 3,000 feet of waterfront. It was a beautiful setting for 85 to 90 girls, ages 7 to 18. Herbert B. and Eleanor Downs were the last owners when the camp closed. The town of Limington now owns the property. This postcard is dated 1923.

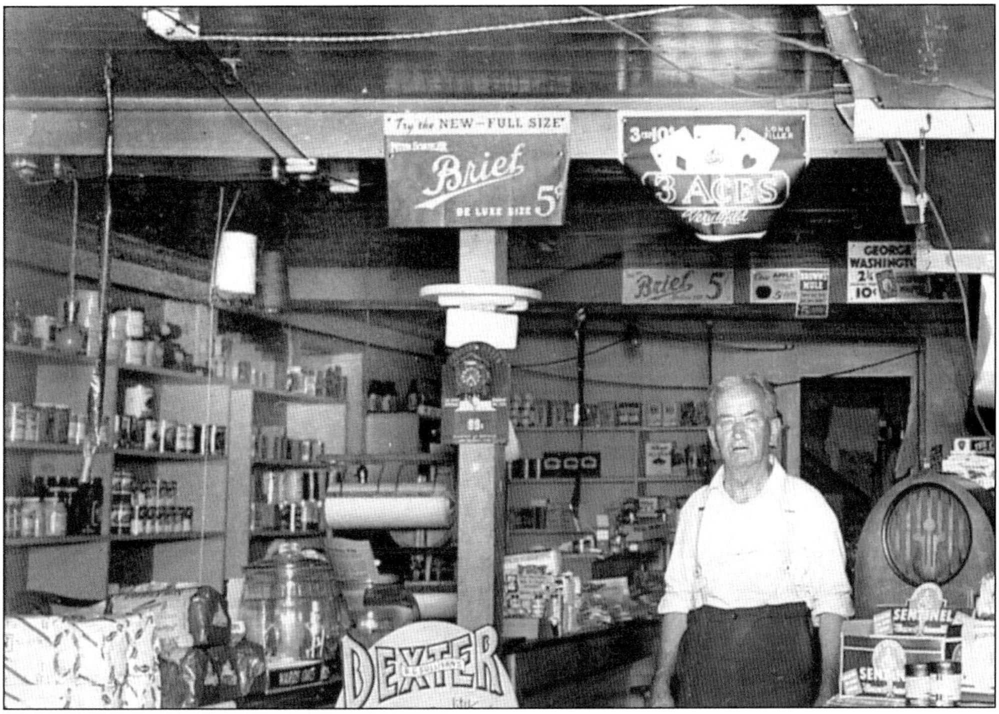

Ed Peter Chick is ready to help in his General Store (Nationwide Products) located on the first floor of the Masonic hall in the 1930s.

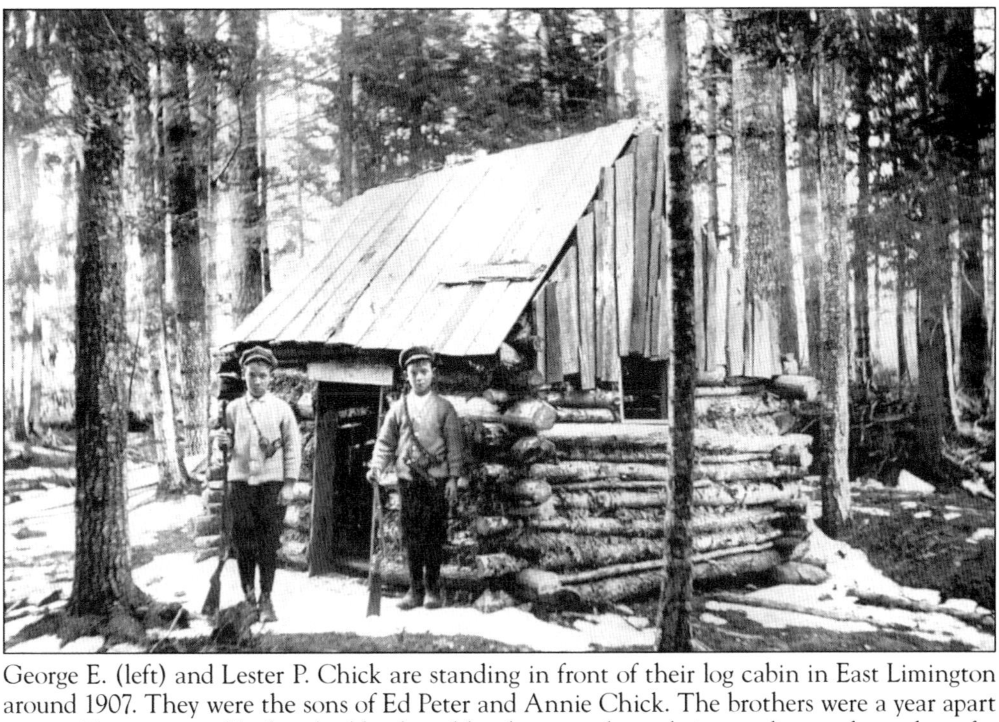

George E. (left) and Lester P. Chick are standing in front of their log cabin in East Limington around 1907. They were the sons of Ed Peter and Annie Chick. The brothers were a year apart in age. Trappers would often build cabins like this one along their trap line and use them for storage and as a shelter.

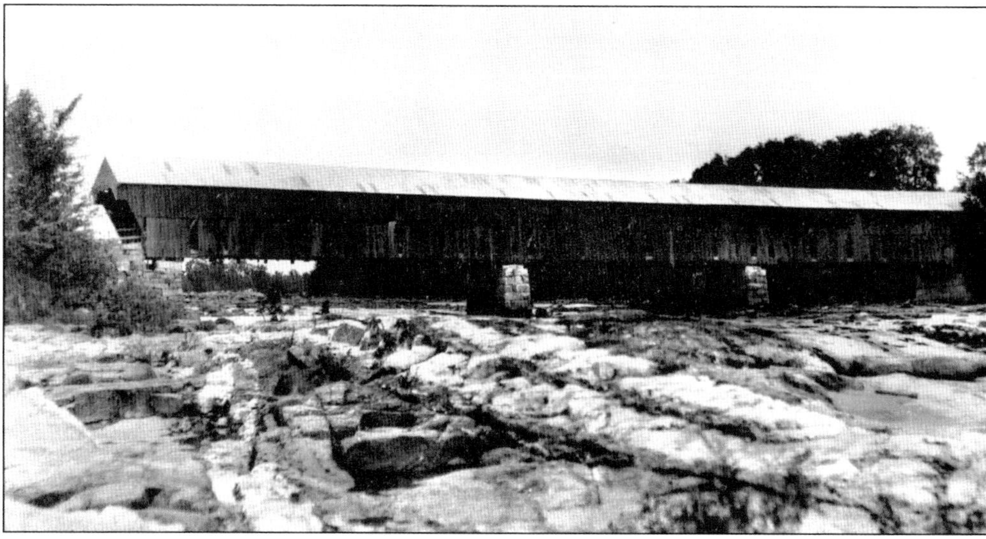

The covered bridge over the Saco River was built about 1894. It was replaced in 1927. The town used to pay men to snow the bridge to make it easier for horse drawn sleighs to go forward.

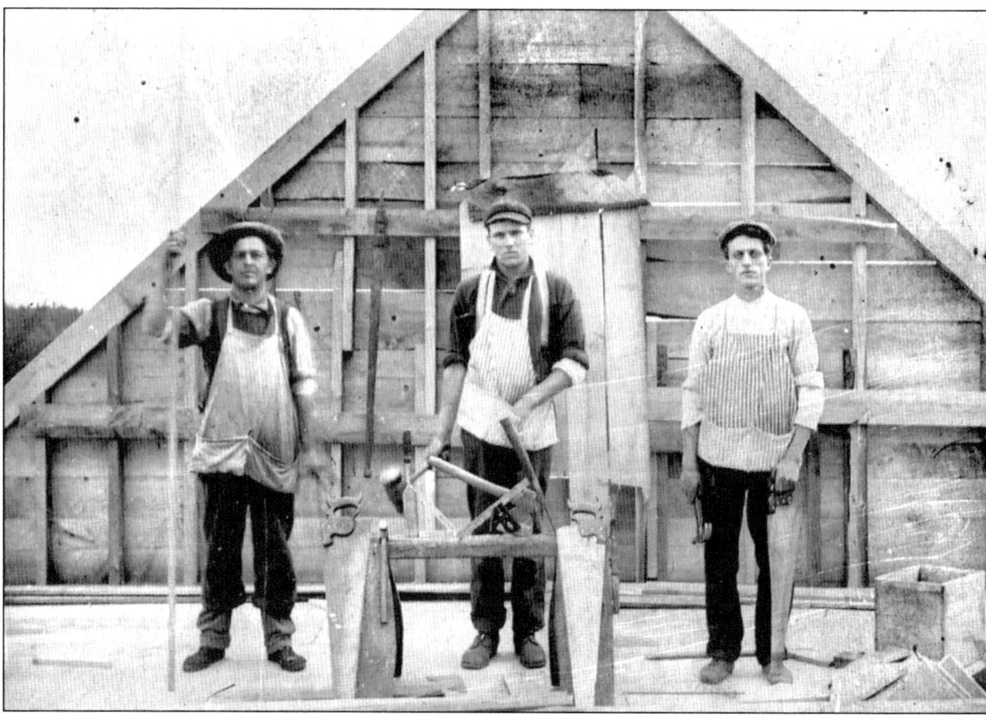

The year was 1910. These farmers and woodsmen would help each other as carpenters. Shown are Rudy Burnham, Will Meserve, and John Boothby.

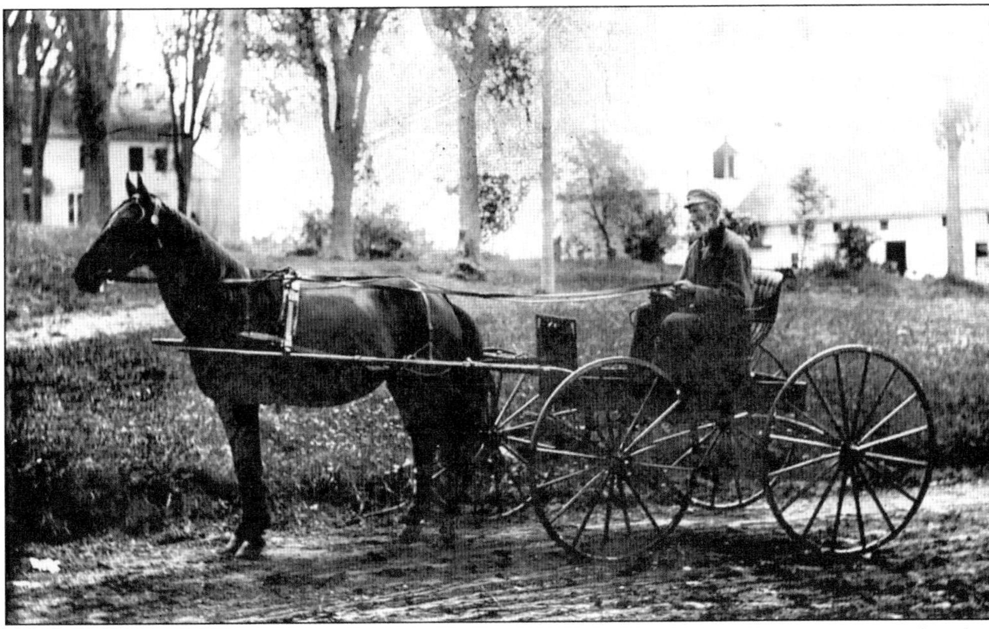

Martin Richardson, shown here, was the father of Bill Richardson. Bill was the town butcher and never married. The Richardson's place is two houses below the Congregational Church. At times during Sunday services, pigs could be heard squealing. He always wore a Mackinaw and an old felt hat no matter what the season. He loved to listen to the dance music while leaning against the porch outside the Grange Hall.

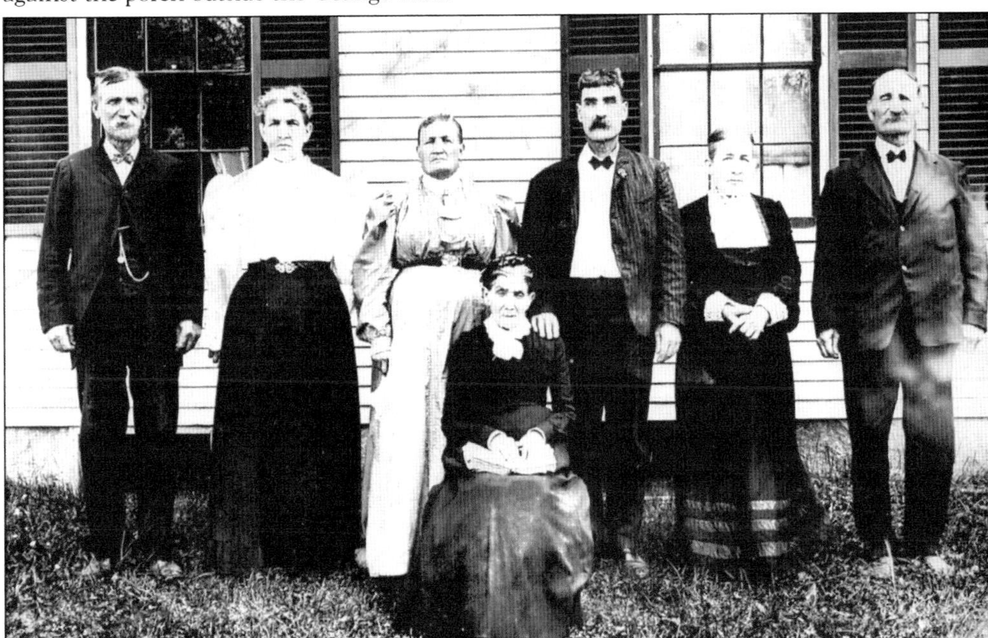

The Joy family posed for this portrait. From left to right are, Joseph Allen Joy (who died on the old home place), Ellen Joy (née Lady), Sabra Joy Wentworth of Saco, Grandmother Joy, Wendell Joy, Ellen Joy Warren, and Samual Woodbury Joy. The Joy house is still standing on Joe Joy Road. It was first settled in 1808.

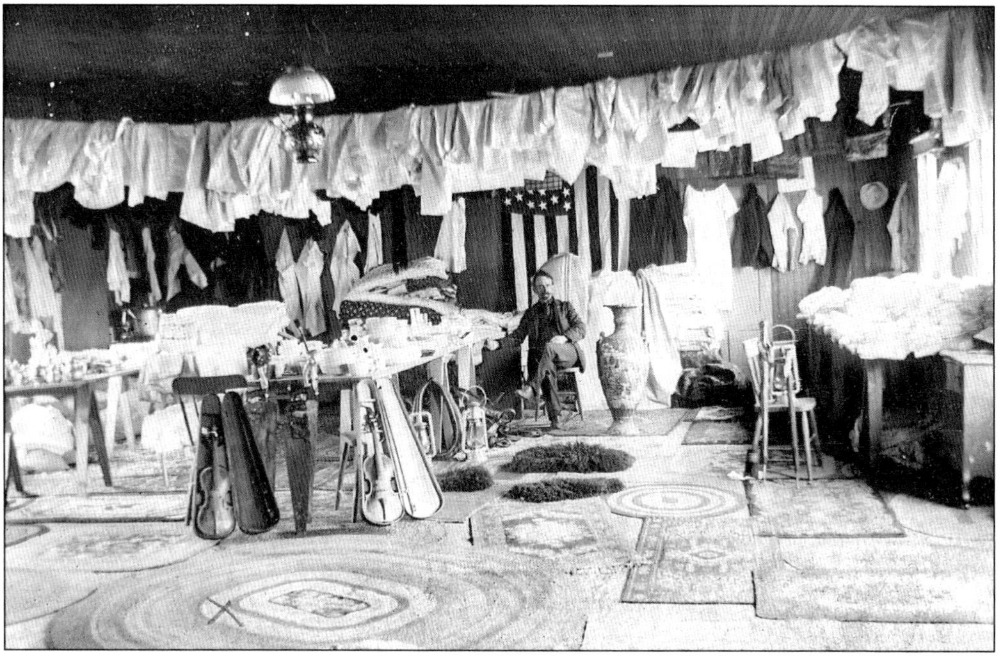

The picture was handed down from Will Meserve. It was from his wife, Hattie Belle Burnham's grandmother and is called Stolen Goods. The "x" in the lower left of the photograph points out the rug referred to as the "Grammie Moses rug stolen from her home." We can only guess the rest of the story.

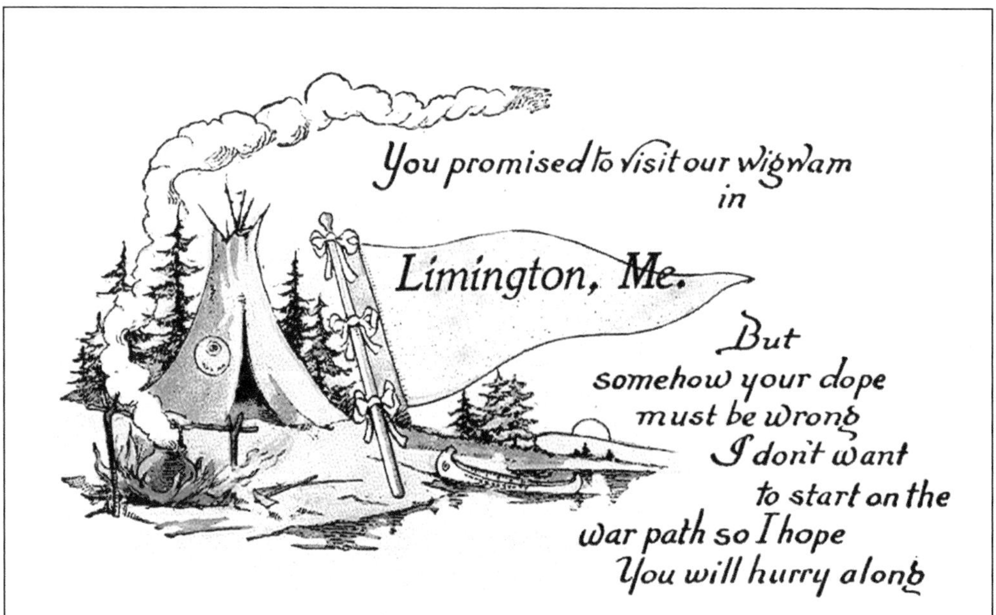

Was this a broken promise or a miscommunication?

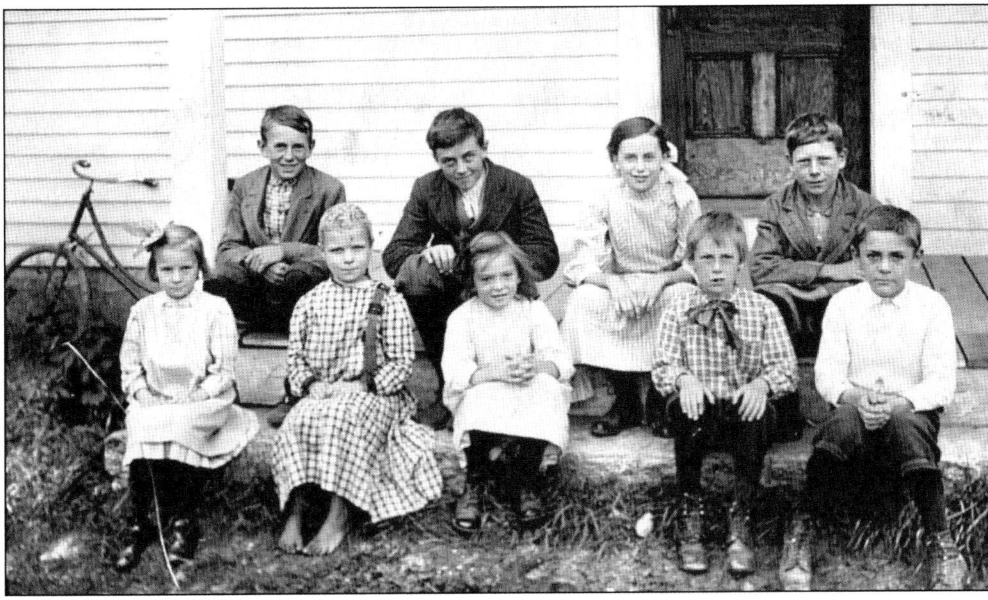

Shown here is a class of students that was typical of Limington's rural schools, of which there were as many as 17 at one time.

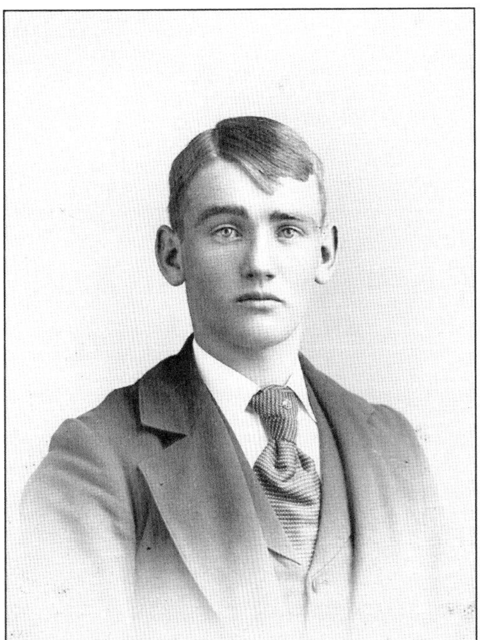

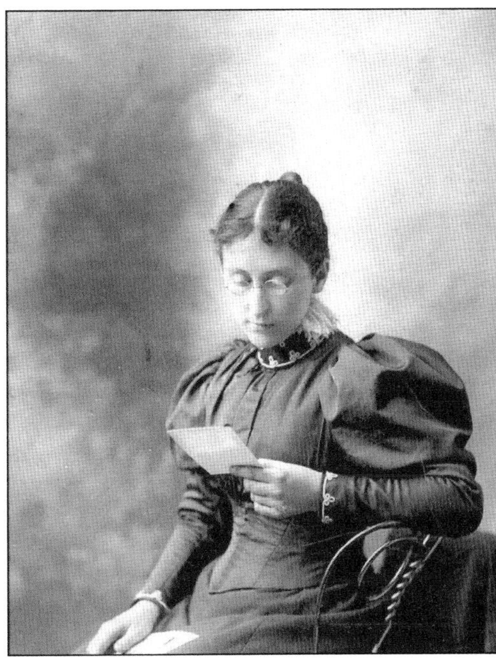

When Leander J. Moody died in July 1961, he left one quarter of his estate to be set up as a trust fund for the academy. He was survived by grandnieces and grandnephews Beverly Ann Moody, James L. Moody Jr., Winship H. Moody, Elaine J. Libby, and Helene J. Thalen, all of Gorham, Maine. Emily Mary Jones (1865–1937) was a Quaker and lived in the house across from the Village Cemetery on Pine Hill Road. As a missionary, she went to Palestine in the 1930s. She died in an automobile accident in Gorham. She was driving to Portland with friends when her hat blew off, and as she reached to catch it, she lost control of the vehicle.

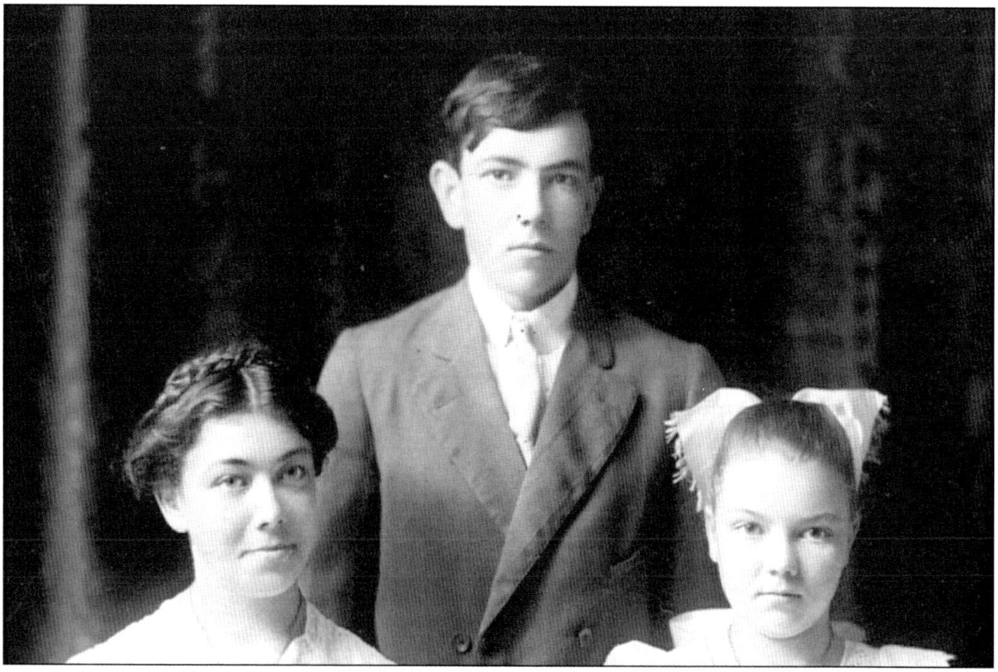

John, Pearl, and Ruth Meserve lived as children on Route 11 up on the hill near where Bob Taylor used to live. John and Ruth never married. Pearl married Elson Norton and lived in South Limington. John was a farmer and Ruth did housekeeping.

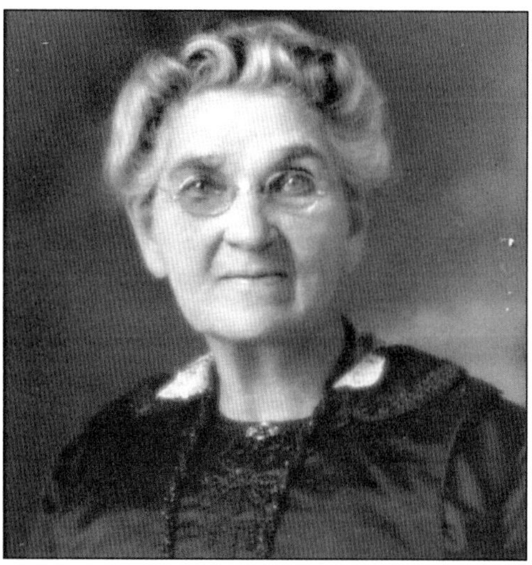

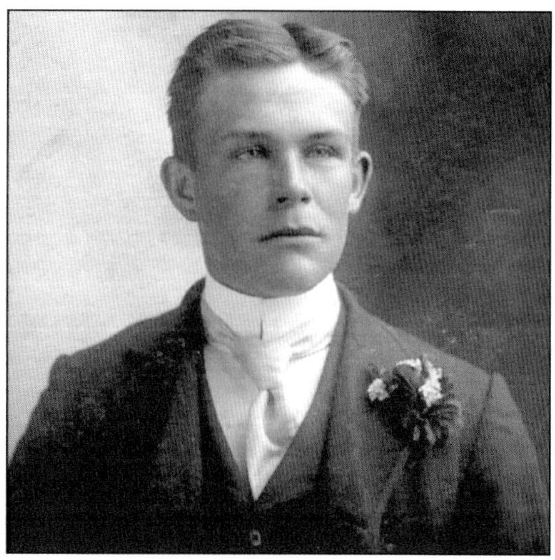

Harriet Ann McDonald (1853–1955) lived to be 103. She had married William P. Marr, a descendant of John Erskine, Earl of Marr, a Scottish nobleman who had an estate in Newcastle, Scotland. Arthur McArthur was sent to collect some inheritance after the Earl died, but was unsuccessful. Harris Paige Ilsly was born on January 12, 1887, son of Gilman S. Ilsley and Georgiana Ilsley (née Brackett). He graduated from Limington Academy in 1899 and received his medical degree from Bowdoin Medical School, with certification in 1909. Dr. Ilsly earned his college expenses by teaching school in Limington and as a conductor for the Portland Railroad Company. His practice had been wholly in his native town of Limington, but he was known throughout York County. He died in 1941.

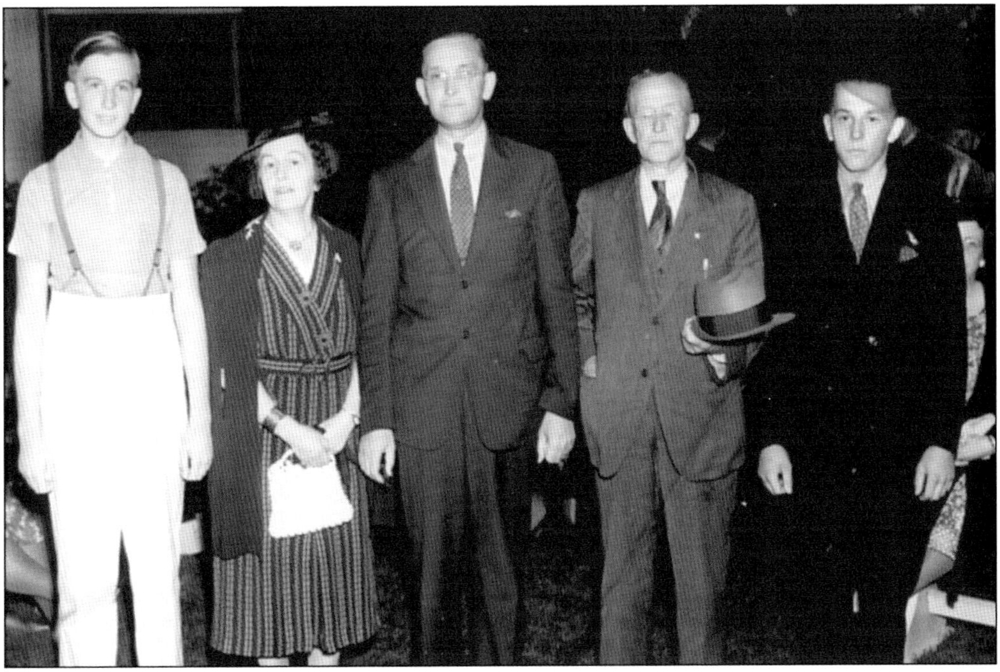

Seen here, from left to right, is Harold B. Emery Jr., his mother Gladys, his father Harold B. Emery Sr., his grandfather Charles, and Harold Jr.'s brother Edwin. Harold Jr. died in World War II and the elementary school in the village is named in his memory.

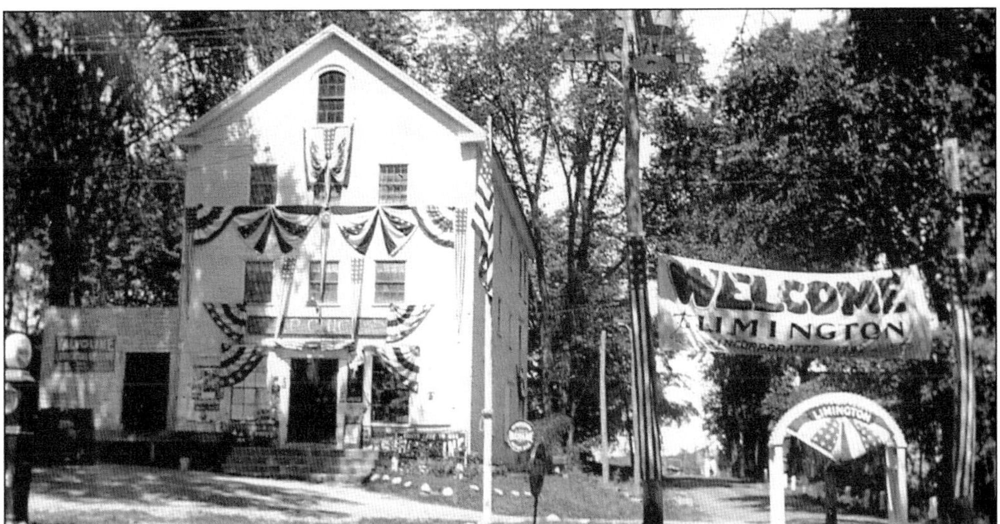

The first recorded meeting of Adoniram Lodge No. 27 had been agreed upon for December 3, 1816—the day before the full moon. The full moon helped on the journey home. The meeting was held in the chamber of James McArthur. Selected brothers were to be sent to Fryeburg in January to obtain membership. A year later in February 1817, the by-laws of the Pythagorean Lodge were signed in Fryeburg. In the summer of 1818, the brethren proceeded to build suitable quarters. The Masonic hall was decorated for the 100th anniversary celebration of Limington Academy in 1948.

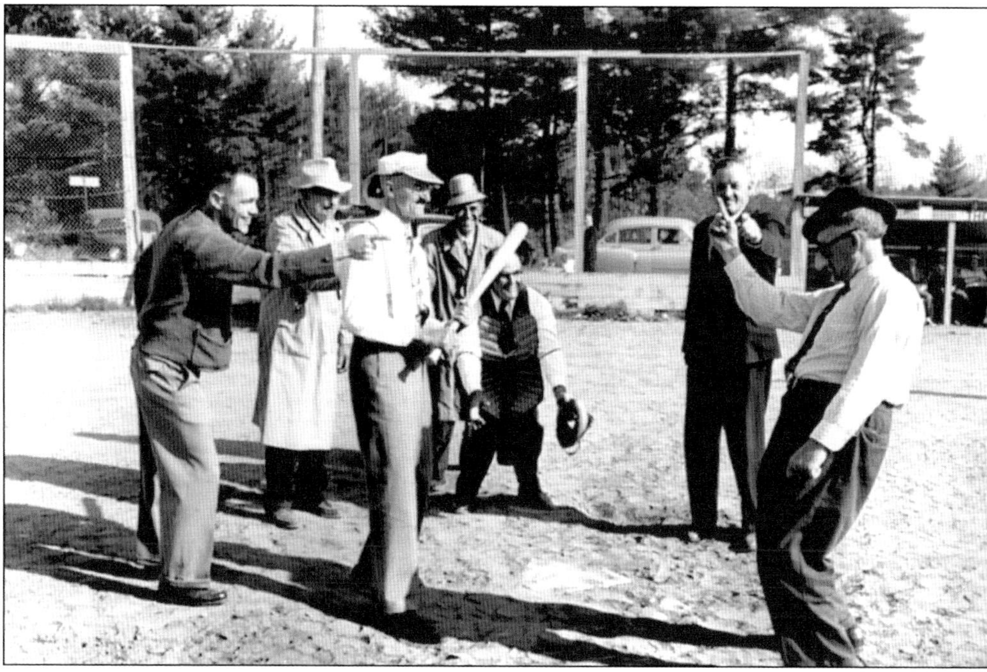

A 1948 baseball game is in full swing. Players are, from left to right, Harry Maxim, Ernest McLucas, Howard Blake, Alvah Weeman, Leon Blake, Dennis Graffam, and Rob Haley.

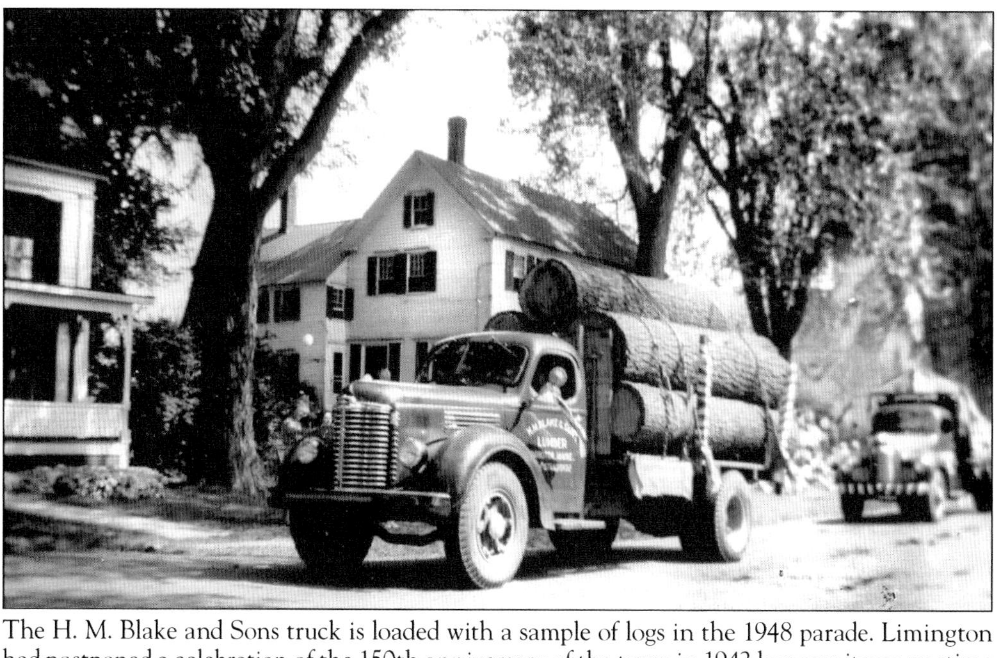

The H. M. Blake and Sons truck is loaded with a sample of logs in the 1948 parade. Limington had postponed a celebration of the 150th anniversary of the town in 1942 because it was wartime and there was gas rationing. The 100th anniversary of Limington Academy was in 1948, so both occasions were celebrated that summer.

Four

NEWFIELD

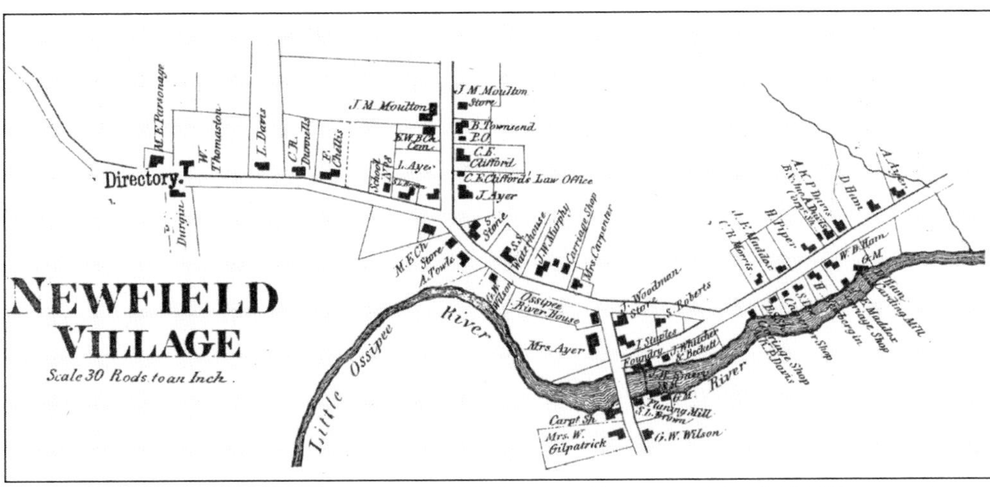

In its pioneer days, the town was known as Washington Plantation. Newfield Village was known as Dam's Mills and West Newfield Village was called Adam's Corner. On its incorporation by an Act of the Massachusetts Legislature on February 26, 1794, it officially became Newfield. Nathaniel Doe first cleared land in Newfield. In June 1777, Paul McDonald and Zebulon Libby began clearing their land. Libby, having fought in the French and Indian War, came seeking a place of peace.

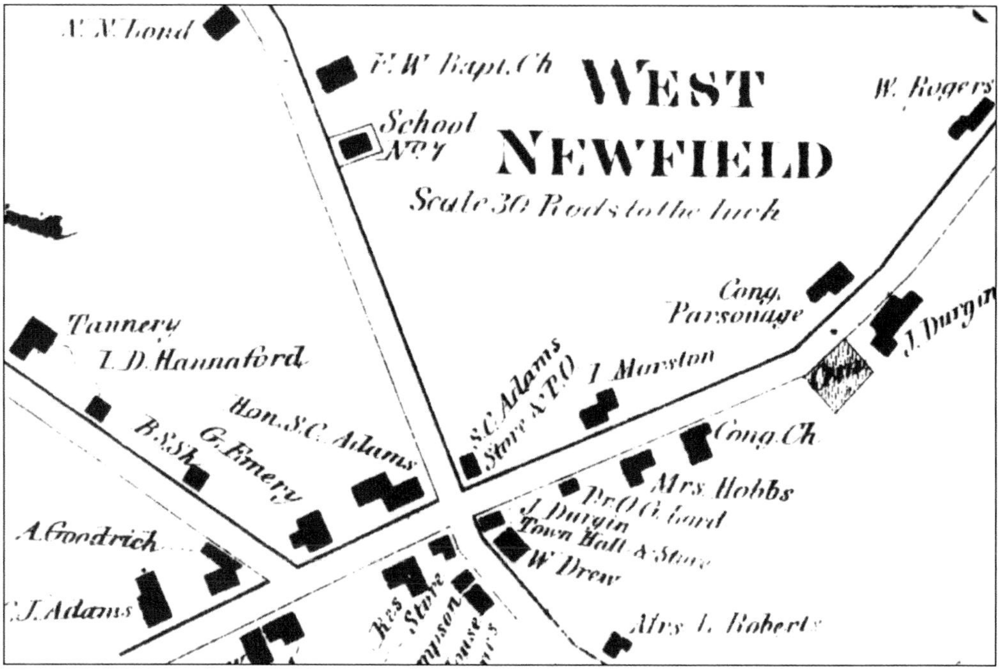

The above map shows the West Newfield Village in 1872. Many of the first settlers came directly from service in the Revolutionary armies.

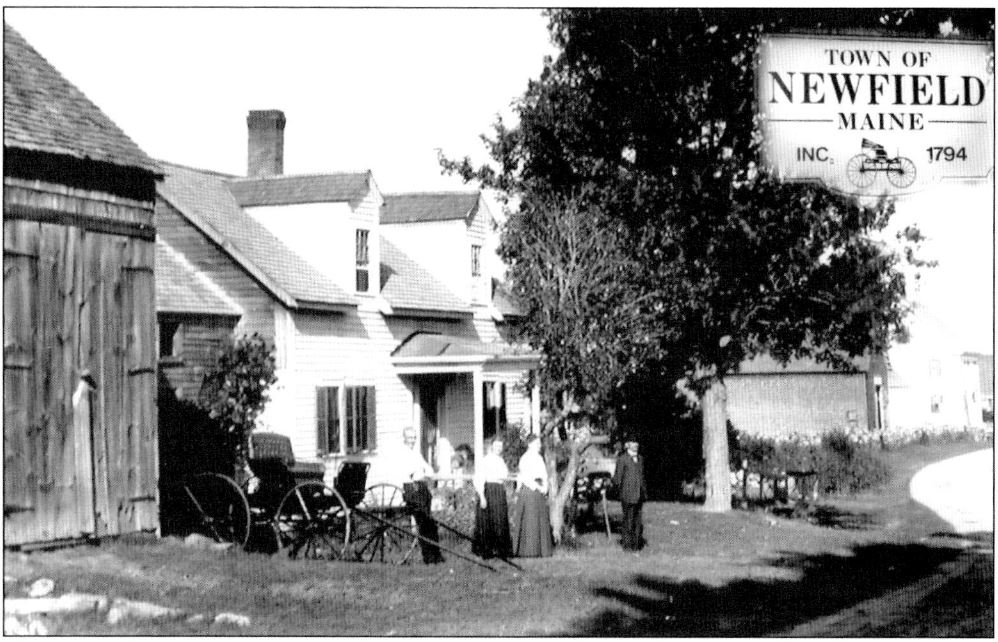

During the latter half of the 19th century, there were numerous Newfield shops employed in the manufacture of carriages. Saws were water powered, planing was done by hand and the shafts and wheels were shaped with steam. Once the carpenter shops were finished, the carriages went to the foundries for ironwork and finally to paint shops. Buggies, two-seated wagons, and sleighs were made.

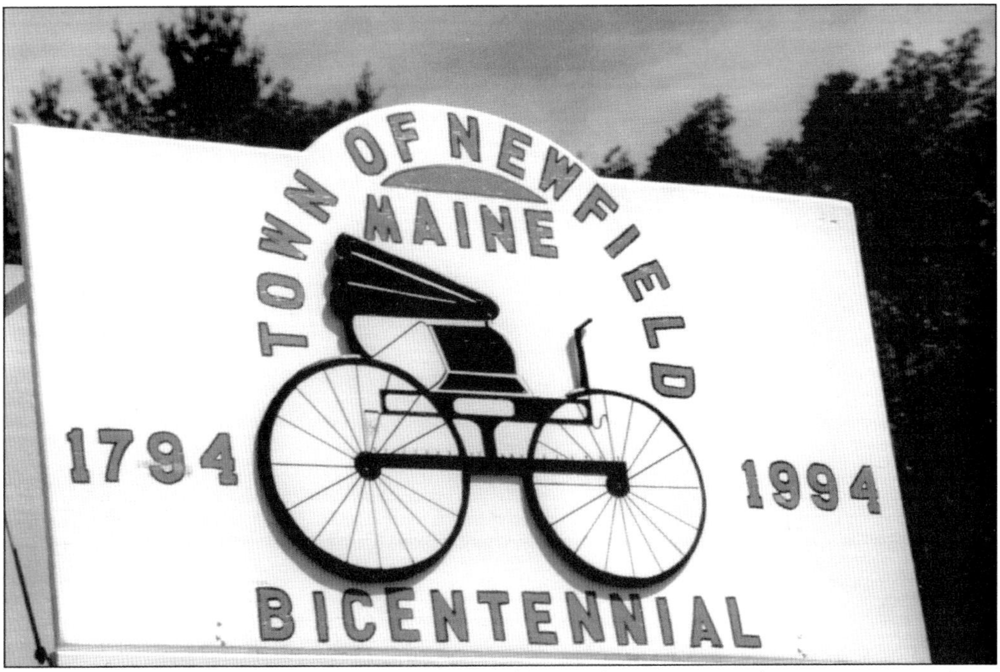

This Bicentennial Seal was created for Newfield's 200th anniversary by a summer resident, Gordon Demeritt, and his students at a Haverhill, Massachusetts, technical high school. It represents a long-ago industry here in manufacturing carriages. This logo is used on various town projects and on the stationery of the Historical Society of Newfield.

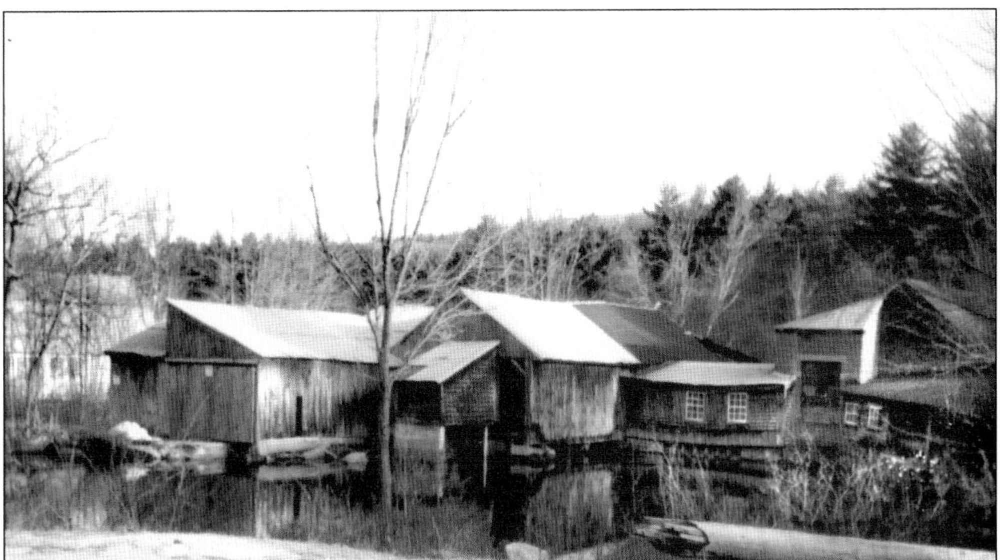
The old Moulton Mill, located near the intersection of Routes 11 and 110, is over 200 years of age. It was operated by the Moulton family for over 100 years but is no longer in use and has been sold. This landmark has long been the focus of artists and photographers. Moulton Lumber Company now operates a building supply business a short distance east of this site.

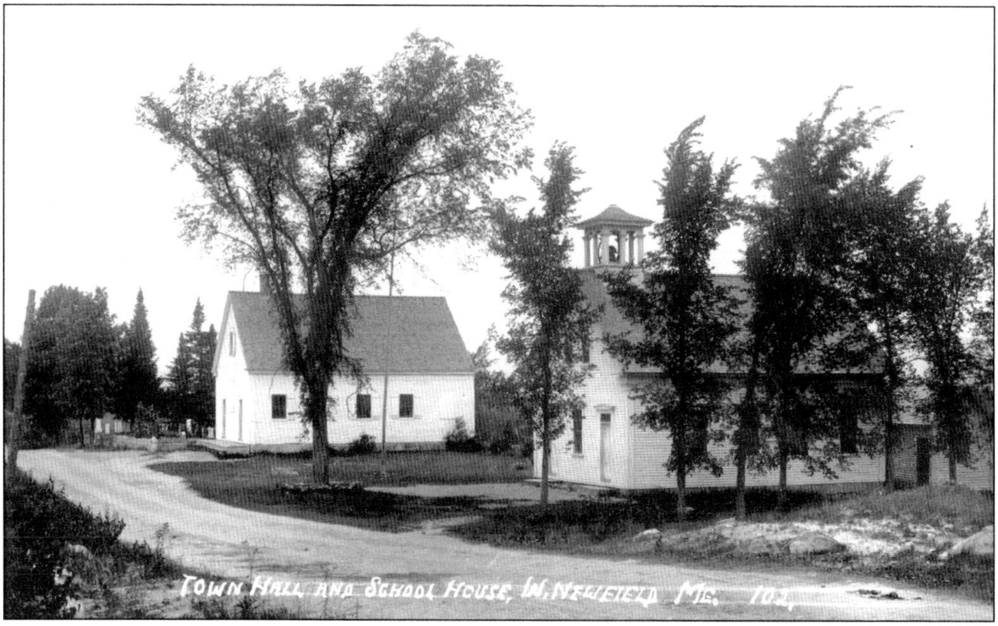

The town hall and the West Newfield School are pictured here as they stood on South Effingham Road before the 1947 fire destroyed them. According to Clayton Weymouth's 1924 Salutatorian speech, the school could not hold all of the pupils, and so classes were held for some students in the town hall.

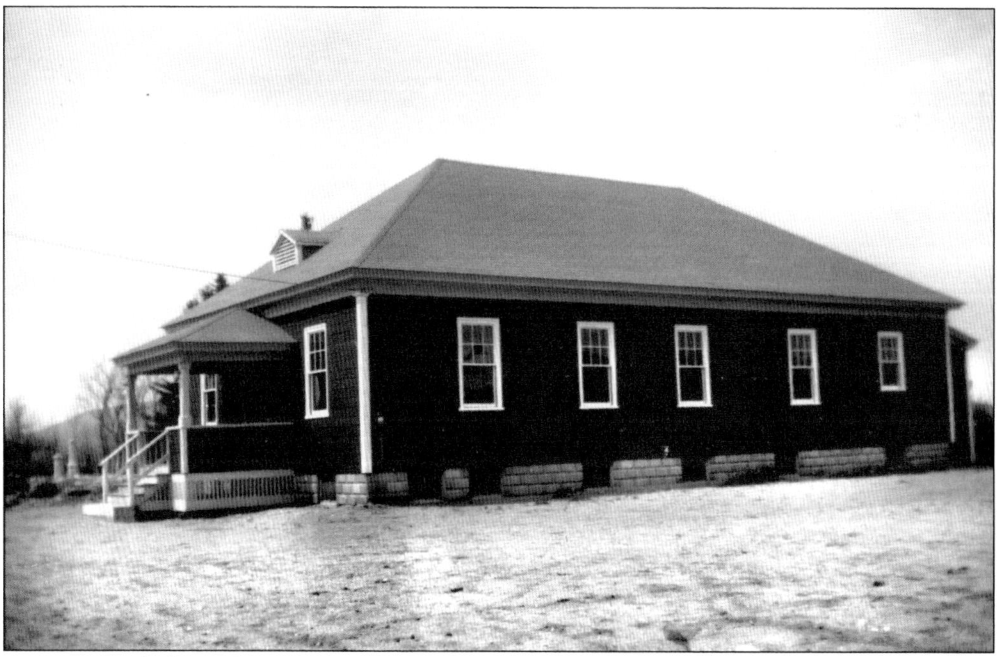

A new town hall was built on the same site as the former hall and was dedicated in 1951. The West Newfield Fire Station was built where the school had been. That building is now used as a recycling station, the scene of much activity on Wednesday afternoons and Saturday mornings during the warmer months of the year.

The town safe was a victim of the fire that destroyed the town hall. A great deal of the town's history went up in flames with the loss of this safe and also the loss of the town vault. Many town records were lost in the disaster. Records that were salvaged were so charred that they were too delicate for much handling.

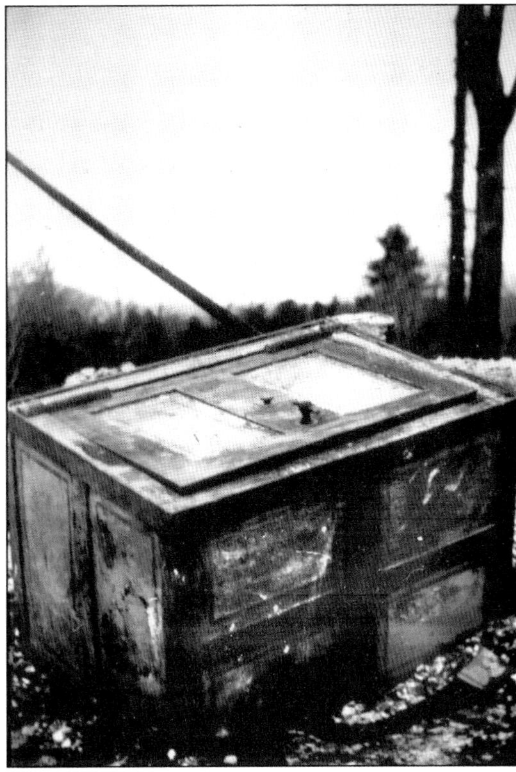

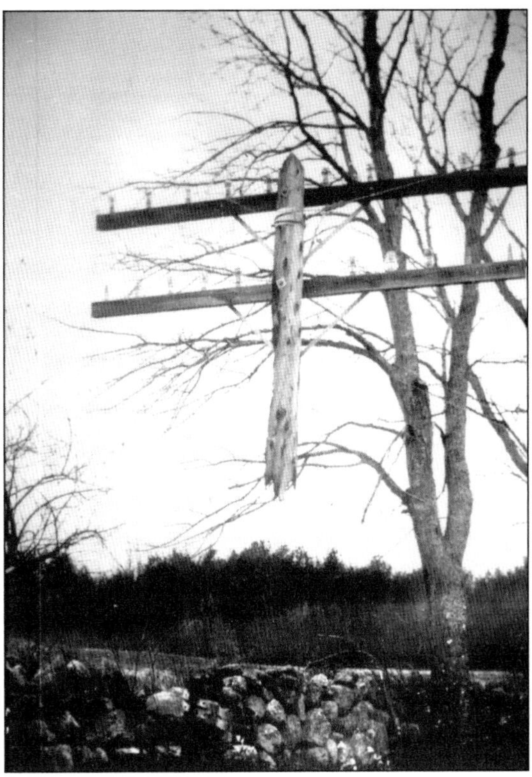

Another casualty of the 1947 conflagration was utility poles hanging on the wires after the raging fire had burned away the lower portion. This one was located near the Carlton home in West Newfield. The fire left the land desolate, farms in smoking ruins, pine and hardwood growth blackened and dead.

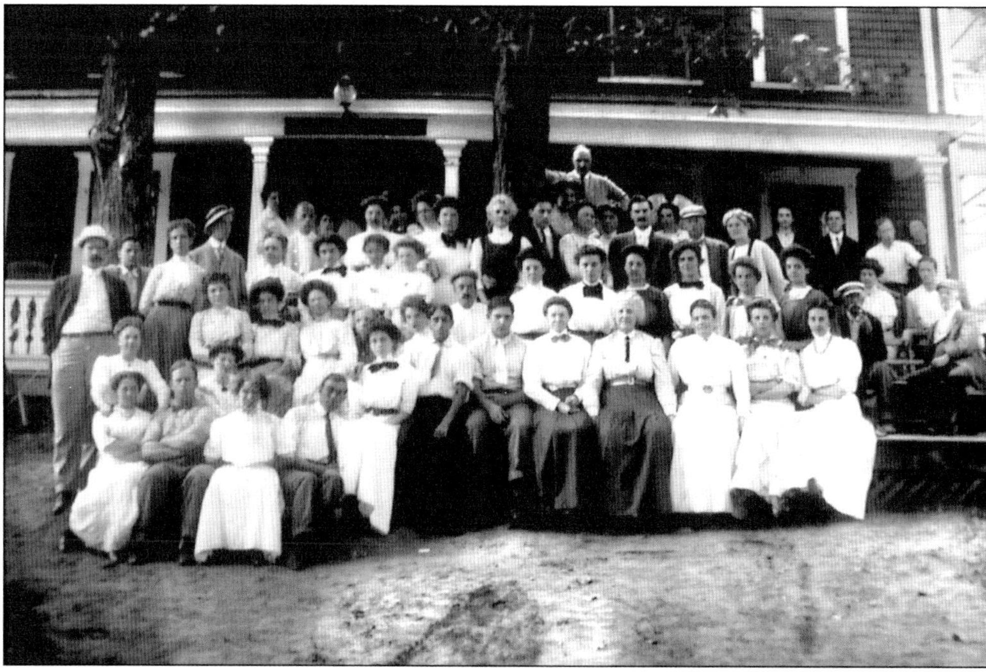

A group of Shady Nook visitors pose for a moment with owner Florence Howe (woman in front of tree). Shady Nook Farm could accommodate up to 90 guests. The hotel, located on Shadynook Road in West Newfield, burned on April 20, 1914.

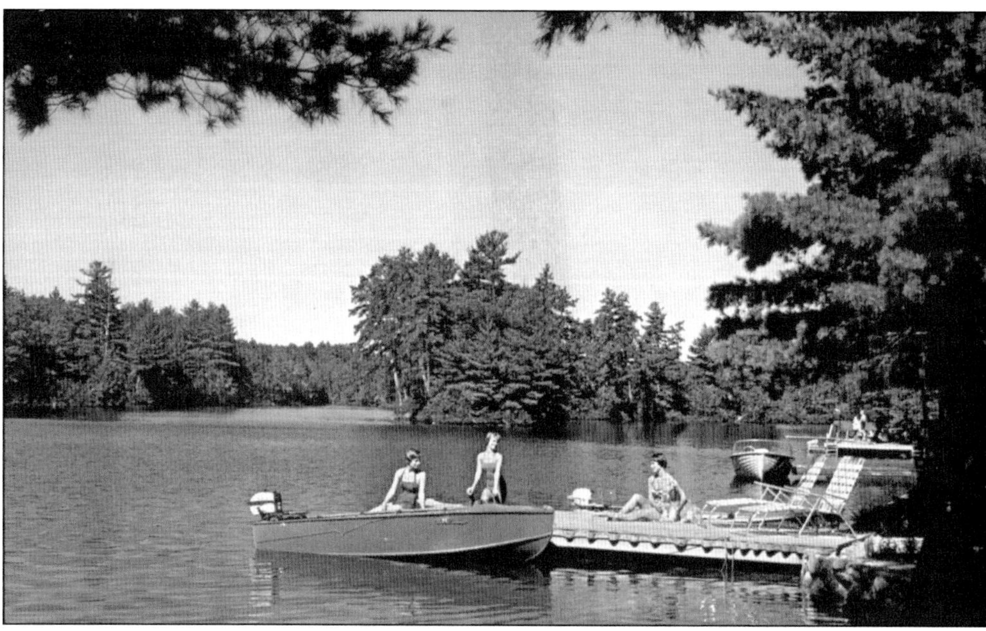

Kingdom of the Pines, also known as Pine-De-Mere, is the locale of the Shady Nook Camps in the Davis Section of Balch Lake. This area was long owned by the late Earle H. (Steve) Davis. This is still a bustling place of summer activity, as is the portion of Balch Lake known as the Whitehouse Section, where there are also many cottages and year-round homes.

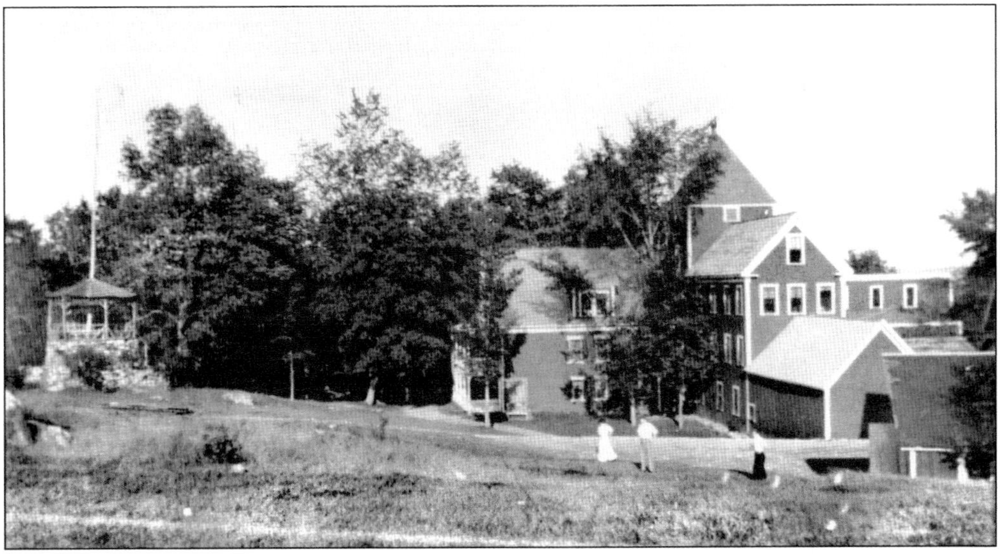

Shady Nook Hotel was situated on Shady Nook Road, West Newfield. It was developed when Shady Nook Farm was enlarged by Florence Howe, mother of Ray and Steve Davis. Howe often did much of the work herself, adding on wings, a bowling alley, dance hall, a tower, and a gazebo. Many summer visitors vacationed here. The buildings are no longer standing but the remains of the gazebo are visible. Brochures for the hotel stated that its carriages met Boston trains at Burleyville (East Wakefield, New Hampshire) for 50¢. It was also stated that "We take Protestants only—no children, no invalids, no cranks, no dogs, no cats."

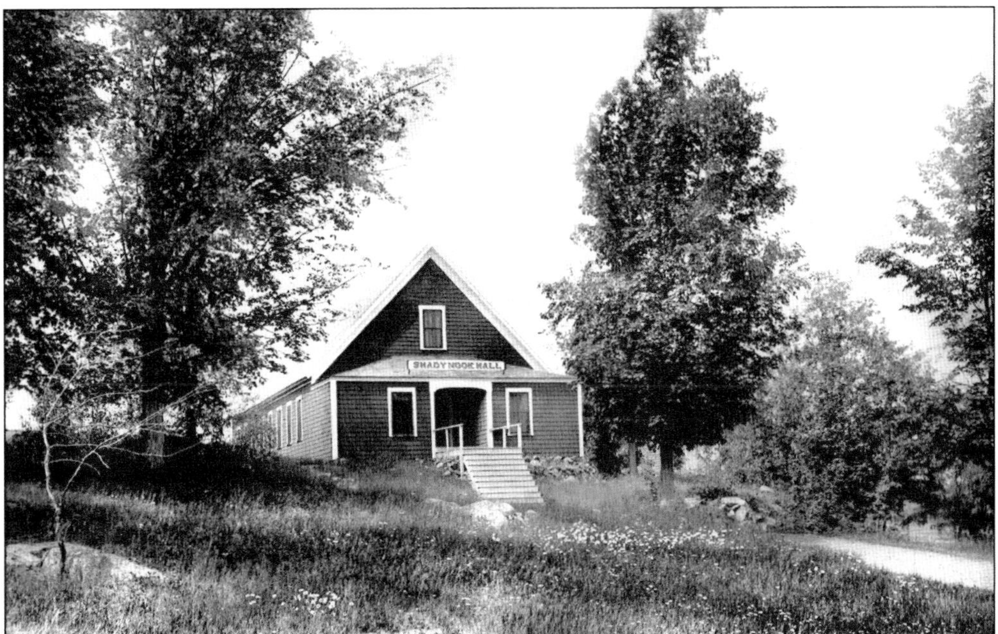

Shady Nook Dance Hall was the scene of many lively gatherings throughout the years. It is located across the road from the spot where the old hotel was located. The building is still standing. An old poster advertising dances there stated that admission was 40¢ on a Thursday evening in 1933 with a 10-piece orchestra.

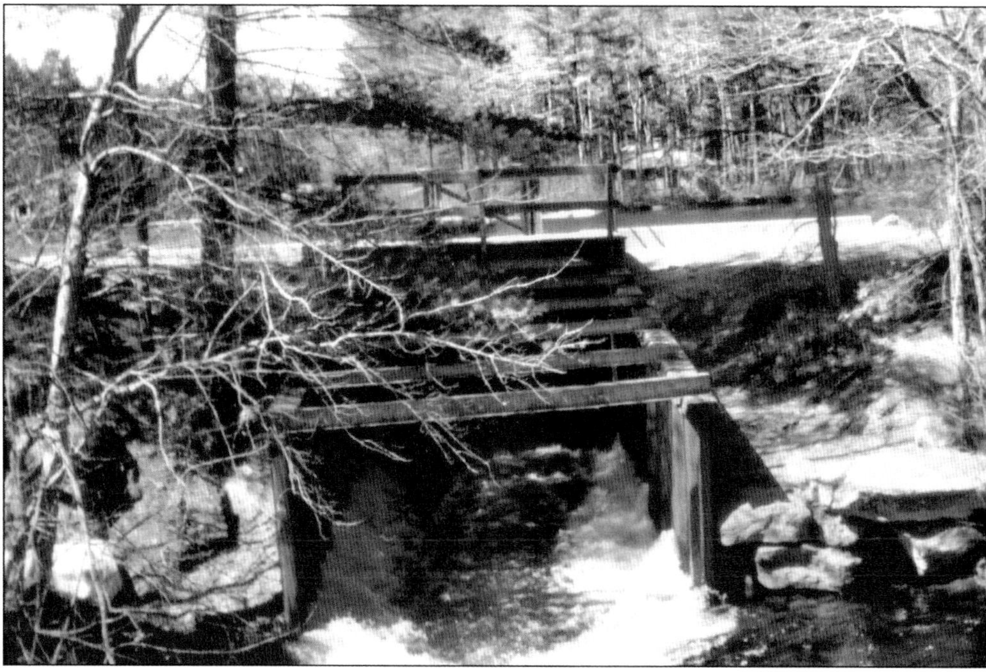

At the start of the Little Ossipee River, the water runs over the dam at man-made Balch Pond, part of which is in Maine, and part in New Hampshire, but also part in Newfield and part in Acton. The pond was dammed to power a sawmill, which was operated for many years.

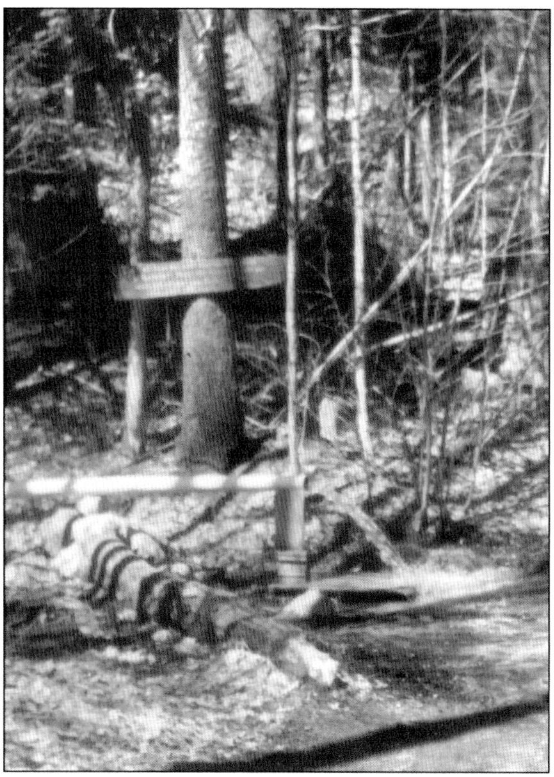

Located on Bond Spring Road (Route 11), West Newfield, is Bond Mount Spring, which has supplied crystal clear water for countless numbers of people for many years. When driving through the area, one can usually see folks filling containers at the spring. This land has been owned by Bond family members since 1790.

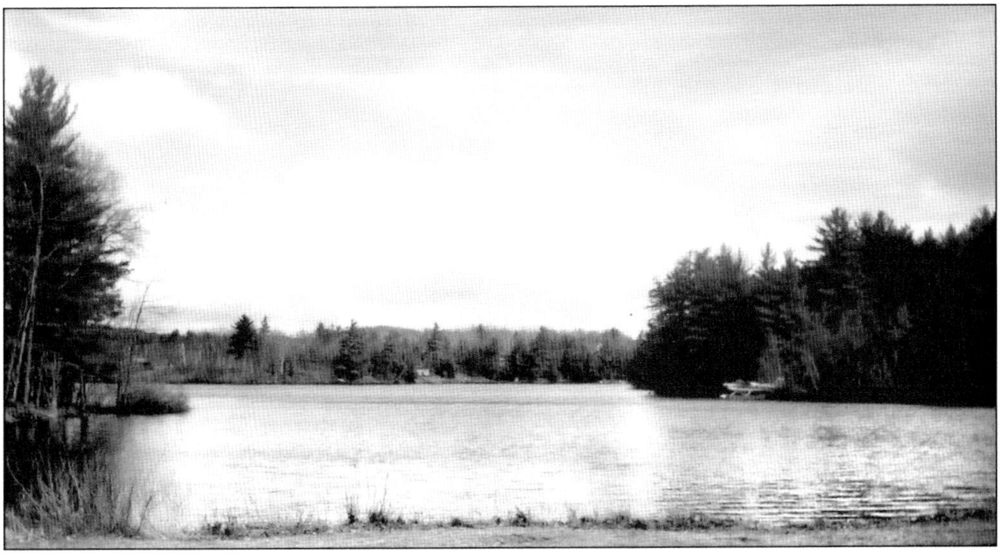

Rock Haven Lake, once known as Adams Pond, is accessible from Route 11, Route 110, the Maplewood Road, and the Stone Road. It has had many summer cottages over the years but is now populated by several year-round residences.

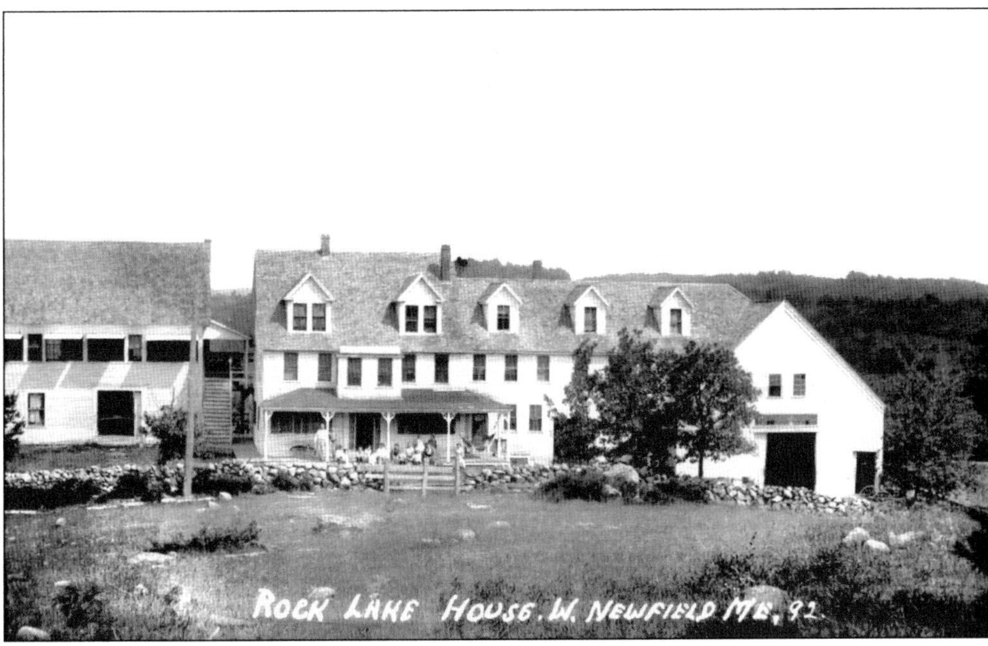

Rock Haven Lake House was operated as a hotel for summer visitors in the early 1900s by Bert Patch and his mother. It was located on a magnificent spot overlooking Rock Haven Lake. They enlarged the property to serve more boarders and also ran dances there. Eventually the buildings were destroyed by fire. Later Bert ran a hotel in Springvale, Maine.

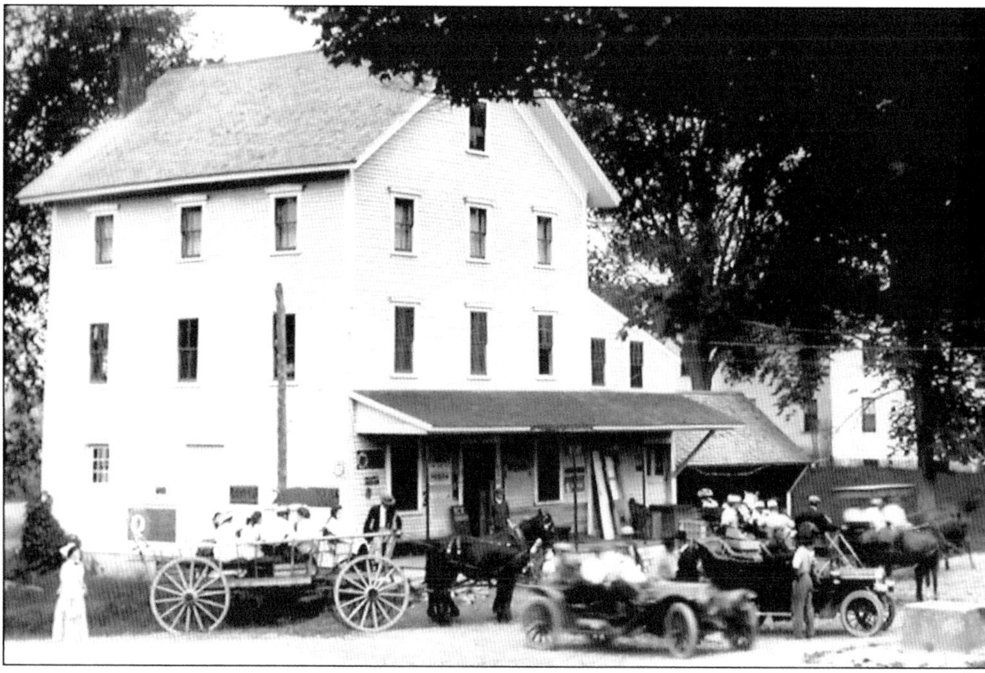

In 1874, this building housed a store on the first floor, the town hall on the second, and the Masonic hall on the third.

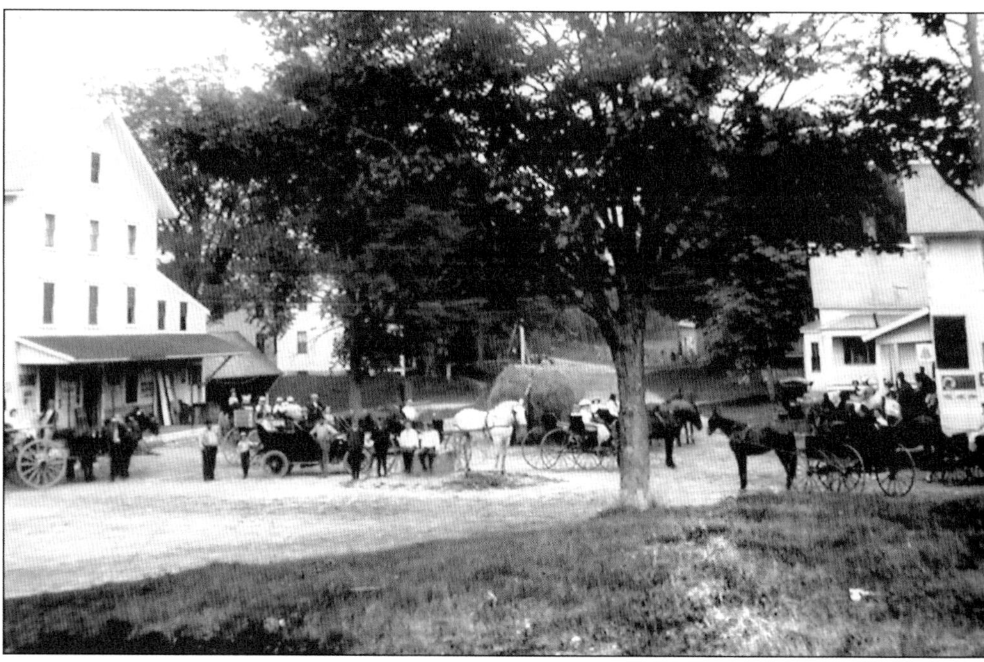

The four corners at the West Newfield Square lead to Maplewood, Parsonsfield; South Effingham, New Hampshire; Province Lake; and Newfield Village.

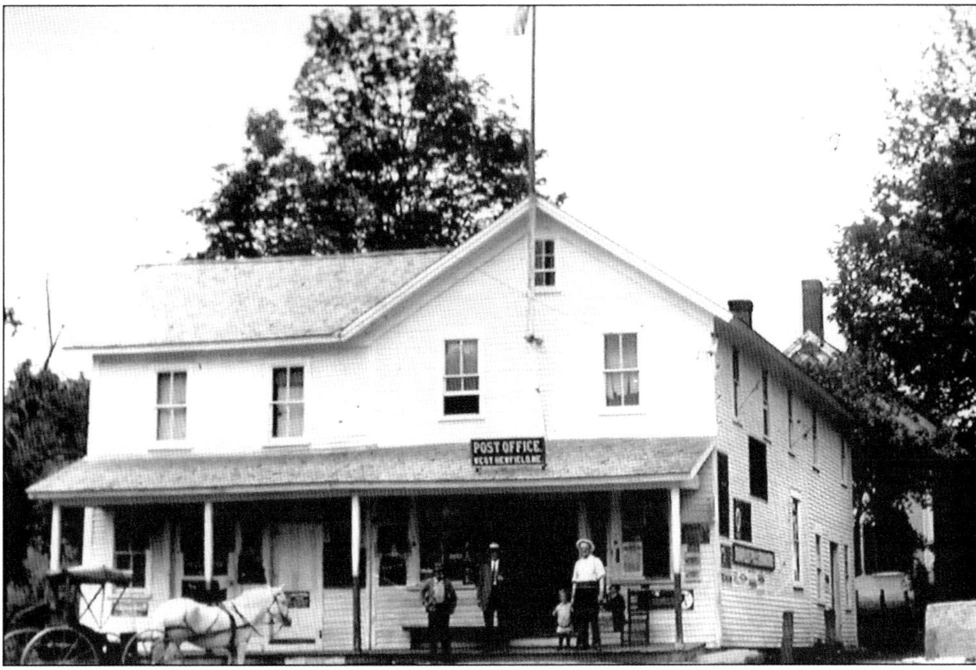

The West Newfield Post Office for many years was situated in the Hannaford Store Building in West Newfield Square. It was run by George Hannaford in 1898, later by his son, Carl, and still later by Carl's daughter, Doris, who served for 40 years. The post office is now located in a building owned by Moulton Lumber Company on South Effingham Road.

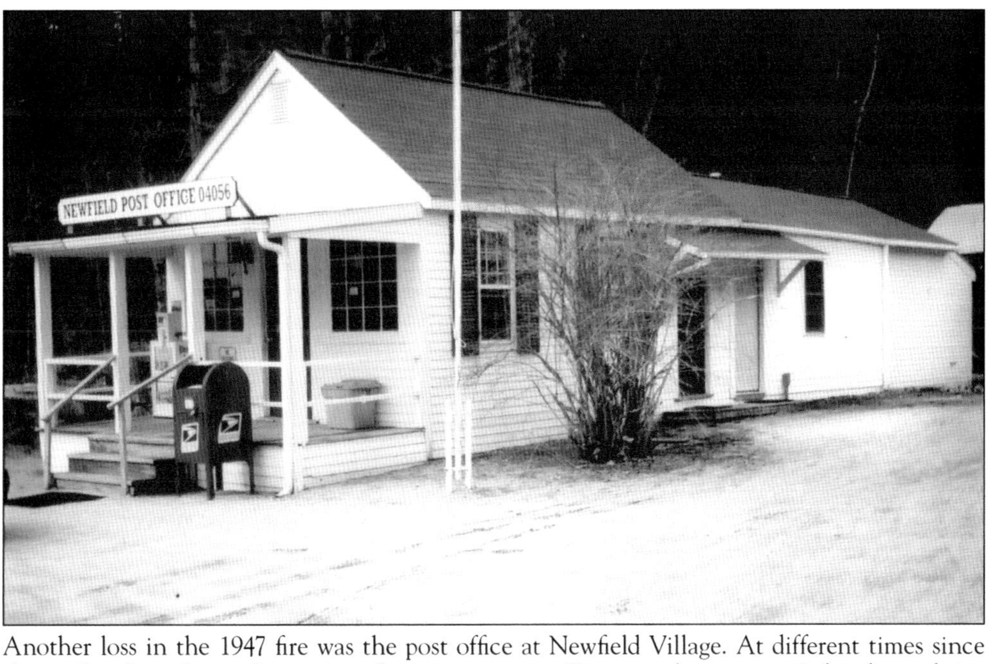

Another loss in the 1947 fire was the post office at Newfield Village. At different times since then it has been located in private homes or a store. For several years now it has been doing business in a building owned by the Willowbrook Village Museum.

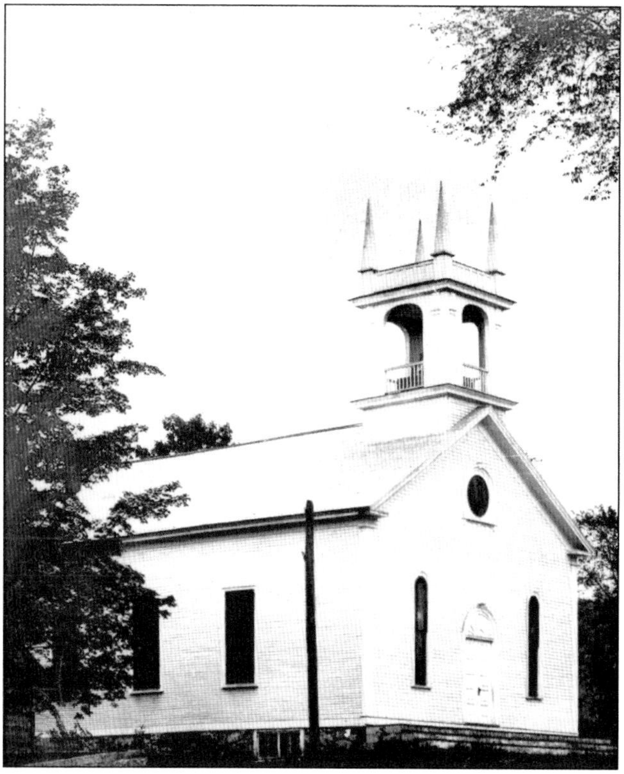

West Newfield Congregational Church, UCC, fortunately escaped the 1947 fire, and still stands today. Memorial Hall was added at the rear and dedicated in 1969. It accommodates church and Sunday school activities and other meetings, and allows the Historical Society of Newfield to hold its annual Christmas party there.

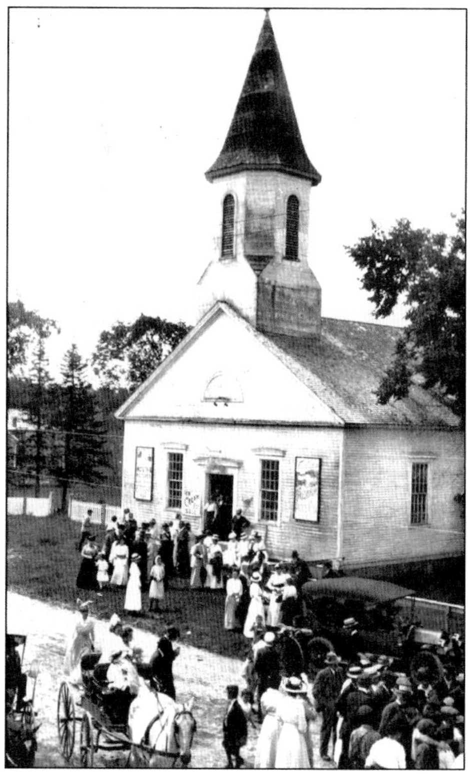

In 1914, a grand social event took place in the form of Old Home Day. Here is a scene at the auditorium in Newfield. The building had previously been a Baptist church. When it was no longer used as a church, weekly silent movies were shown and plays were also performed. It was located beside the old Baptist cemetery. This auditorium also succumbed to the 1947 fire.

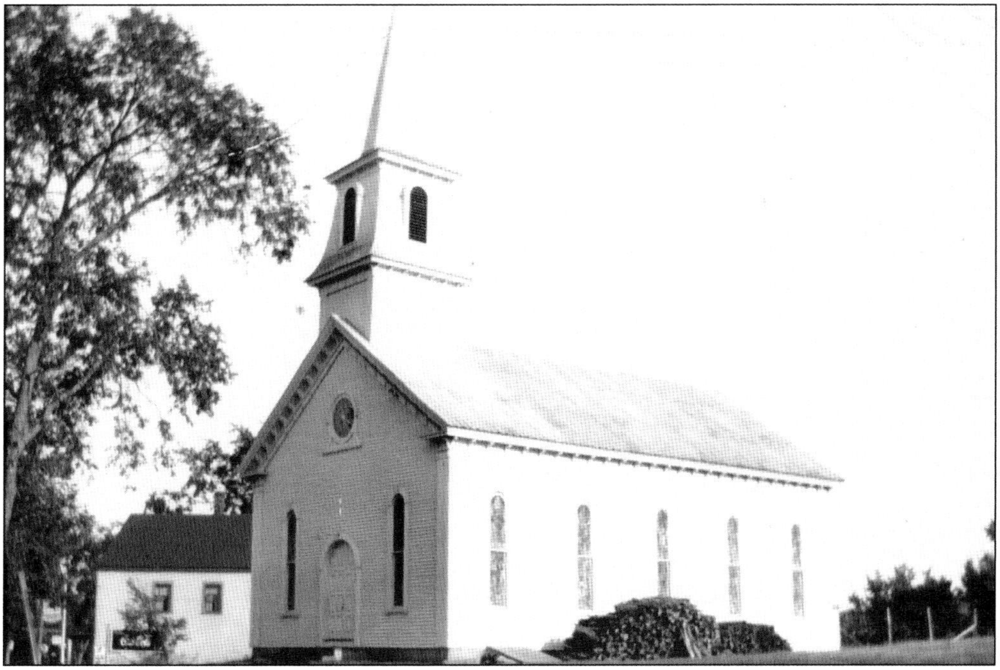

Pictured here is the Newfield Methodist Church as it stood before the devastating fire of 1947. It had been built in 1872. The church had been served by many fine ministers over the years, one born in England, another in Australia, and another in Canada.

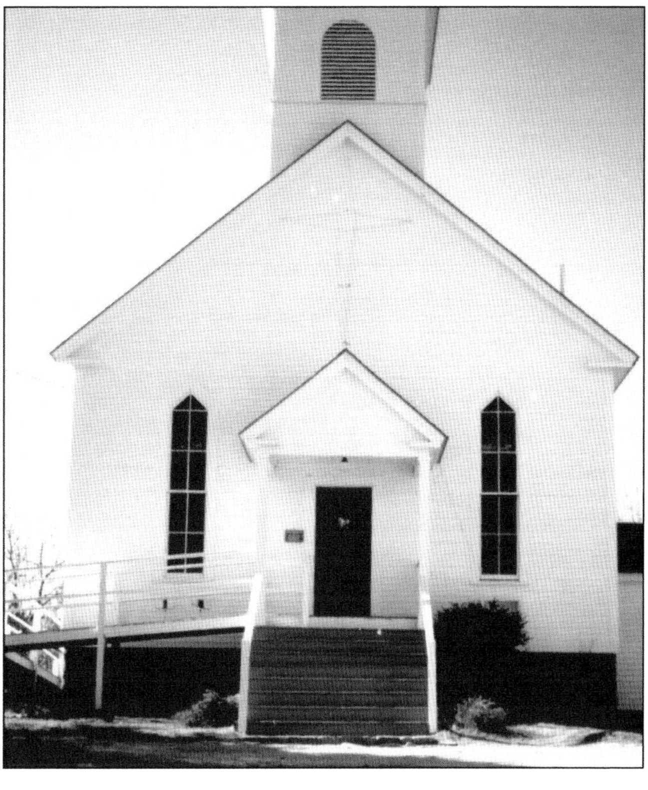

After the fire disaster, the Merriland Ridge Church of Wells, Maine, along with its contents, was given to the Newfield Methodist Church members for their new house of worship. It was transported to Newfield and secured on the site of the former church. Many church people and local citizens worked together to set up the edifice. It was dedicated in 1949.

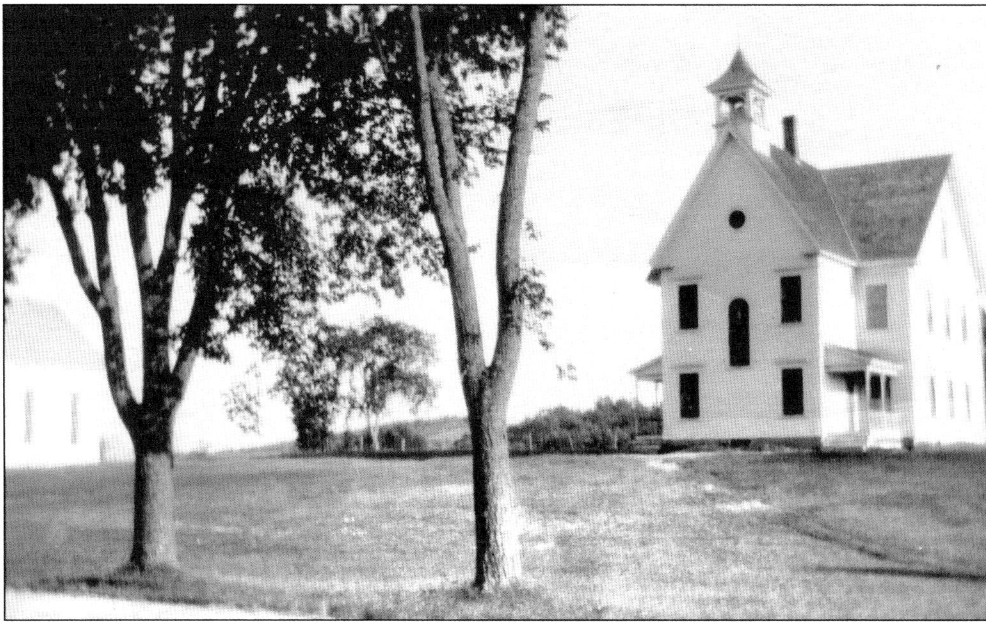

The school at Newfield Village consisted of elementary grades on the first floor with the Ethan Stone High School occupying the second floor. This school, too, burned in the 1947 fire, causing many changes in schooling and transportation schedules. In 1966, Newfield joined five other towns to form School Administrative District 57. The middle and high school students attend the district schools for their grade levels situated in Waterboro. Elementary students attend the Line School on Route 11 on the town line.

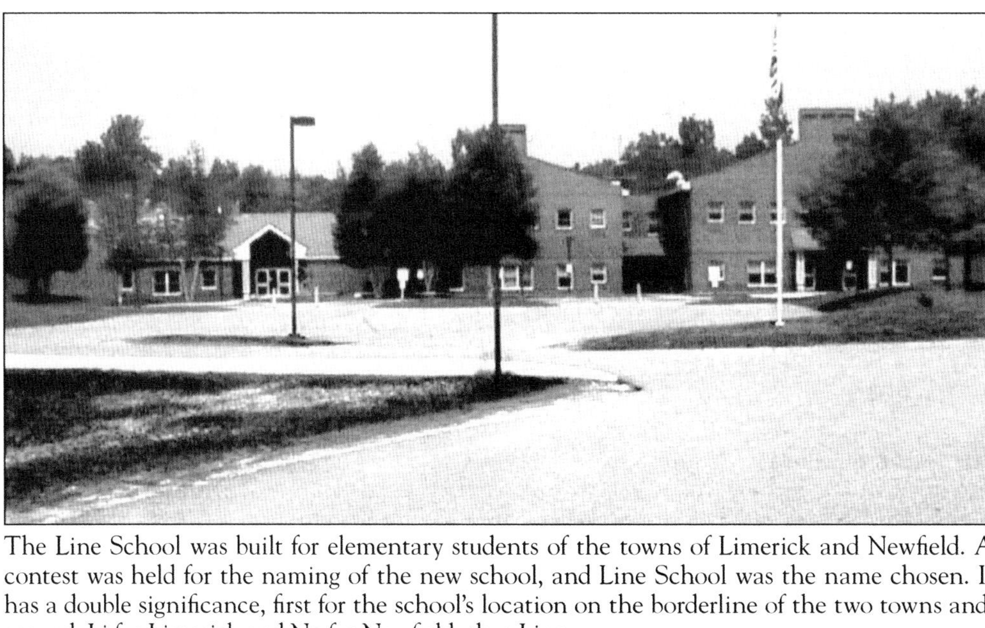

The Line School was built for elementary students of the towns of Limerick and Newfield. A contest was held for the naming of the new school, and Line School was the name chosen. It has a double significance, first for the school's location on the borderline of the two towns and, second, Li for Limerick and Ne for Newfield, thus Line.

A prefabricated structure was installed to replace the school at Newfield lost in the fire. After the new Line School was completed, this building was turned over to the town and it now houses the offices of the selectmen, town clerk–tax collector, and the code enforcement officer. The Newfield Library uses one former classroom.

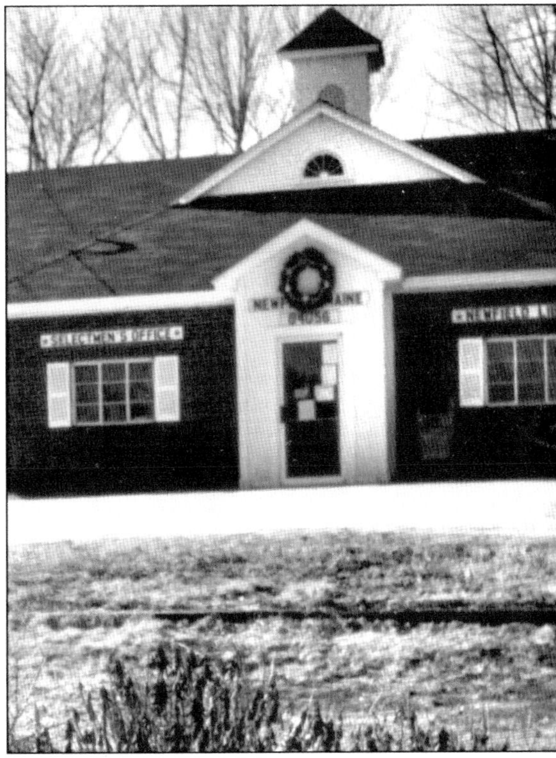

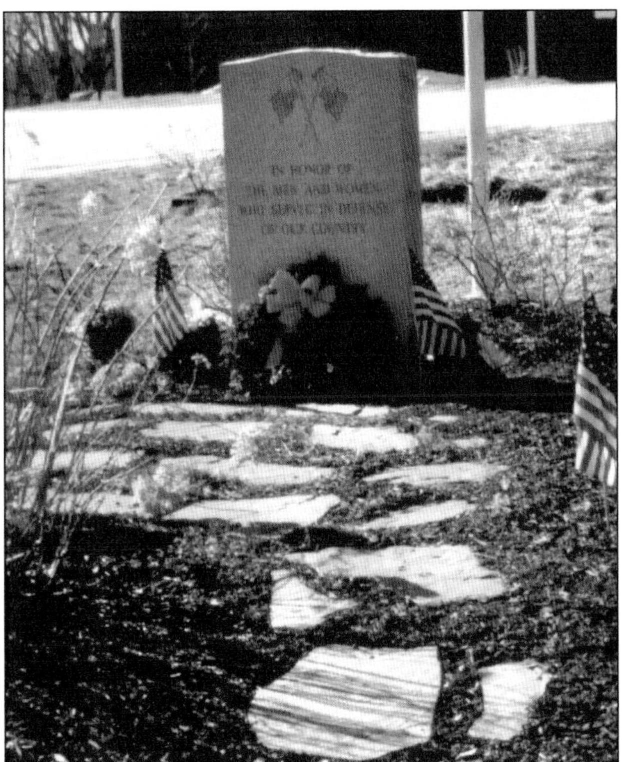

A memorial stone was placed on the grounds of the town office building and was dedicated on November 11, 1999. This was a joint project between the historical society and the town of Newfield in memory of all men and women who have served in all United States conflicts of war. Each November 11, at 11:00 a.m., a memorial service is held here.

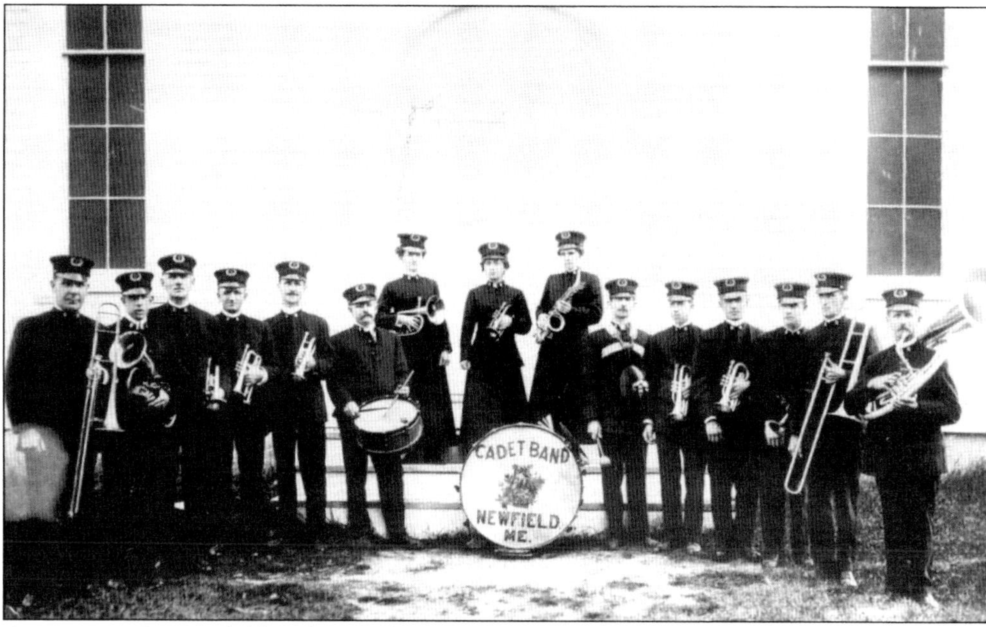

At one time the Newfield Cadet Band was an active community group. They were instrumental in having the grandstand constructed at the intersection of Elm Street and Route 11, but it, too, went in the fire. A replica of the bandstand is on the grounds of Willowbrook Village Museum.

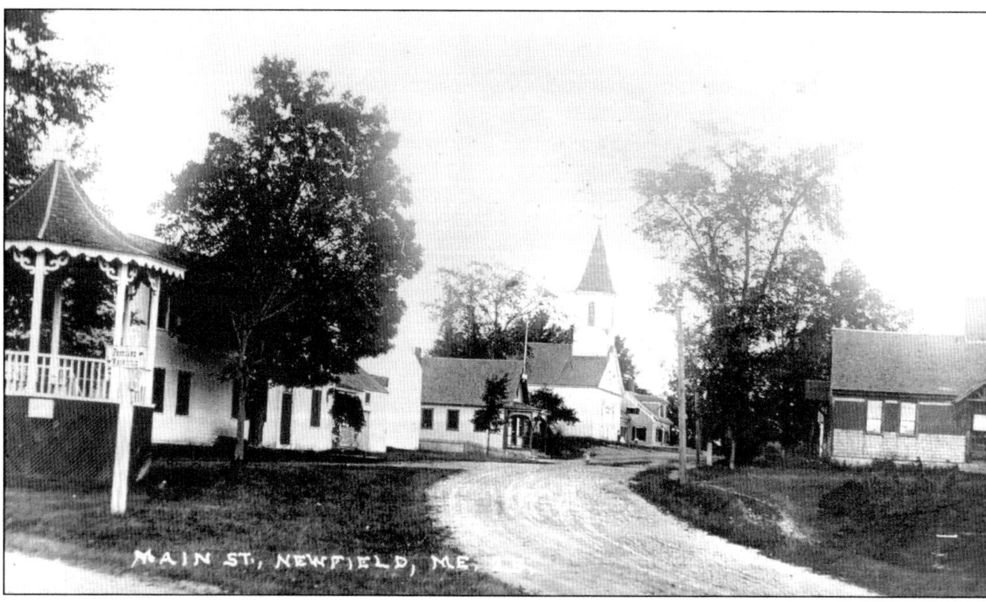

At Newfield Village the bandstand, along with the Captain Falker place, Newfield Post Office, Old Baptist Church (auditorium) and the Polly Moulton home, all on the left side of the road, were wiped out in the 1947 fire. Also lost was the Joe Heald place on the right. However, somehow, other buildings beyond were saved.

The Newfield Library building has had an interesting history. It has served as a doctor's office and a law office. It is believed that lawyer Nathan Clifford had his law office here while residing in town. He went on to become an outstanding statesman, serving in many public offices. He was a justice on the U.S. Supreme Court and also a minister to Mexico. This building served as a library for about 100 years beginning in 1890, and is currently being used as a storage facility. The Village Library and Reading Room are now located at the town office building.

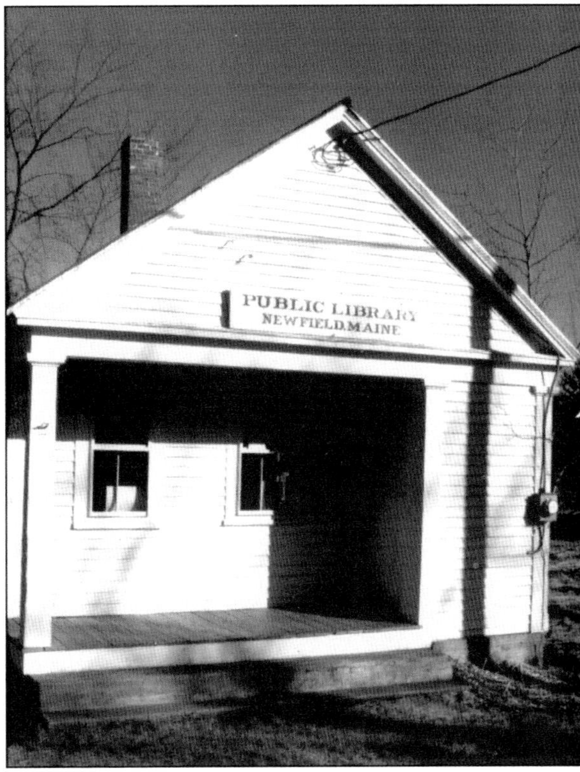

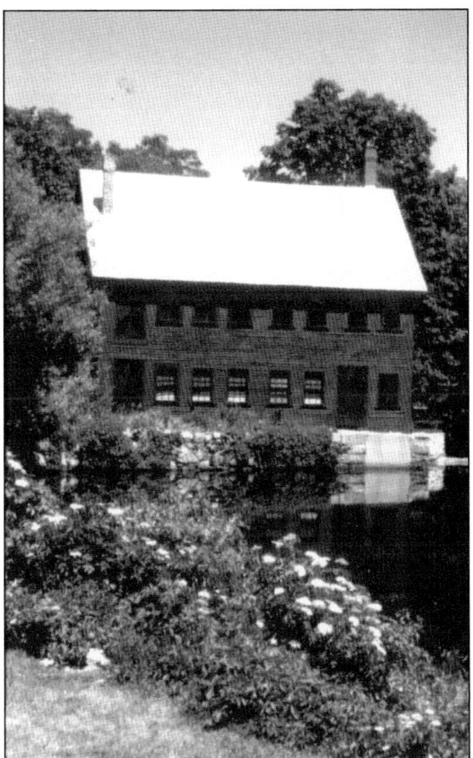

This former mill is located in a beautiful setting by the Old Mill Pond on Elm Street. In recent years it was converted to residential living. When it was owned by Denise Carpenter, current president of Newfield's Historical Society, she did considerable reconstruction work herself to enhance the living quarters. She has since sold the property.

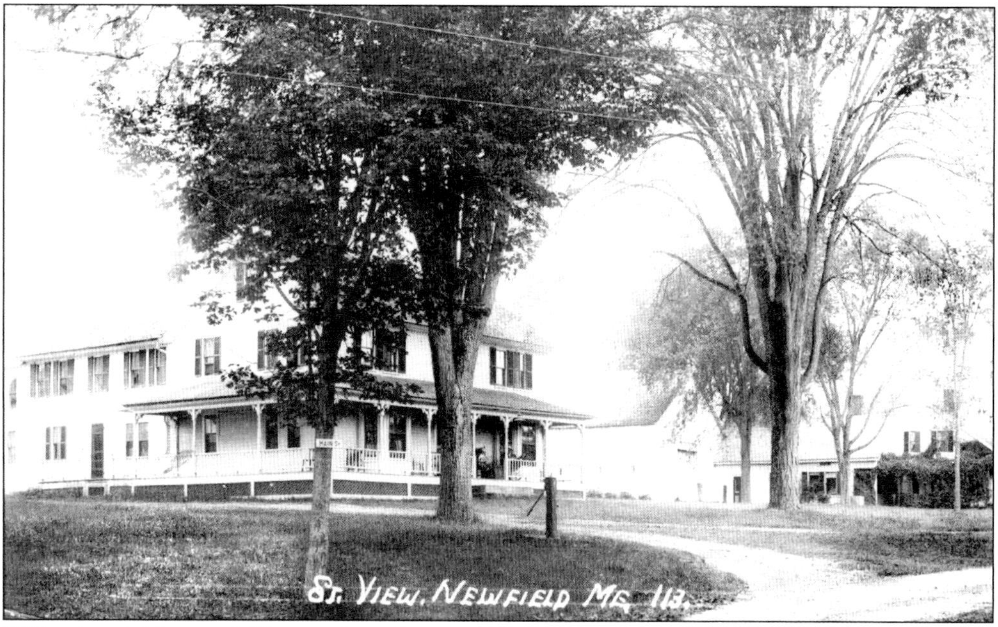

Willowbrook Museum Village is the culmination of the dreams of the late Donald King, his wife, and their family. Open from spring until fall, it is visited by tour bus groups, school classes, and folks of all ages. The buildings are situated near the Old Mill Pond in a very picturesque country setting. Nineteenth century living is displayed among the buildings with many artifacts of the era. The King family has recently formed an agreement with the Historical Society of Newfield allowing the Historical Society to have a building constructed on land of the museum to house the Society's archives and to hold its meetings and displays. This home was built in 1813.

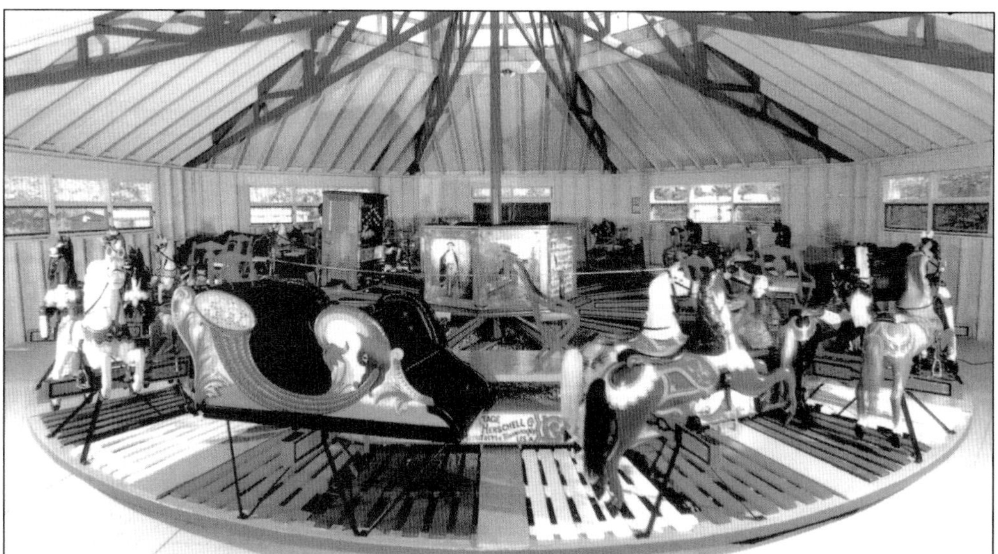

An inviting attraction at Willowbrook Museum (especially to children) is the 1894 Armitage-Herschell carousel that is located in a building crafted especially for its display. It is generally only open for viewing, but one day in the season is set aside for rides with tickets available at a booth nearby.

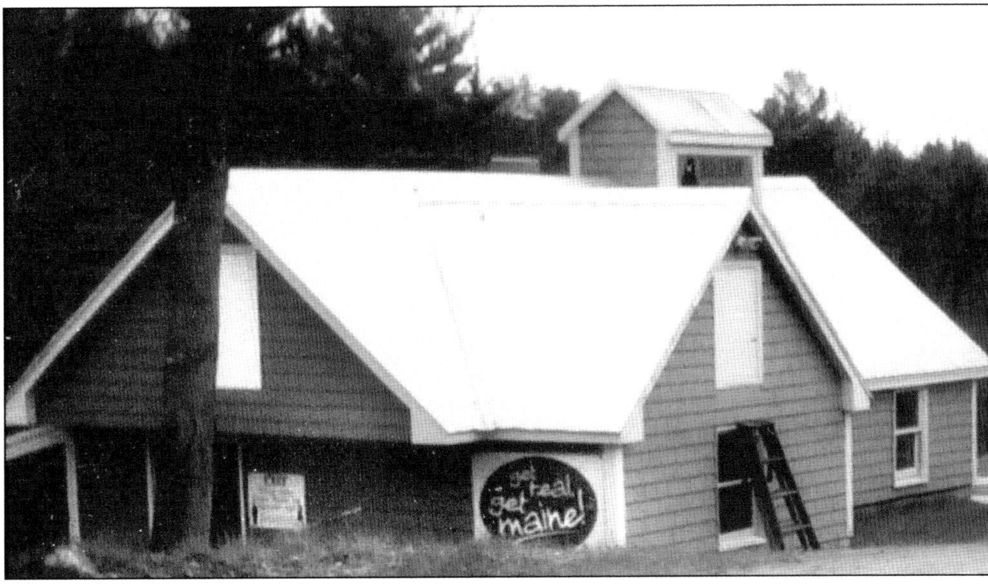

Long a tradition in Newfield is the production of maple syrup. Maine Maple Sunday is presently observed by Newfield's two local maple syrup producers each spring, generally on the last Sunday of March. Bryant's Hilltop Boilers on Elm Street has many attractions to interest all ages, especially the sample tasting of maple syrup or cream. Children can participate in suggesting names for newborn farm animals, or sit on farm tractors, or watch sap being boiled down to the syrup stage.

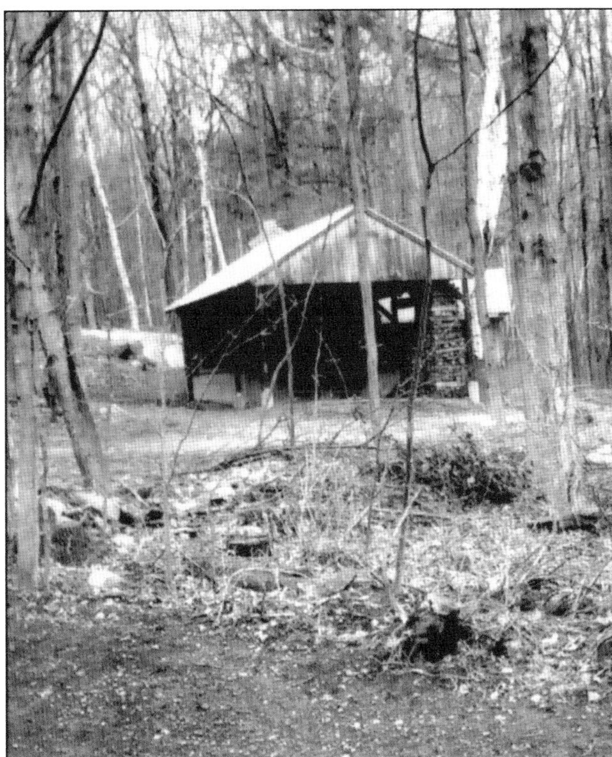

Delicious spun maple sugar may be sampled at Ashley Gerry's Sugar Hill operation on Route 11. Demonstrations take place and there are hikes to the maple orchard nearby. Sometimes there are wagon rides to the site.

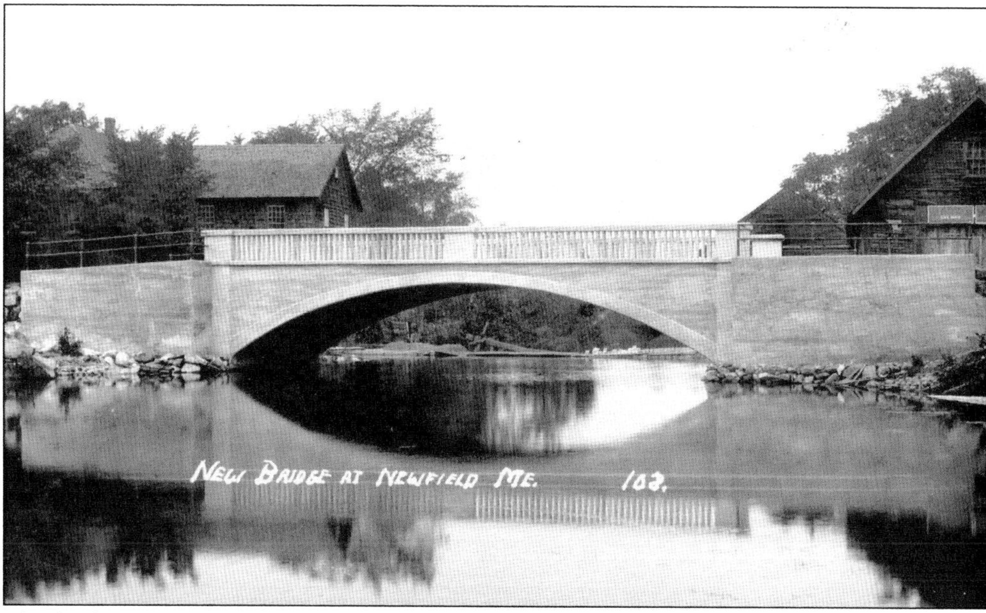

This bridge on the Ross Corner Road (or Bridge Street) crosses over the Little Ossipee River that begins at Balch Pond, runs to the edge of North Shapleigh, winding its way on through Newfield Village, and continuing on to Limerick and Limington. In the past, many mills operated along the banks of the river. Today canoeists and fishermen and even a certain representative to the U.S. Congress from Maine frequent the river, which is shown around 1924.

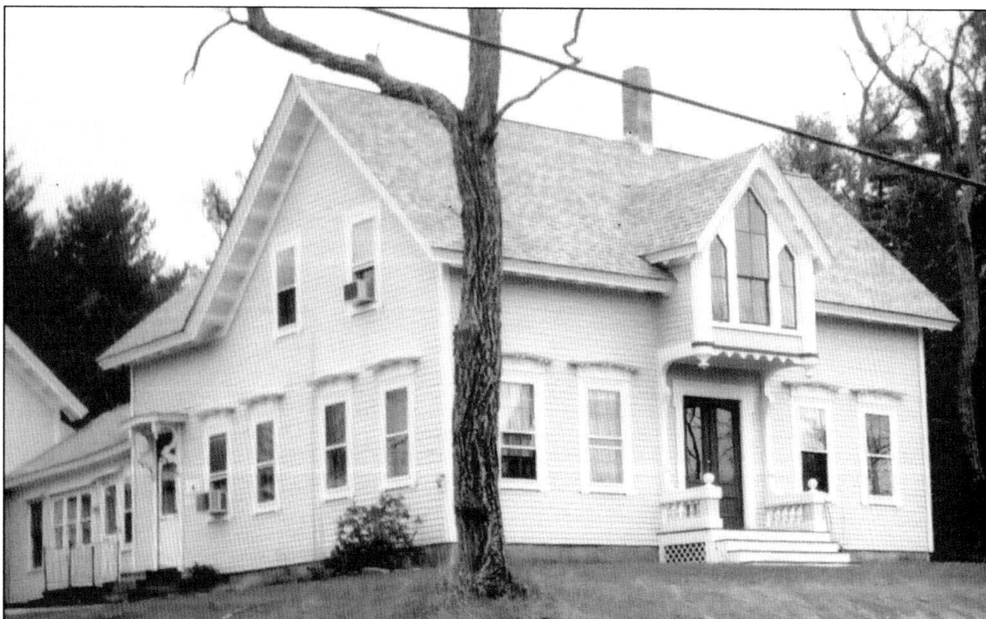

At various periods over the years, there have been funeral homes located here. The last one was on the corner of Route 11 and Elm Street in Newfield Village. It later became the home of Carl and Hilda Perry, where Hilda held her real estate office. At the present time, a radio network business is on the premises.

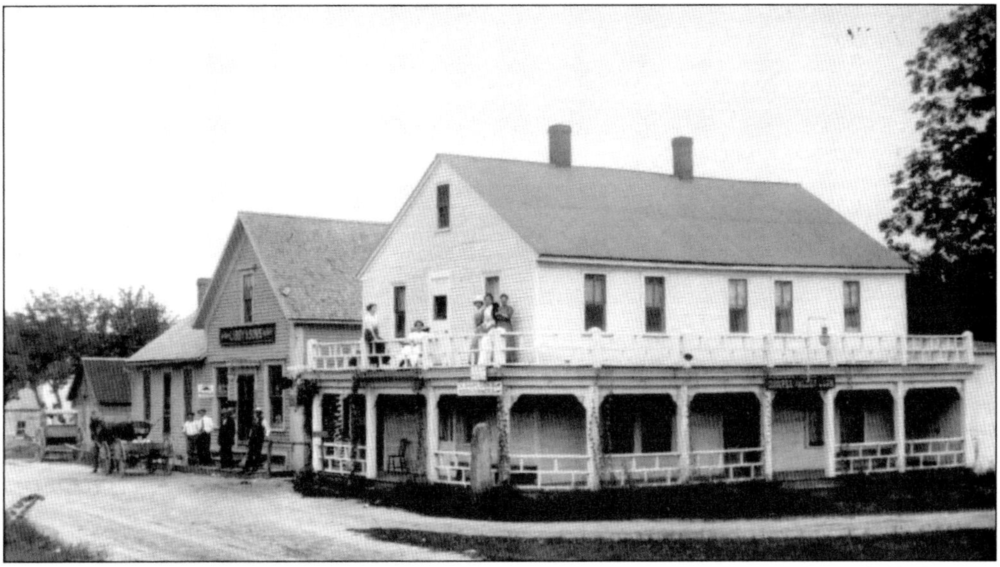

Many homes served as boarding homes, inns, or hotels during the early days of Newfield's history. One popular place was Mirror Lake Farm, located just off Route 11, on Shady Nook Road. There was also the West Newfield House. Another guesthouse was the Ossipee River House, later known as The Maples, on the corner of Route 11 and Bridge Street, and now occupied by Sunflower Crafts. On the same street, a short distance beyond the bridge was Echo House. Pictured above is the Ossipee Valley Club that served as a social center. It was across the street from the Maples.

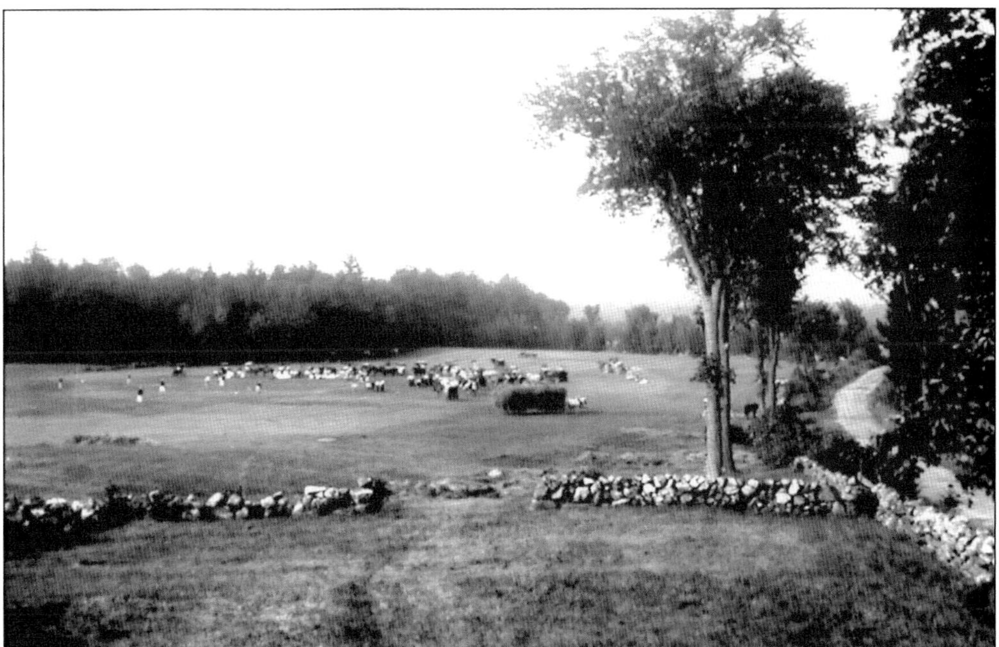

Tucker Field, located on Maplewood Road, West Newfield, was the scene of a baseball game around 1905.

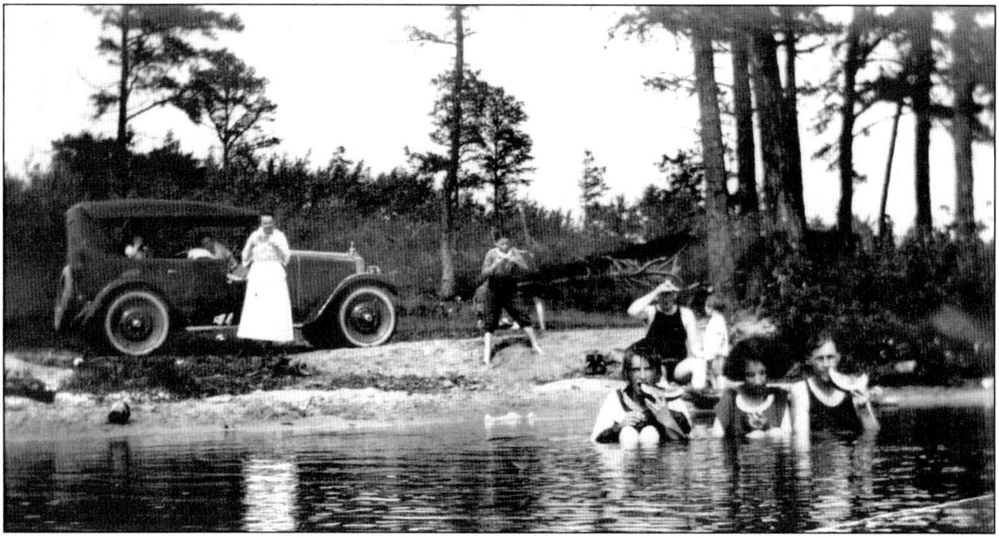

Poverty Pond, known by some newcomers as Silver Lake, is situated near Waterboro and Shapleigh, just off the easterly side of the Ross Corner Road. This pond boasts a pleasant sandy public beach, thanks to the late Ada Hawkins. Here, too, are many year-round residents.

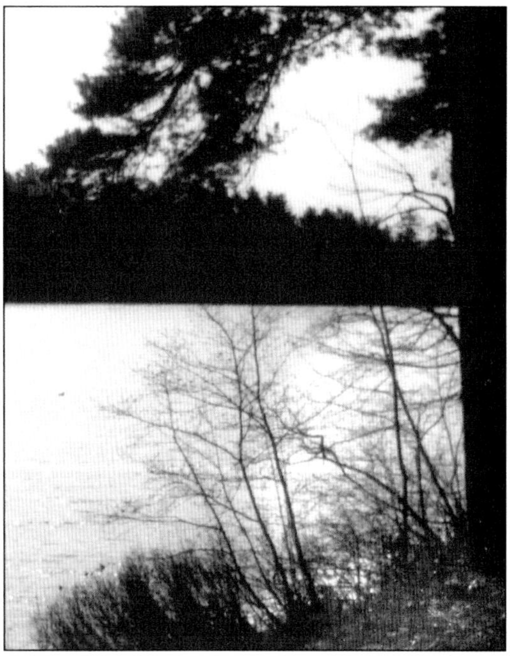

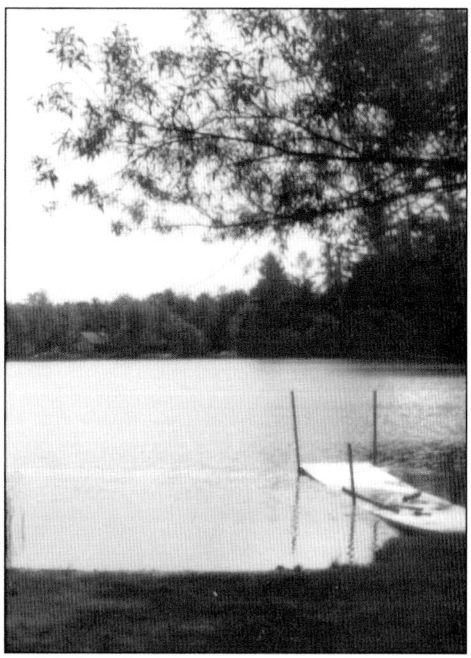

Hidden Lake (once known as Pinkham Pond) is a small lake off Libby Road. It is in a very quiet, secluded area. It also now has some winterized homes in this peaceful country setting. Mirror Lake, once known as Turner Pond, is located just off Bond Spring Road. There have been a few cottages on its shores for years. Now there are year-round homes around the lake.

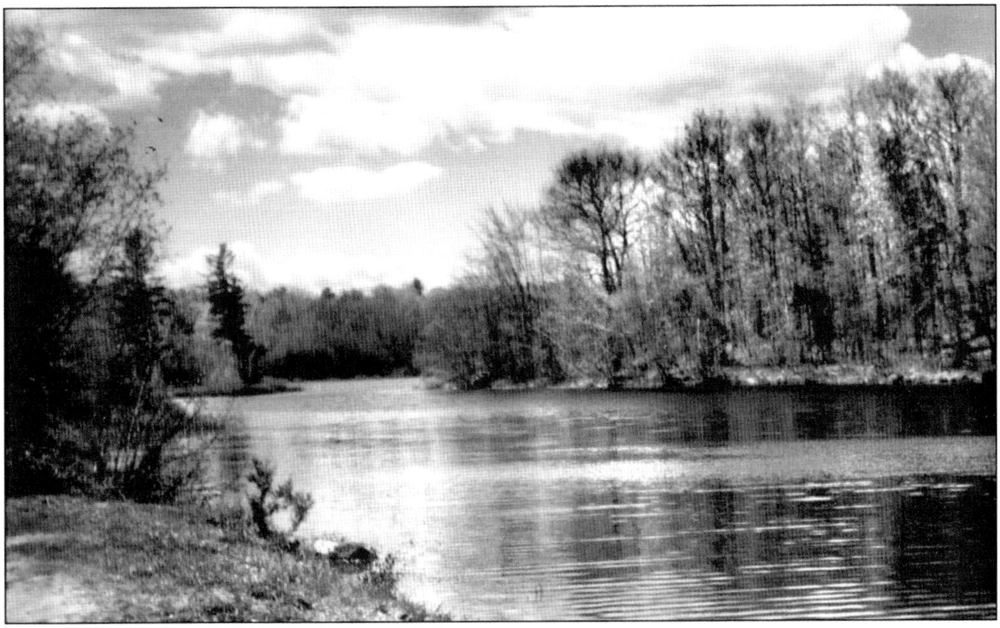

Symmes Pond, located on Route 11 between West Newfield and Newfield, has only a few homes. Fishermen often visit it. In the winter a few fish houses can be seen there when the pond is frozen over. Across the road where a stream runs from the lake under the road, a rare aquatic plant can be seen growing with red blossoms.

This chapter could not conclude without a tribute to Newfield's first woman doctor, Marion King Moulton, who married a local young man, Arthur Moulton, in 1941. They built their home near Rock Haven Lake on Route 110 and here she maintained her office, serving patients from near and far. She was affiliated with H. D. Goodall Hospital in Sanford, Maine, and there she delivered many babies as well as at her home, or at the patient's home. All the while, she was raising her own family. She retired in 1984, but continued to be active for a time on various medical boards. Although no longer practicing medicine, and now 91 years of age, she is still busily occupied with church activities.

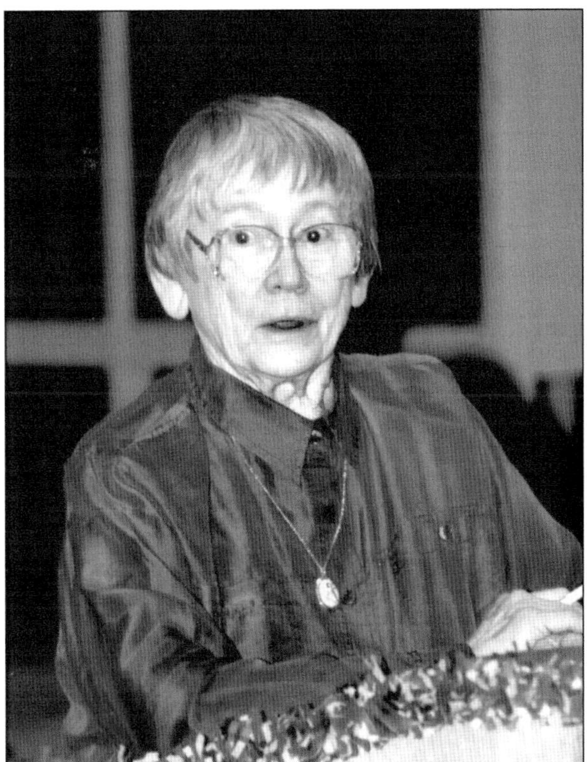

My State of Maine

The first of the states to the east
The last of the states to the west
Her emblems—spruce and the pine tree.
Her standards—the truth is the best.
Lake-dotted, indented and charming.
Pine-studded with forest and fern
Maine is the Mother of Mountains
Maine is the Mother of Men.

Her rivers flow fast to the ocean
Her ships float staunch on the sea,
In tradition her history is grounded
From corruption her annals are free.
When war clouds descend on the nation
Quickly she answers again
Maine is the Mother of Mountains,
Maine is the Mother of Men

Rock-ribbed, unchanging and steady
Hospitable, cool-minded and calm
A sentinel state in the Northland
Her children from forest and farm.
Strong is the strength of their vigor
Still young at three-score and ten—
Maine is the mother of Mountains,
Maine is the Mother of Men.

The first of the states in the sunrise
The last of the states in its time
In summer a nation's wide playground,
Green-swarded, majestic, sublime.
Pine-jeweled, sea-bound and hoary,
Proud parent as always she's been
Maine is the Mother of Mountains,
Maine is the Mother of Men.

The late Earle H. Davis, enterprising developer of Shady Nook Camps on Balch Lake, West Newfield, wrote this poem. Davis graduated from Columbia University and taught for a time at Freedom Academy. During World War I, he served as a captain at a New Jersey Arsenal. He was a member of the 87th Maine Legislature and was a 50-year member of Day Spring Masonic Lodge. He also served on the board of selectmen for Newfield.

Five

PARSONSFIELD

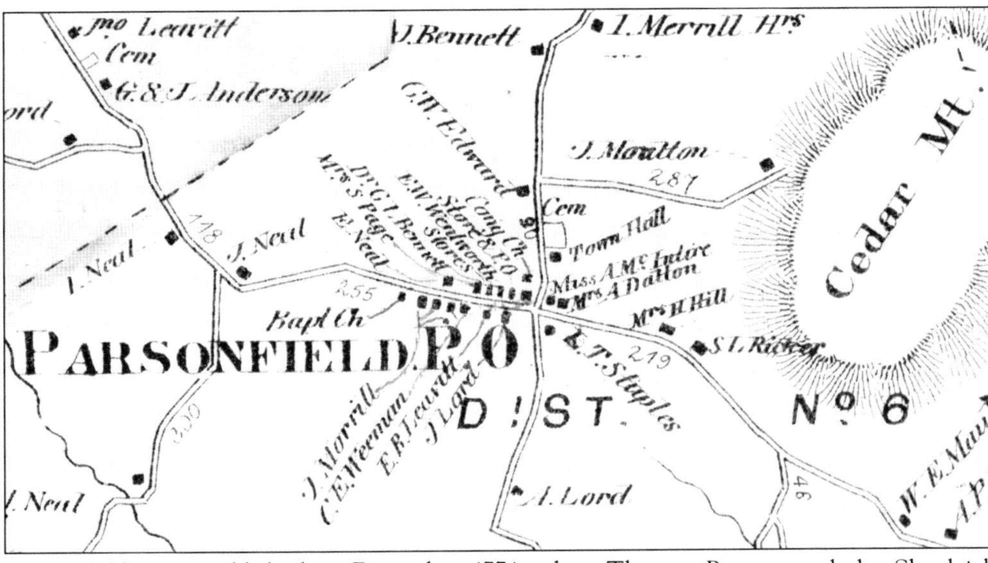

Parsonsfield was established in December 1774, when Thomas Parsons and the Shapleigh proprietors finally agreed upon a deed. Incorporation occurred March 9, 1785. Being a large town of 64 square miles, inhabitants were often strangers with widely differing views. Although 10 acres was set apart at Middle Road Village, designated for public buildings and town meetings, there was no one business center. Town officials were elected, but no man or group of men had controlling influence from border to border. Instead several small villages developed with neighborhood leaders whose purposes were often local and frequently conflicted with those of other neighborhoods. This section of an 1872 map shows Parsonsfield or Middle Road Village at the intersection of Middle Road and Merrill Hill Road, the geographic center of town. It was here that the church-meeting house was built in 1790 as specified in the deed to Thomas Parsons. Only the school, church, town house, and some homes remain today.

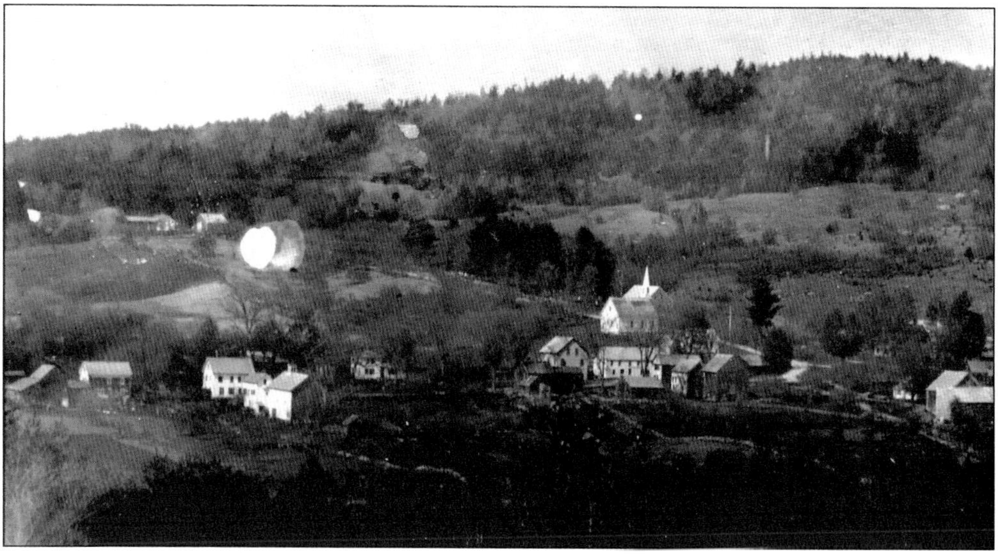

This birds-eye view of Middle Road Village from the south, with Cedar Mountain in the background, shows the back of the Congregational Church on Merrill Hill Road. Just the roof of the town house can be seen across the road and the school is barely visible through the trees below the church on the corner. The horizontal row of buildings on Middle Road included stores, a post office, and private homes.

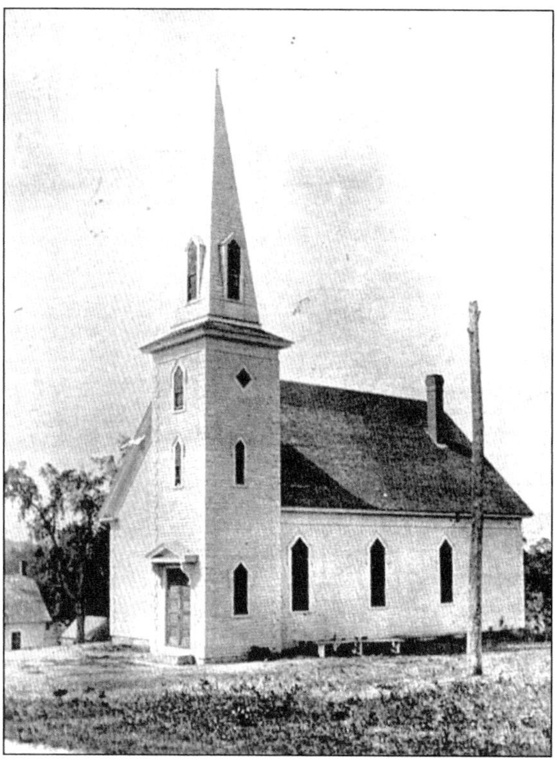

The Union Church located across from the town house at Middle Road Village is where the second Congregational Church once stood. In 1899, the Congregational Church sold this property to the Union Church Society. Society volunteers of several denominations, who wanted a convenient location in which to worship, built a new church. Although regular services ceased in 1920, an annual service is held here each August.

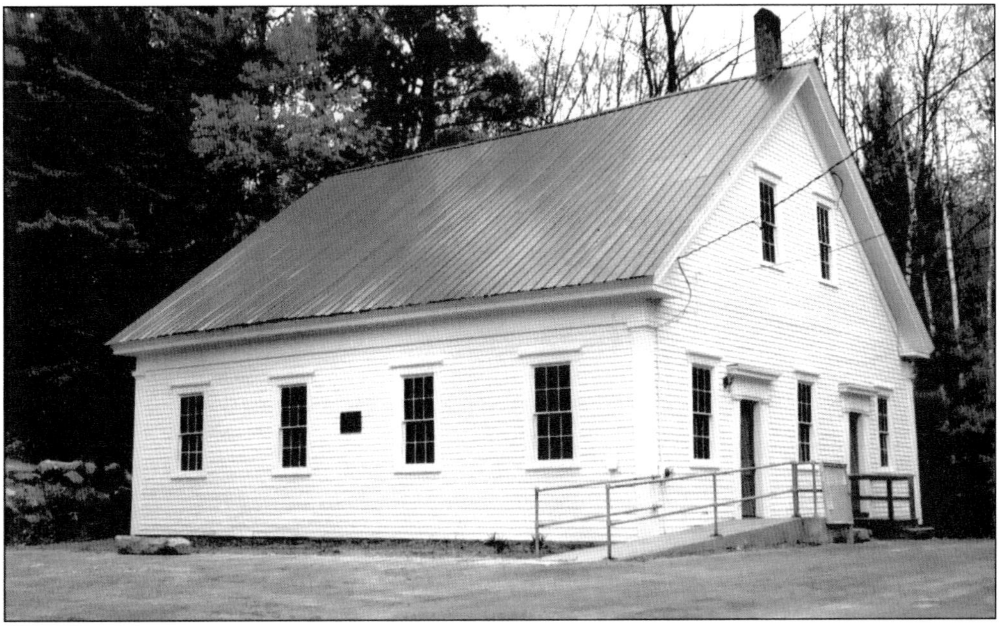

The Parsonsfield Town House on Merrill Hill Road was built about 1832 when the town and Congregational Church could no longer agree about sharing the church as a meetinghouse. It is being restored by ROOT, a group of interested citizens, and is on the National Register of Historic Places. Although Parsonsfield's municipal offices moved to Kezar Falls Village, all residents south of North Road still vote here.

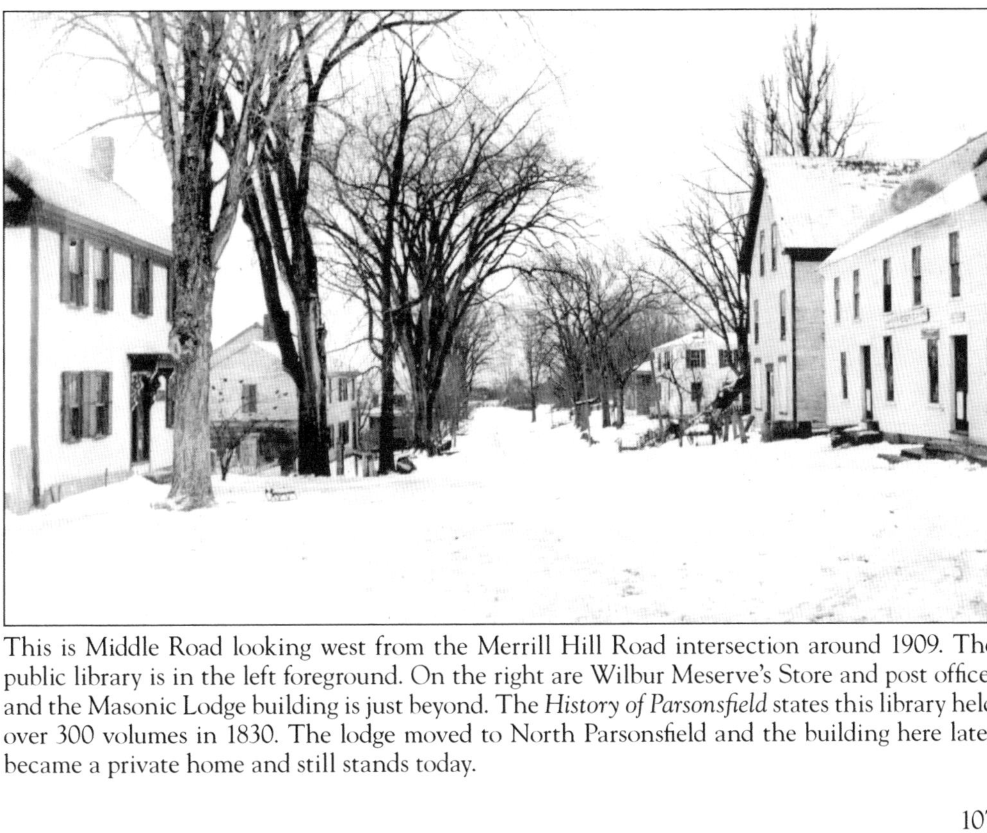

This is Middle Road looking west from the Merrill Hill Road intersection around 1909. The public library is in the left foreground. On the right are Wilbur Meserve's Store and post office, and the Masonic Lodge building is just beyond. The *History of Parsonsfield* states this library held over 300 volumes in 1830. The lodge moved to North Parsonsfield and the building here later became a private home and still stands today.

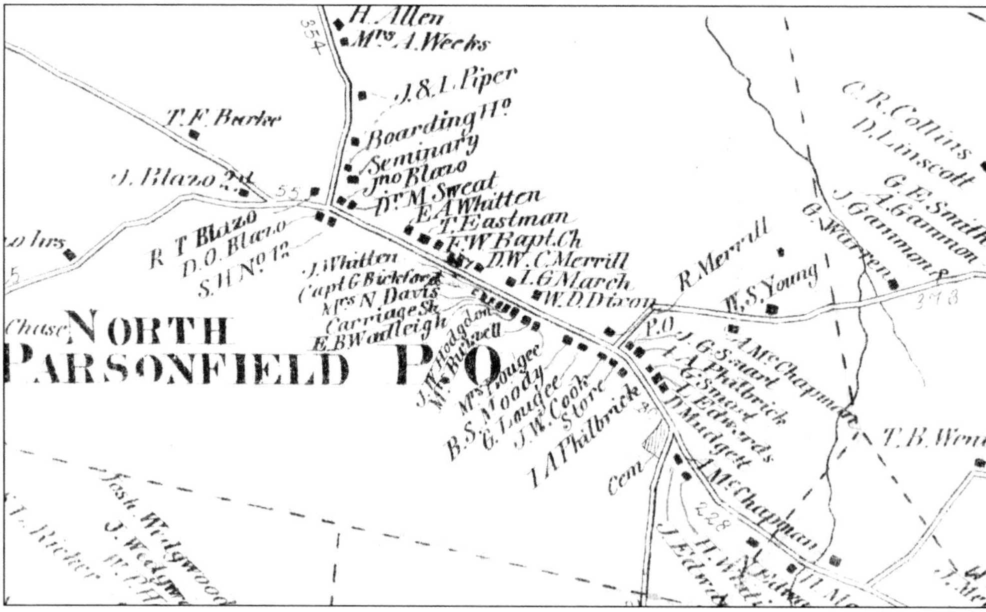

Not the usual compact village, North Parsonsfield was a broad straight street about a mile in length that turned north a short distance toward Porter. In 1872, a cluster of houses, stores, a church, and a school started at the cemetery and ended at Parsonsfield Seminary on the northern end. About 40 families lived here then, and many beautiful homes were built in this area.

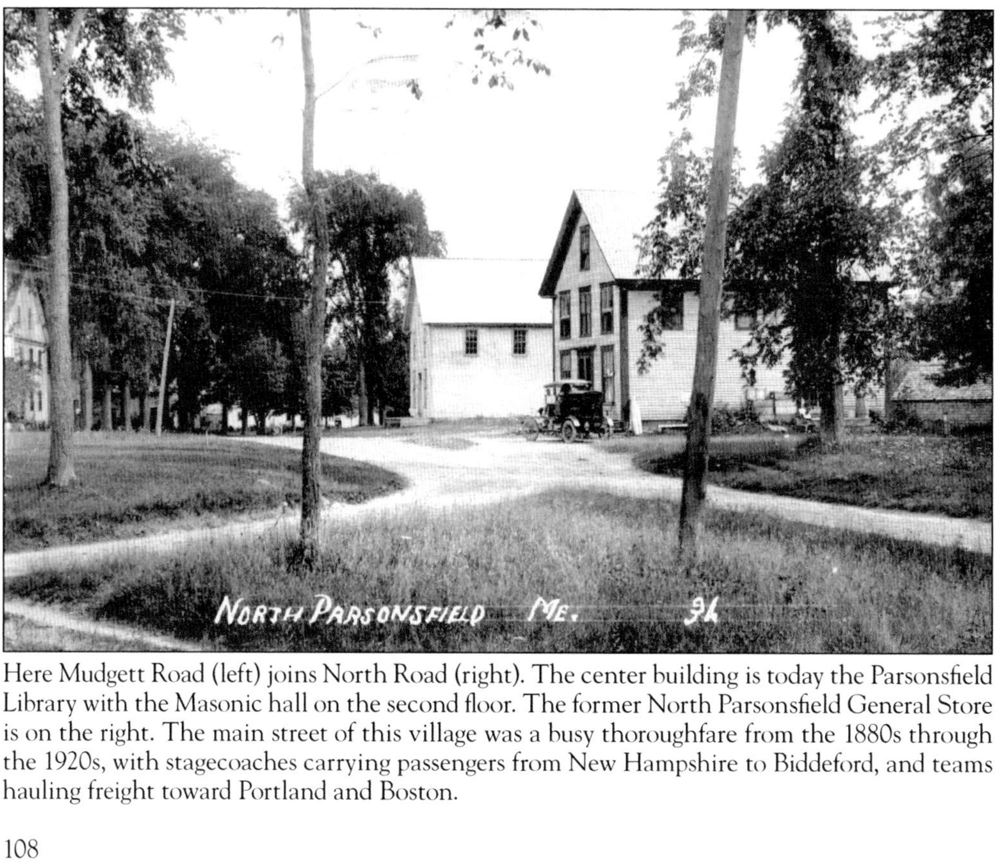

Here Mudgett Road (left) joins North Road (right). The center building is today the Parsonsfield Library with the Masonic hall on the second floor. The former North Parsonsfield General Store is on the right. The main street of this village was a busy thoroughfare from the 1880s through the 1920s, with stagecoaches carrying passengers from New Hampshire to Biddeford, and teams hauling freight toward Portland and Boston.

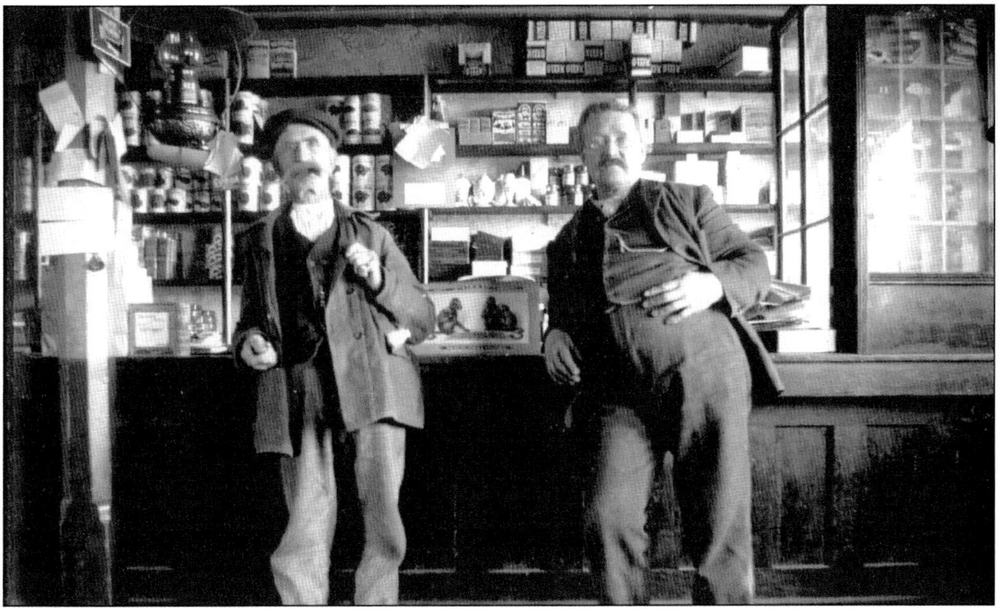

The North Parsonsfield General Store, started by James W. Cook in 1850, served local residents and farmers as well as passersby. It was later owned by John Wentworth, was sold to Sam Pease in 1907, and had a succession of owners ending with the Hammonds sometime after 1958. This 1904 picture is of George Stewart on the left, and John Wentworth, proprietor, on the right.

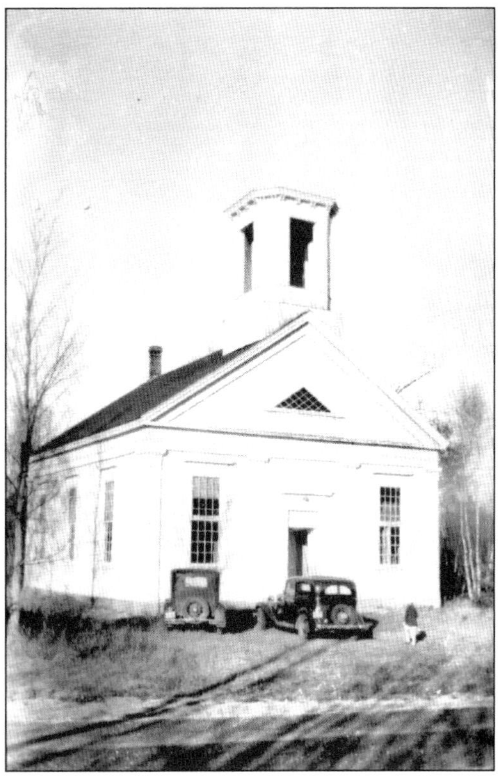

This 1931 picture shows the North Parsonsfield Free Baptist Church located on North Road near the present Fred Morrill Elementary School. The *History of Parsonsfield* states that it was built in 1853, and 13 people met on April 17, 1856, with Rev. B. S. Manson and G. W. Whitney and formed the church. It soon had 37 members. No longer used or maintained, it was taken down in the 1970s.

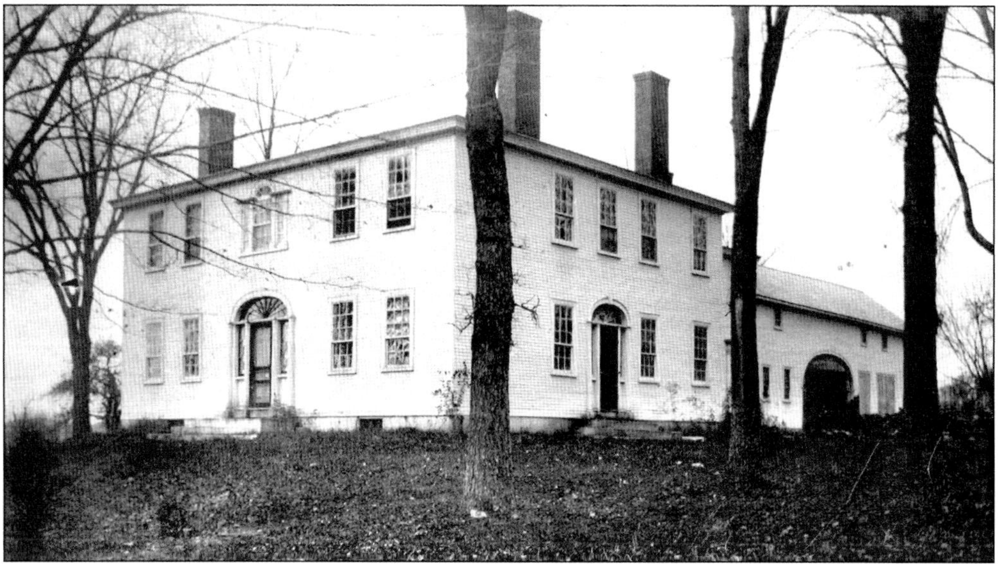

The Robert Blazo house is still located across from Parsonsfield Seminary on North Road. This and the Sweat Mansion below are fine examples of the large expensive homes built by the prosperous residents of North Parsonsfield in the early 1800s. Robert T. Blazo, a respected lawyer, conveyed land for the "Par-Sem" buildings and was on the board of trustees for the school.

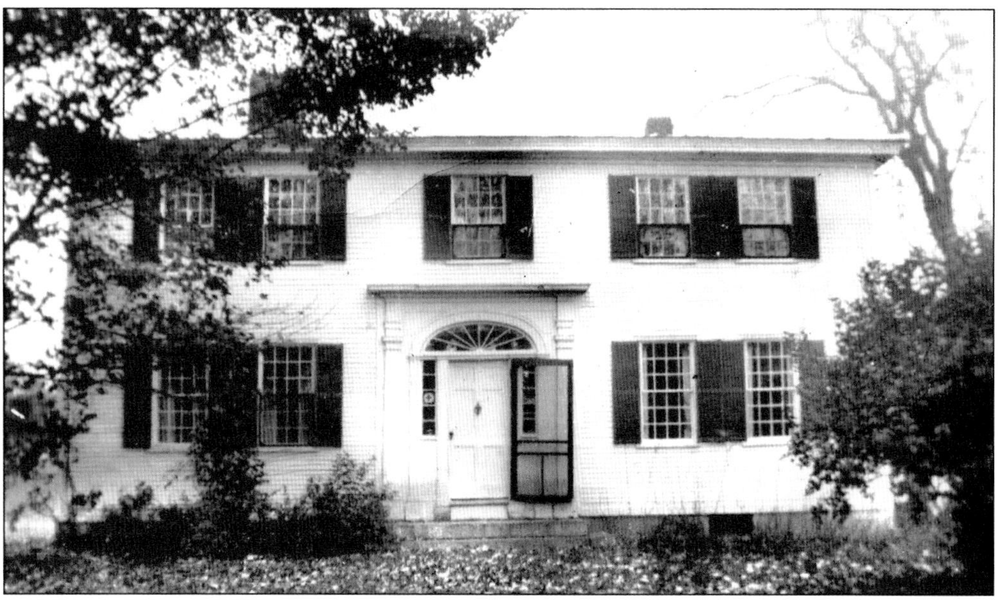

Dr. Moses Sweat built the Sweat Mansion located on North Road close to Parsonsfield Seminary in 1816. It once served as the principal's residence for the seminary. Dr. Sweat was widely known as a skilled physician and teacher of medicine. He was active in starting the original "Par-Sem" and served as secretary of the Parsonsfield Seminary Board of Trustees for many years. It is now a private residence.

This is Seminary Hall at Parsonsfield Seminary that began as a tuition school in 1832 with a strong Baptist Church influence. It offered both classical and college preparatory courses to students from many localities. Eventually it became a free high school for the town, graduating its last class in 1949. It became an elementary school from 1952 to 1986. The Friends of Par-Sem maintain the buildings today.

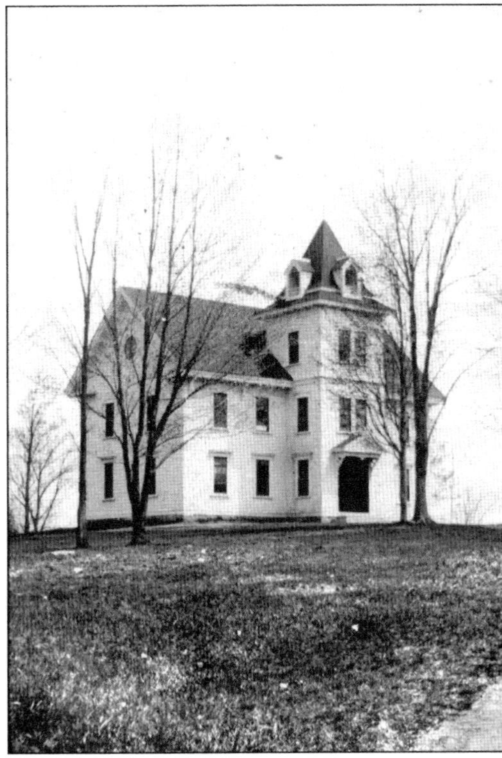

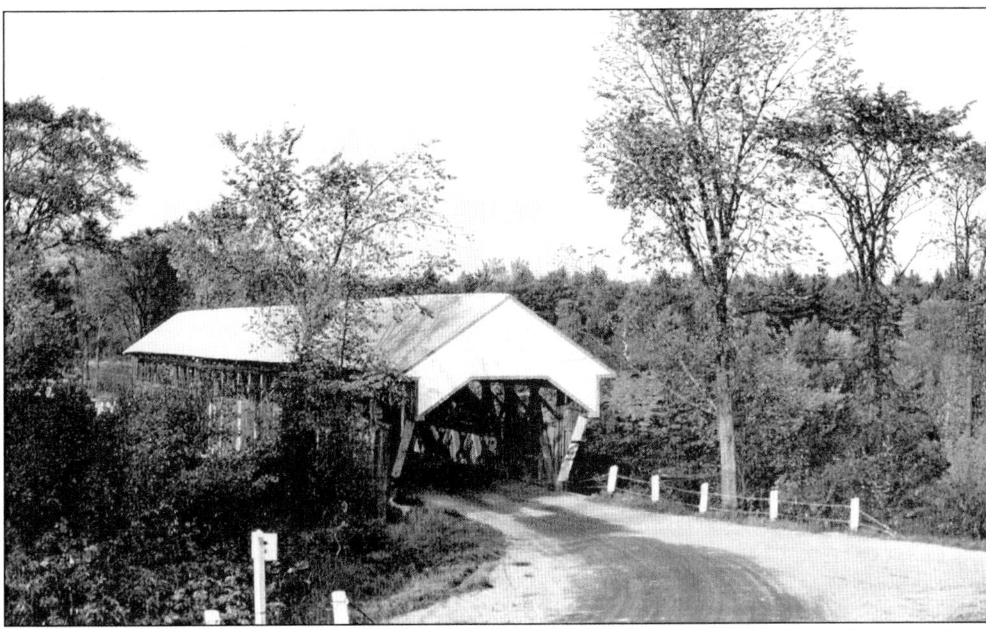

The Parsonsfield-Porter Covered Bridge over the Ossipee River near Porter Village was built as a simple pier bridge in 1798, rebuilt in 1808 and in 1857, then built as a covered bridge in 1876. Both towns maintained it for many years, at times with controversy. In 1964 it was closed to traffic when the new road and bridge were built upstream. The State of Maine restored the bridge in 2000.

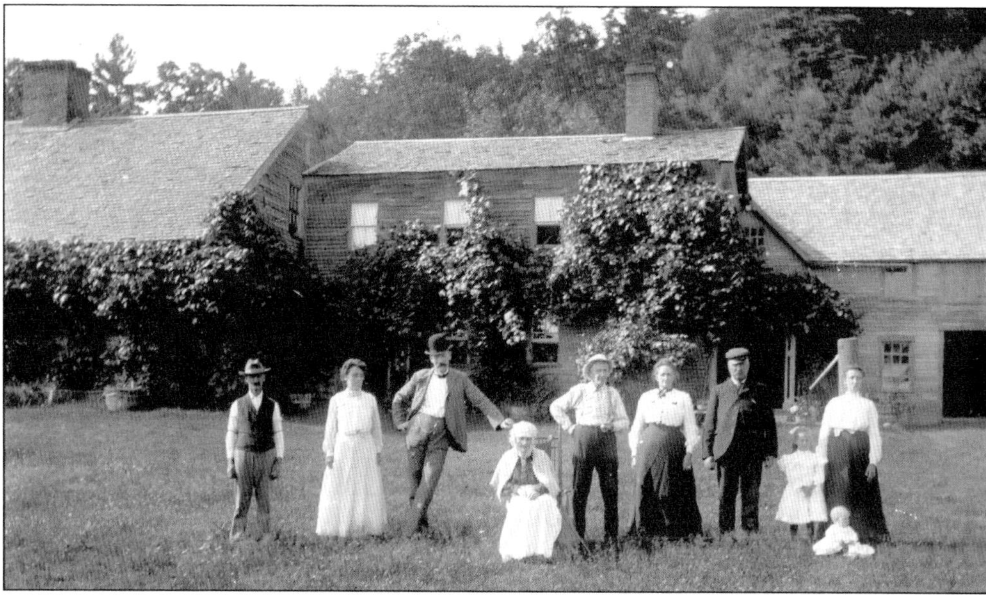

This is the Trueworthy home on Kezar Mountain Road around 1907. J. Woodman Trueworthy, owner, was active in town affairs, serving in several capacities. Seen here, from left to right, are Fred Trueworthy; Helen Trueworthy (née Parker); Ralph Trueworthy (husband of Helen); Angeline Woodman Trueworthy; John Trueworthy; Josie Rounds Trueworthy (née Floyd), wife of Fred; Al Floyd; Mrs. Al Floyd; and children. The Trueworthys maintained a home here for many years beginning in 1806. A new house exists on this site today.

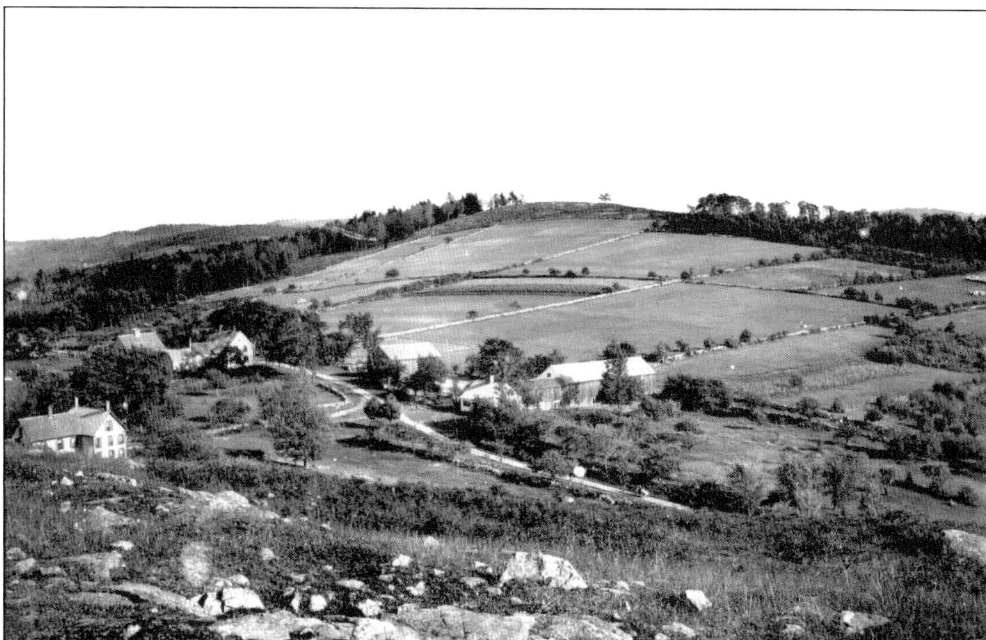

This scene overlooks the farm country around North Parsonsfield from Banks' Mountain. On the left is the Banks' home, next is the Pillsbury home and to the right of Banks Road is the McAllister home, which has since burned. Although fertile, this hilly and rocky land is typical of this area as well as much of Maine. How difficult it must have been for the farmers of the time.

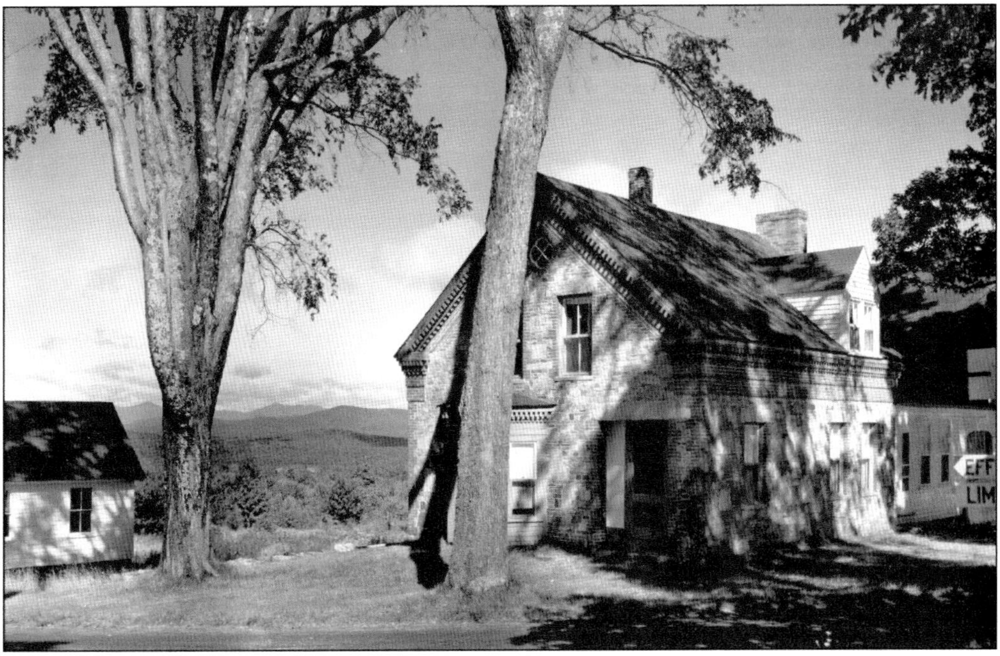

Albion Keith Parris Lougee built this Lougee home on North Road between 1857 and 1860. The Lougee family was one of the earliest to settle in Parsonsfield when three brothers, Gilman, Samuel, and John, came here in 1778. They went on to become prosperous farmers and played an important role in Parsonsfield town affairs and its history.

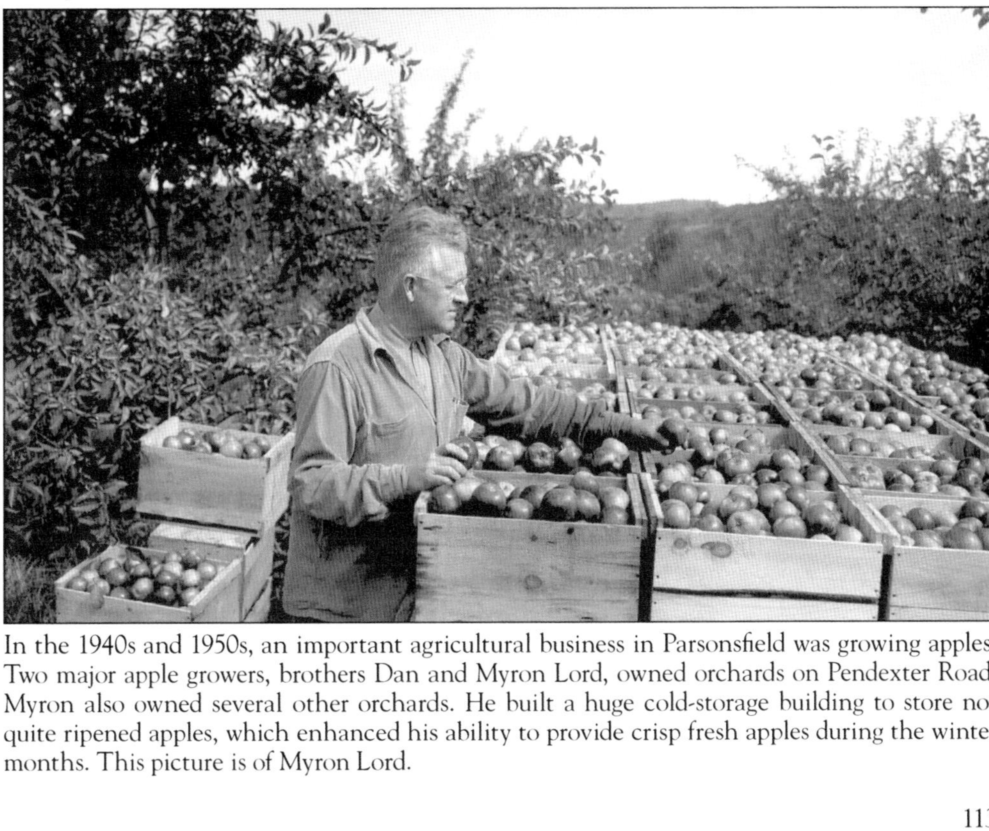

In the 1940s and 1950s, an important agricultural business in Parsonsfield was growing apples. Two major apple growers, brothers Dan and Myron Lord, owned orchards on Pendexter Road. Myron also owned several other orchards. He built a huge cold-storage building to store not quite ripened apples, which enhanced his ability to provide crisp fresh apples during the winter months. This picture is of Myron Lord.

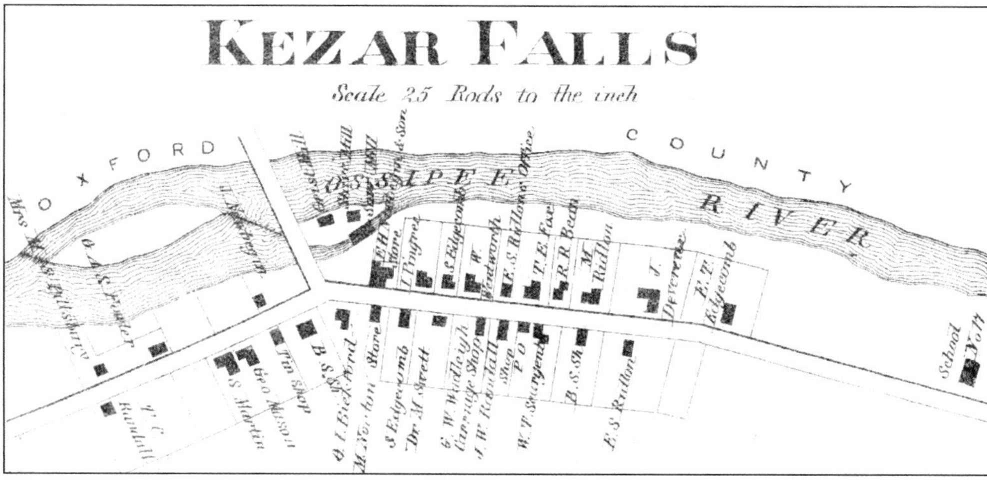

By the mid-1800s the potential of water power was realized and the village of Kezar Falls started to develop on both sides of the Ossipee River, with Porter on the north and Parsonsfield on the south. This 1872 map of the Parsonsfield side shows homes of several prominent citizens and a number of commercial establishments. Today this is Parsonsfield's only business center and the municipal offices are located here.

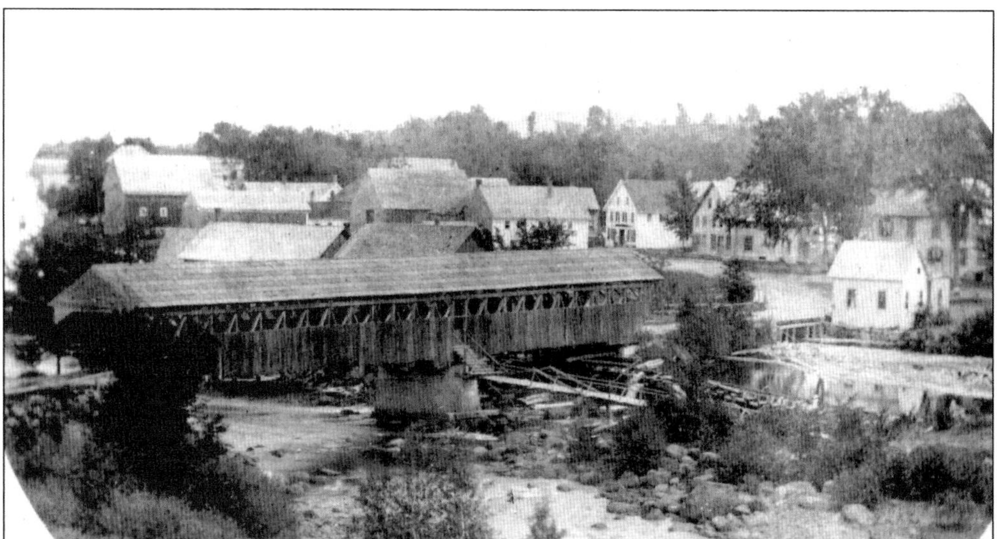

This covered bridge connected the Parsonsfield and Porter sides of the village. The first bridge built here in 1833 was an open bridge, paid for by public subscription. The covered bridge was built in 1869 and was replaced in 1927 by a cement bridge. To the right can be seen a footbridge that led to Garner's Island where a bandstand was located.

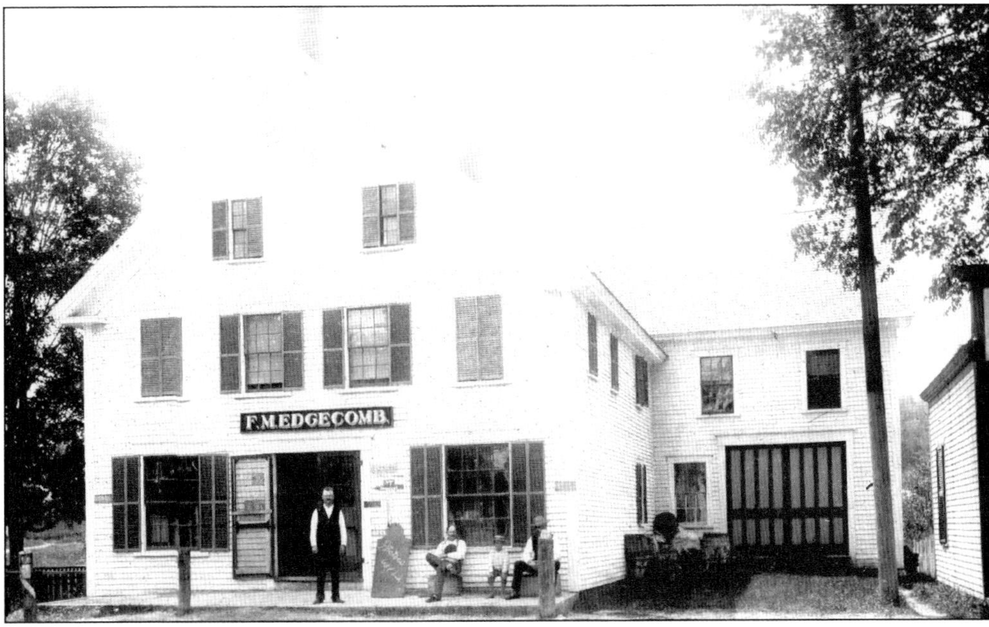

In the mid-1800s, Sutton Edgecomb was the first known occupant of the Norton Hardware building operating a grocery and hardware store. Later Will Norton bought and continued the hardware business. In the 1930s, Clarence Sawyer and Neil Hamilton took over the business and later sold it to Roger Stanley and Charles Mitchell, who ran a hardware and propane business until 2000. Now it is Kezar Falls Hardware owned by Greg Schick.

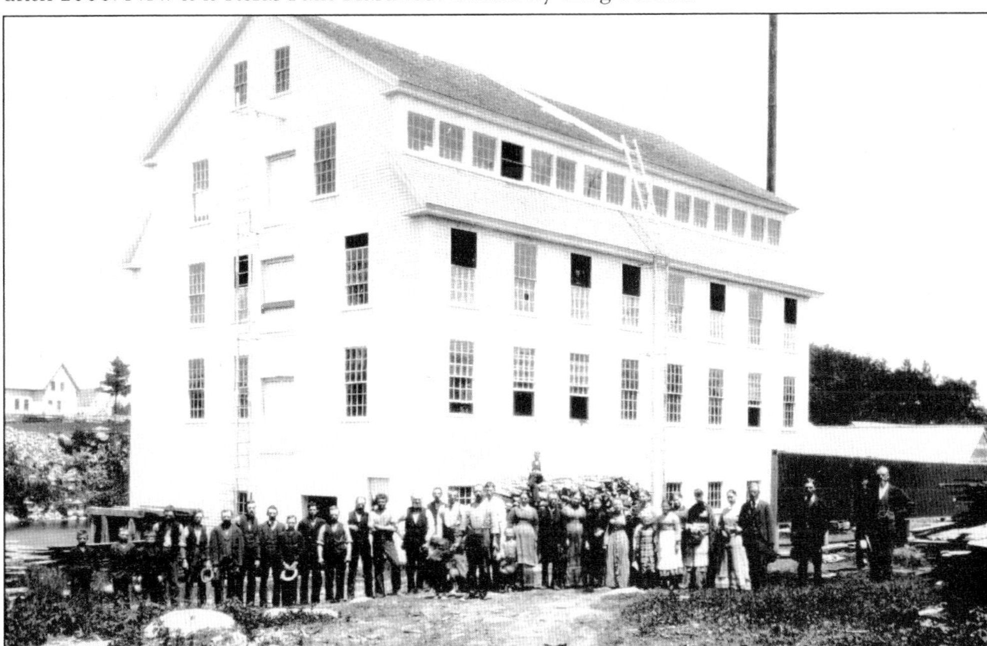

This is the original building of the Kezar Falls Woolen Mill, built in 1880. Three local citizens, George W. Towle, Elijah Fox, and John Devereux, organized the Kezar Falls Manufacturing Company. In 1881, Allen Garner was hired to set up the machinery and run the mill. The success of the mill was largely due to his efforts. The first yard of cloth was woven in July 1881.

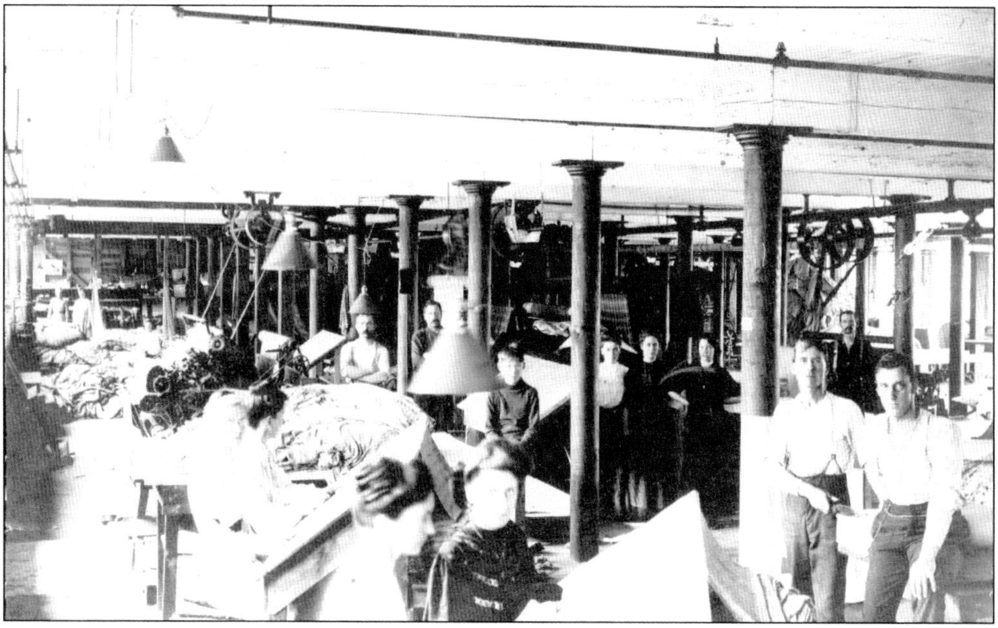

The woolen mill prospered and provided employment for many men and women from the surrounding area. Local citizens who had made their living from farming were then able to leave the farms and work here. The mill was sold several times but continued to remain open until 2000 when Robinson Manufacturing was forced to close its Kezar Falls Division, thus ending an important source of employment for this area.

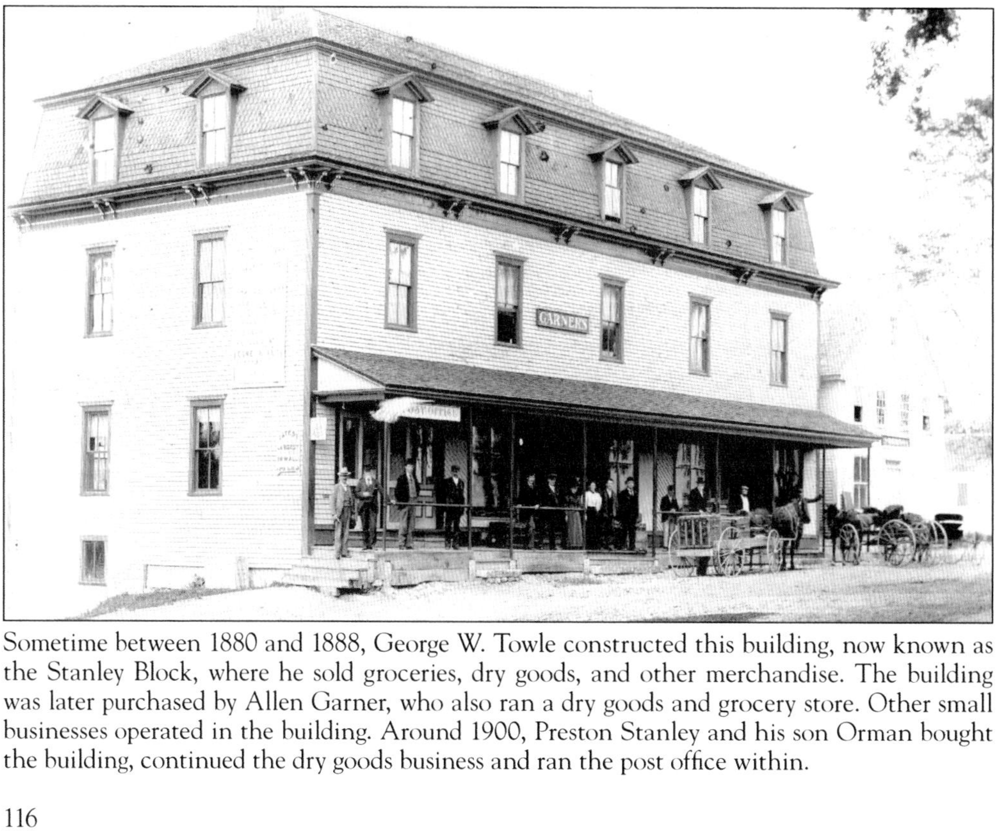

Sometime between 1880 and 1888, George W. Towle constructed this building, now known as the Stanley Block, where he sold groceries, dry goods, and other merchandise. The building was later purchased by Allen Garner, who also ran a dry goods and grocery store. Other small businesses operated in the building. Around 1900, Preston Stanley and his son Orman bought the building, continued the dry goods business and ran the post office within.

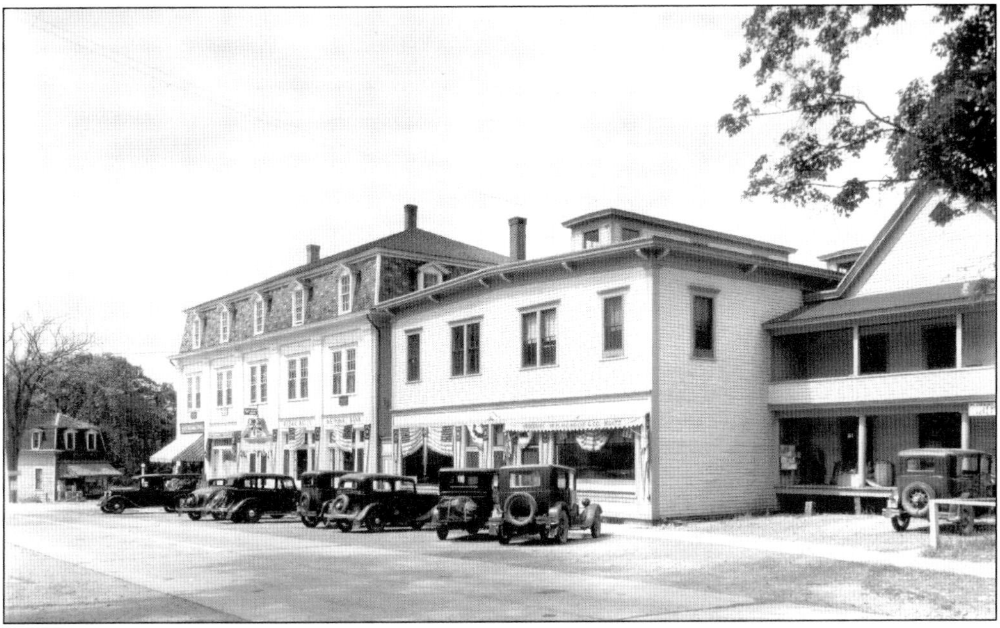

This shows the Stanley Block as it looked in 1927. In 1910, George W. Towle and Allen Garner organized the Kezar Falls National Bank here, connected to the dry goods store by a swinging door. By 1932, the store was sold, the building was remodeled including the bank, and apartments and offices were added. In 1937, a fire destroyed the third floor. The bank has recently been replaced by various shops.

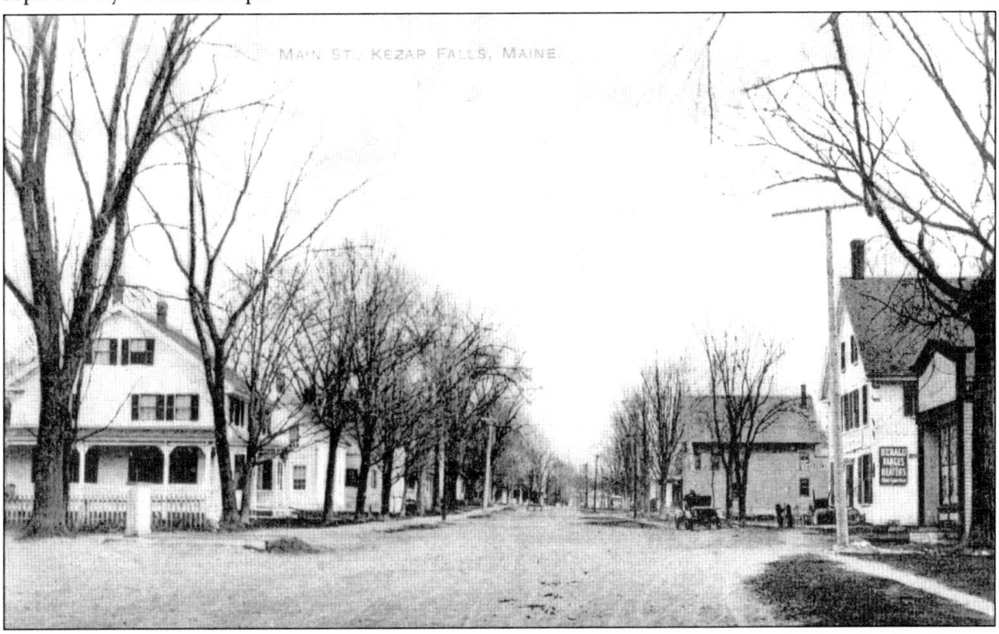

This 1909 scene is looking east on Federal Road just beyond the Stanley Block. The first house on the left, once the Griffith's home, no longer exists, and the next house was Givens' (later The Kezar Falls Wool Shop). From the right are Dr. Ham's drug store (later Dr. Hayden's dental office), Norton Hardware, and an apartment house. Several impressive homes were built farther down including homes for the Garners and Dr. Devereux.

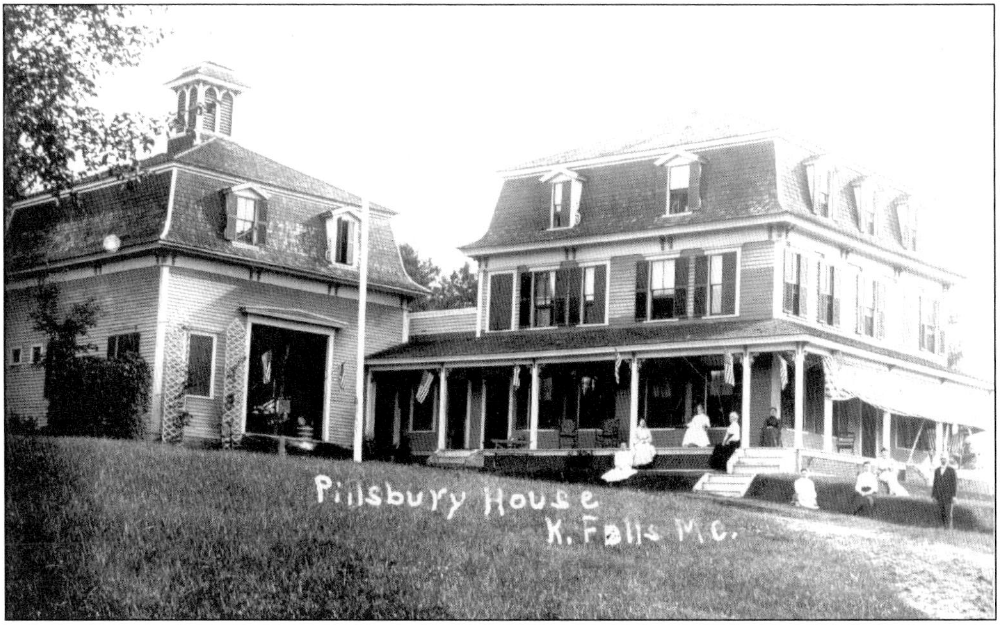

The Pillsbury House was built in 1882 by the three sons of David and Sarah Pillsbury of Boston. It is located on Elm Street in Kezar Falls, overlooking the Ossipee River. The main building was a three-storied square house of 13 rooms capped by a mansard roof. The house was built as a summer boarding house. The Pillsbury House closed in 1911, and is a private residence today.

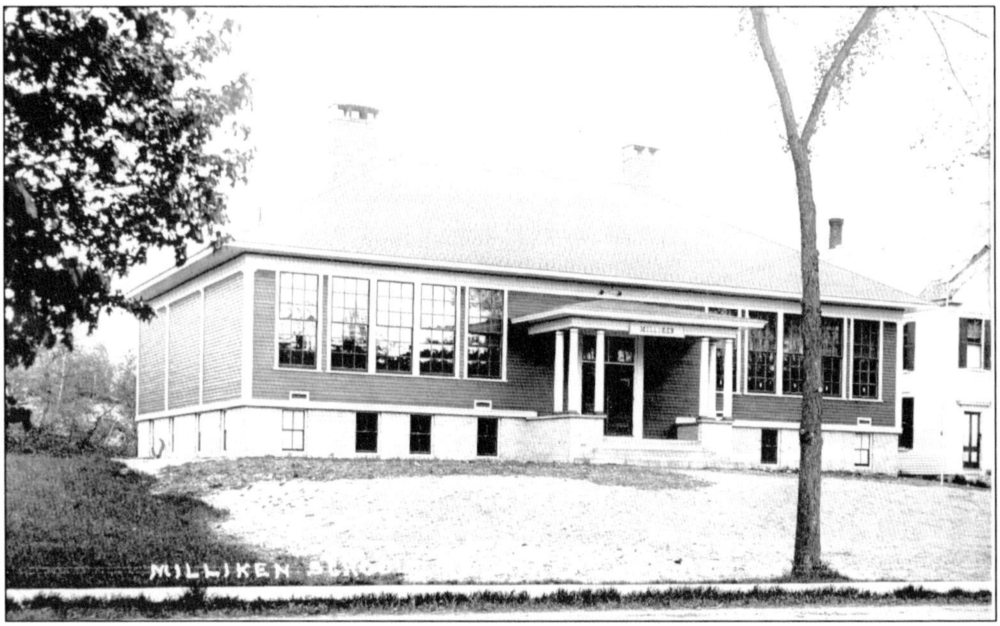

Milliken School on Federal Road was built in 1925 to replace an older building, which was used since 1873. This new modern school had four classrooms housing grades four through seven. A lunchroom, kitchen, and restrooms were located in the basement. A small stage was at one end of the seventh grade classroom with a moveable wall between the sixth and seventh grade classes. In 1988, it was converted to the Parsonsfield town office.

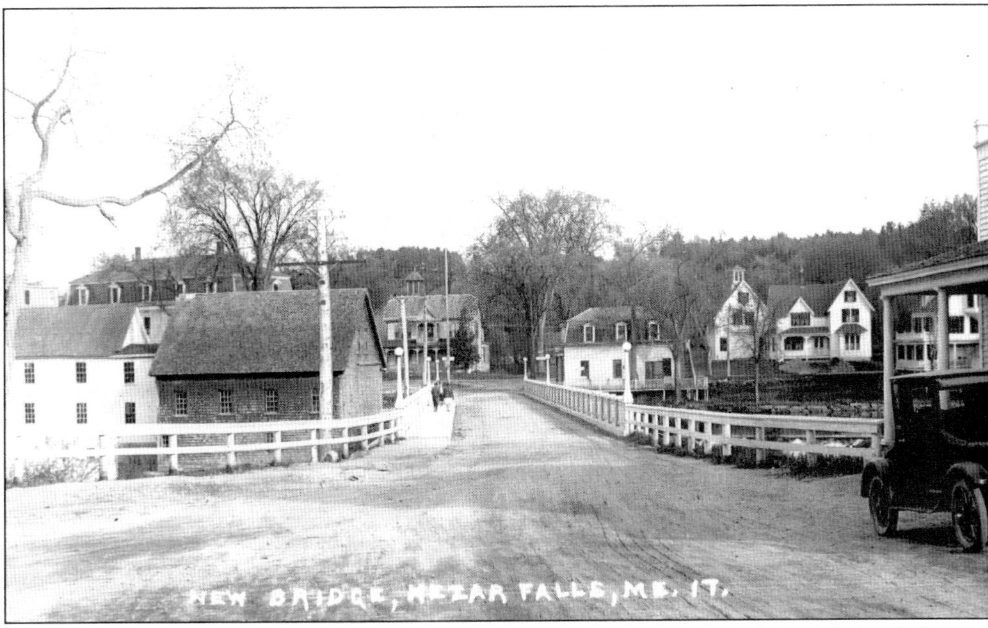

In 1927, a new cement bridge replaced the covered bridge. Shown on the left behind the mill buildings is the Stanley Block and in the center is the Bullock House, (the location of the current post office). To the right is the Newbegin Cigar Shop, post office, and Dr. Ridlon's home and office. In 2001, the bridge was totally replaced with a larger one, which was built to the right of the one above.

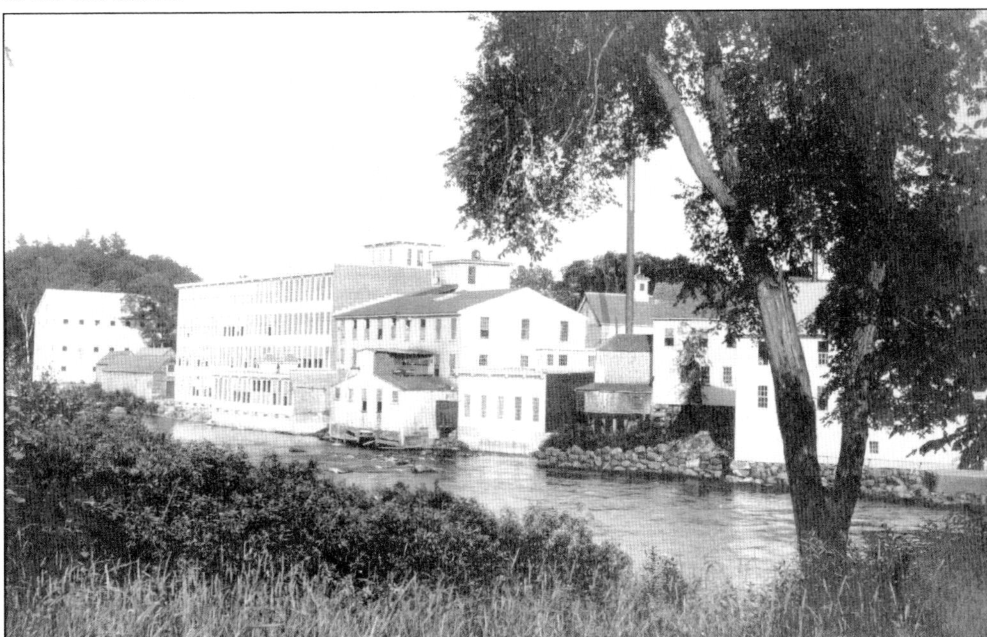

This 1909 picture of the Kezar Falls Woolen Mill, from the Porter side of the river, shows its many additions and extensions. It became the "heart of the village" and had earned a fine reputation for producing quality woolen material for over a century. It played an important role during both World War I and II, producing cloth for military uniforms.

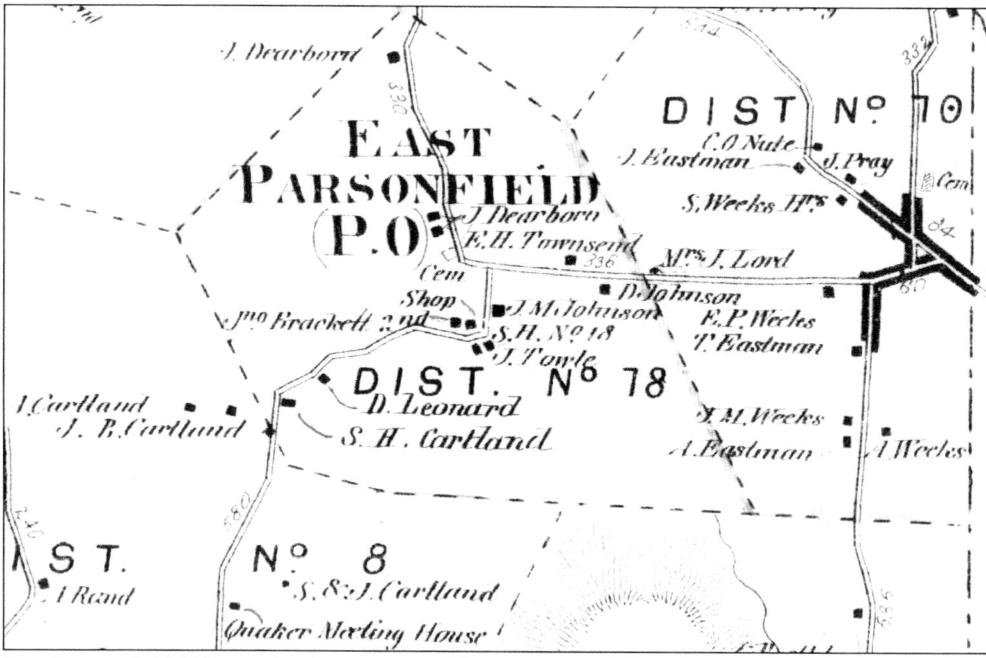

East Parsonsfield Village, also known as Weeks Corner, is located on the east end of North Road near the Cornish town line. Once a thriving village with stores, a post office, school, church, and hotel, it was one of the last Parsonsfield villages to lose its business center. Although there are many residences here today, only the post office remains as a reminder of what it once was.

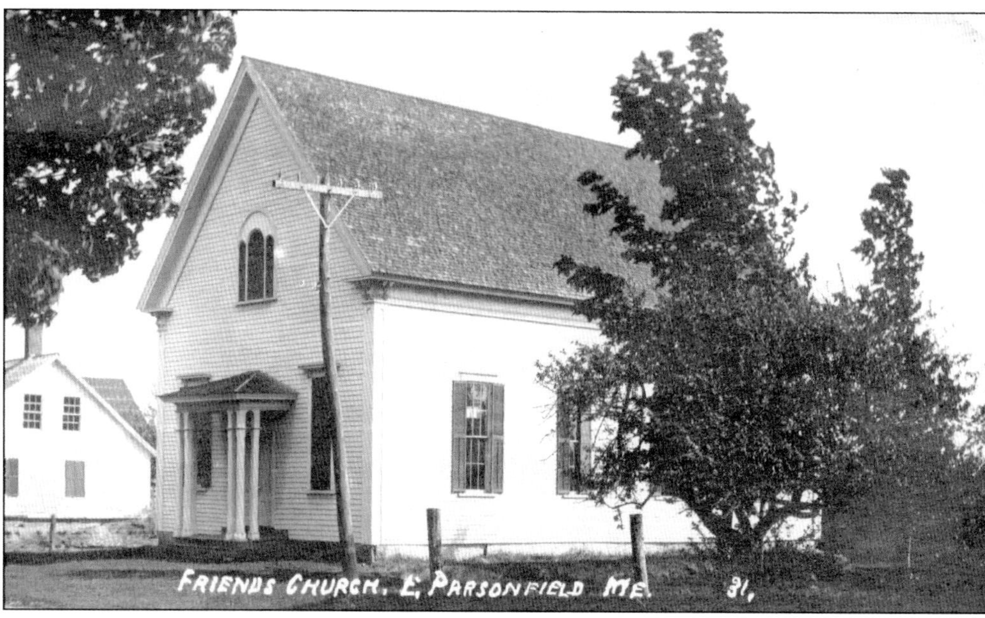

This is the Friends Church in 1928 located on North Road near the center of East Parsonsfield. It was built in 1888 for about 100 members. The first meeting of Friends in Parsonsfield was held around 1798, and the first meetinghouse was built in 1838 with 20 members. This neat little building is now empty and in disrepair. (This is not the Quaker Meeting House on the above map.)

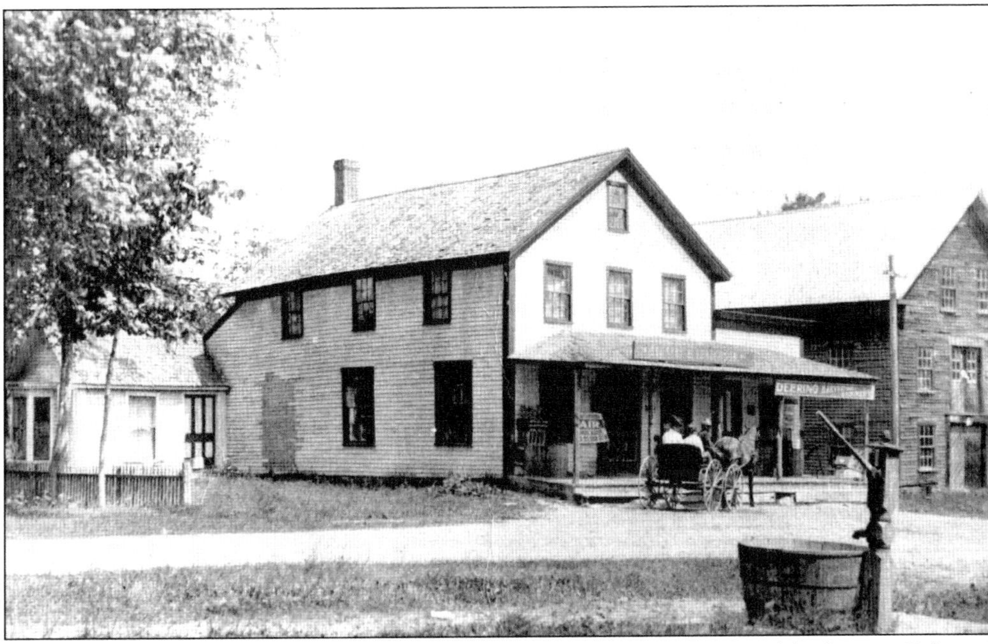

The Boothby and Fenderson store, pictured here in 1906, was once owned by Jerome Cole and Woodbridge G. O. Ridlon. The second floor was once a coat factory and the small, attached building was a village library for a while. Owned by Reuben Fenderson for many years, it burned down in 1940. The carriage shop on the right was owned by Jerome Cole and was torn down in 1930.

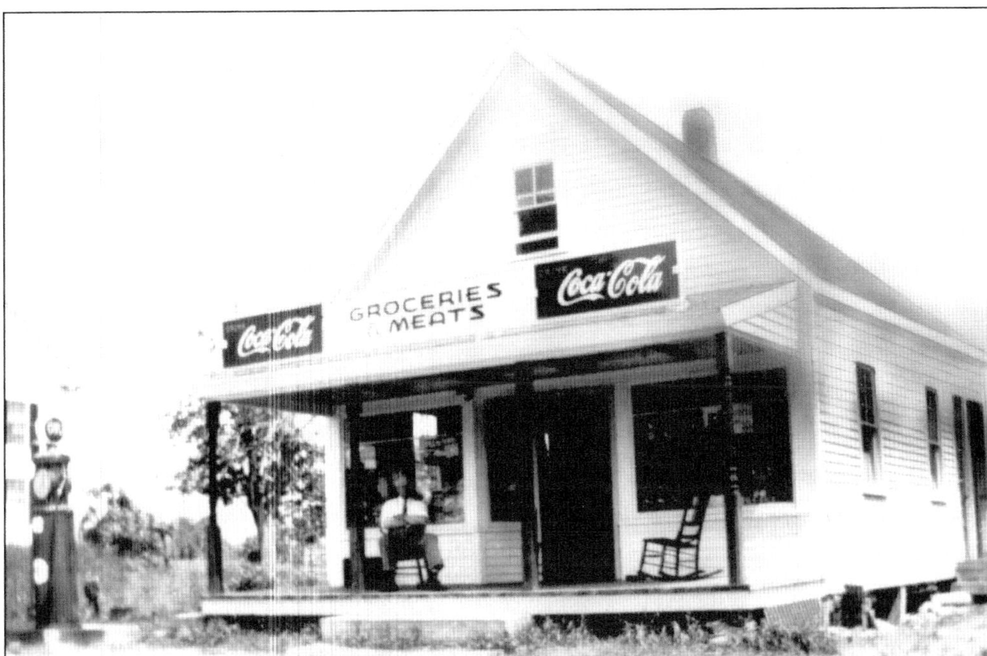

Reuben and May Fenderson constructed this building in 1941 to replace the store that burned. It remains today as the East Parsonsfield Post Office. This is now the only post office in Parsonsfield other than the main post office located at Kezar Falls Village.

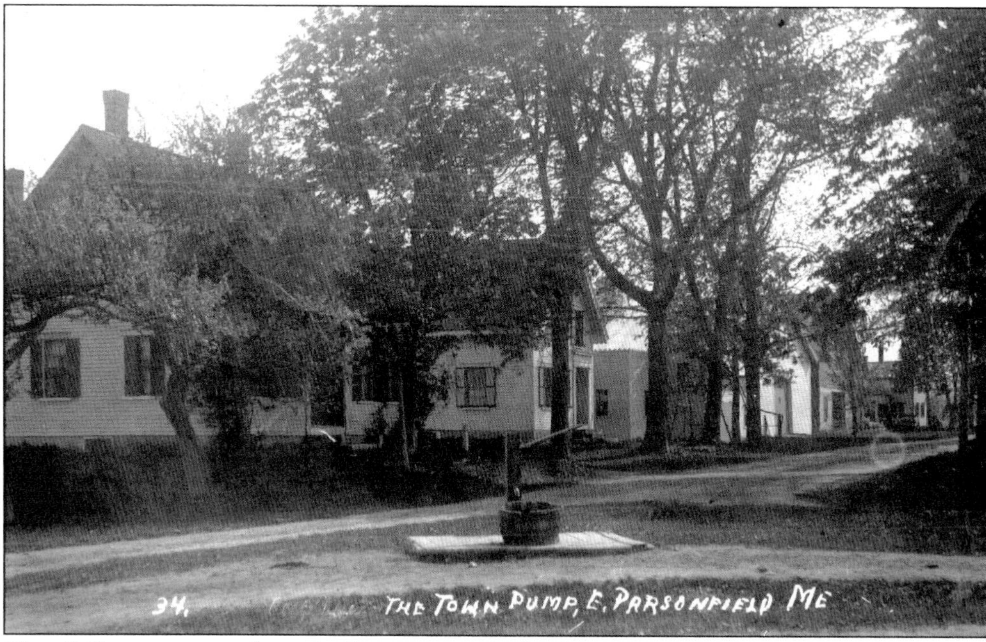

This 1909 scene across from Fenderson's store looks down Maplecrest Road at the intersection of North Road. Charles Dearborn owned the house on the left and followed by the Hansons, who gave it to the Baptist church for a parsonage. Next was Ina and Ormond Watson's home, and farther down, the Dunnell's and Mouradian's. Used into the 1960s, the town pump was an important water supply in dry seasons.

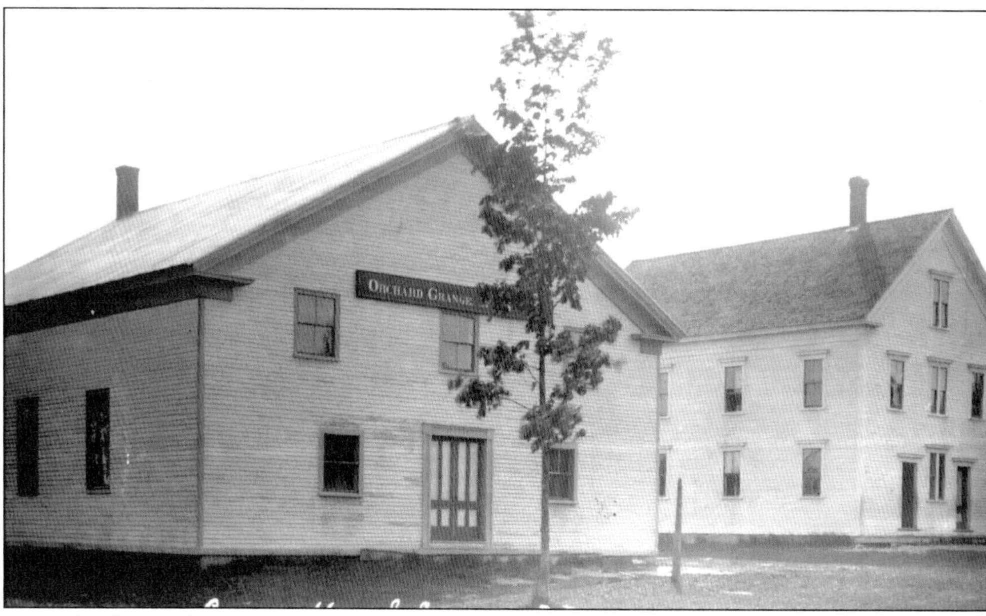

Both the Orchard Grange Hall and District No. 10 East Parsonsfield School are shown in this picture from 1915. The buildings are still located on North Road in East Parsonsfield Village. The school closed in 1952 when the Parsonsfield consolidated school system was established at Parsonsfield Seminary. Both buildings became private homes, and an antique store was located in the front of the school for a while.

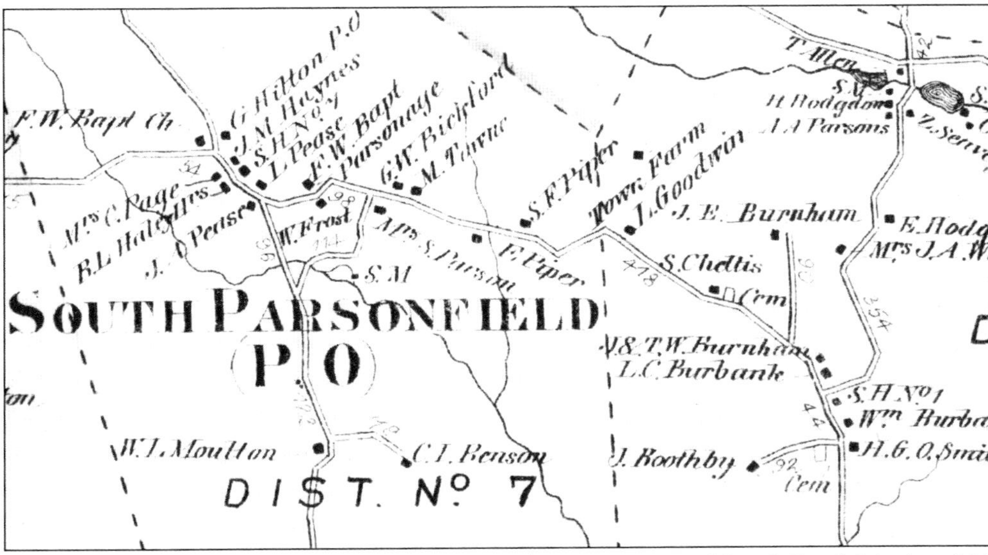

This little village of South Parsonsfield begins at the intersection of South Road, Moulton Hill Road, and Maplewood Road by the Free Will Baptist Church. In 1872, the date of this map, it also had a school, post office, and many large homesteads. Like most of the other villages in Parsonsfield, only the church and some of the homes remain today.

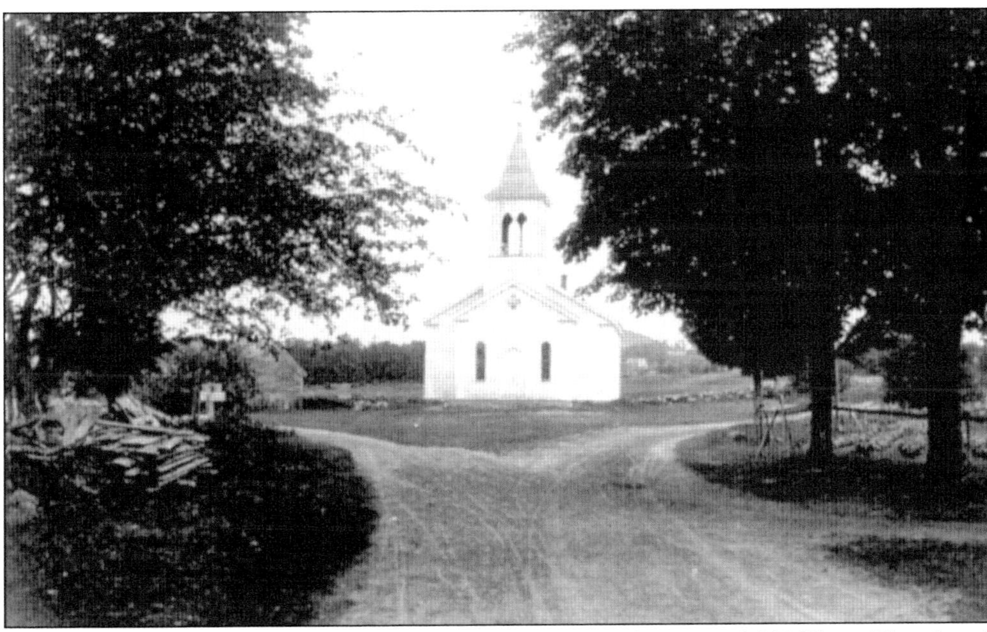

The Free Will Baptist Church stands at the corner in South Parsonsfield Village. The church was organized on July 15, 1830. The first pastor was Andrew J. Foss. This building was built in 1840 and was renovated in 1872. It replaced the first meetinghouse, a low, one-story building that stood where the schoolhouse is located. Today it is the only church still operating in Parsonsfield outside of Kezar Falls.

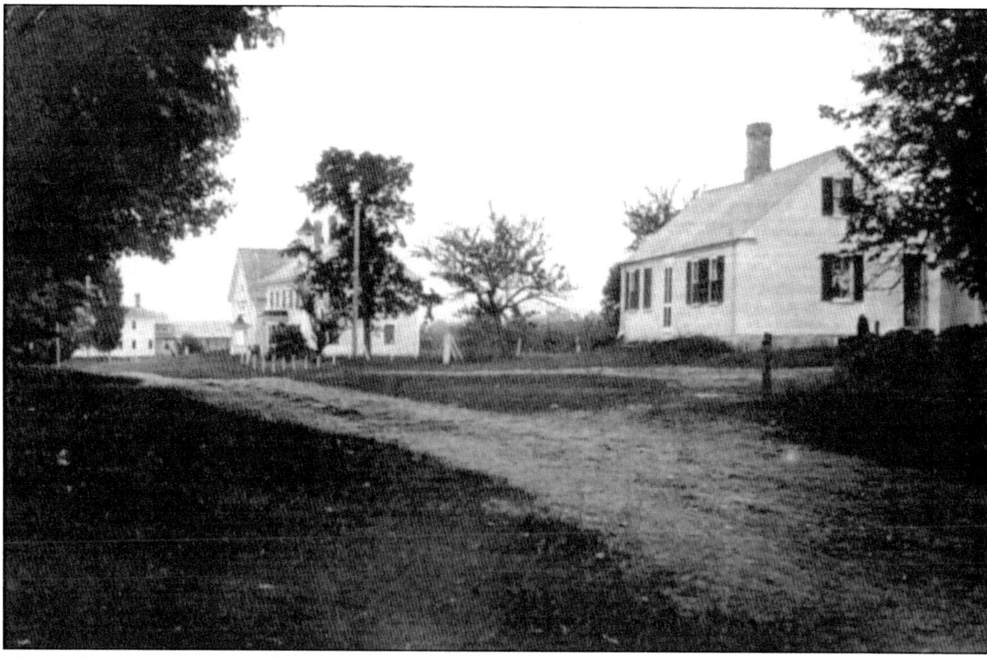

This is South Road around 1910, looking east. On the far left is the Nathaniel Pease house. The middle house that was once the Hale's, then the Guest's, and then the O'Brien's, burned down on March 14, 1942. The O'Briens used to take in boarders. The white house in the foreground is located just beyond the intersection and the Baptist church, and was once a store and post office.

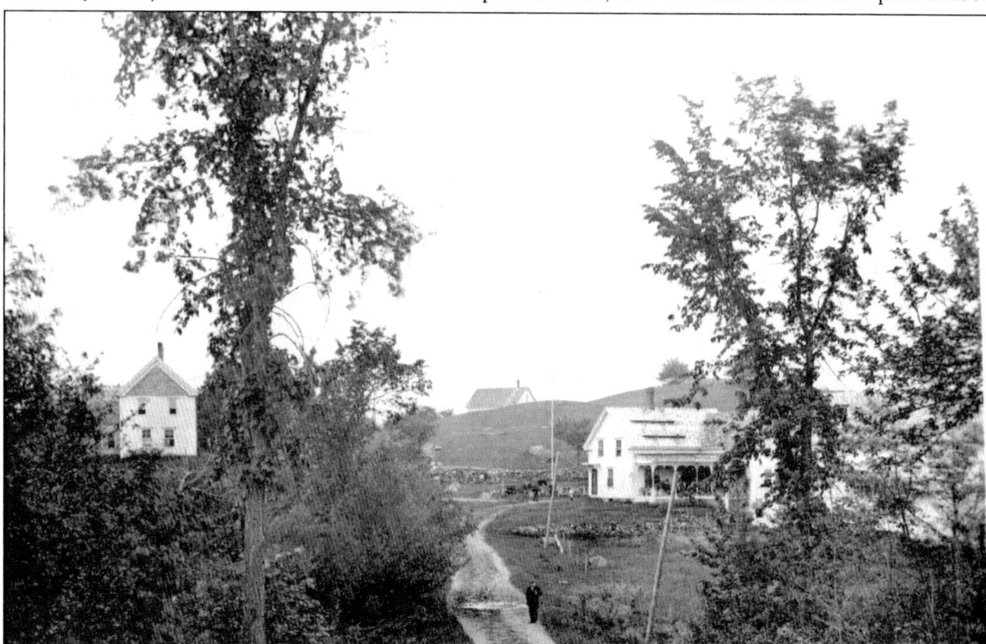

This scene taken at the end of the 19th the century is looking toward South Road where the buildings are located; the Baptist Church Parsonage is on the left, the Bickford House is on the right, and the roof of the South Parsonsfield School House District No. 7 is in the distance. Samuel Pease is standing in the road.

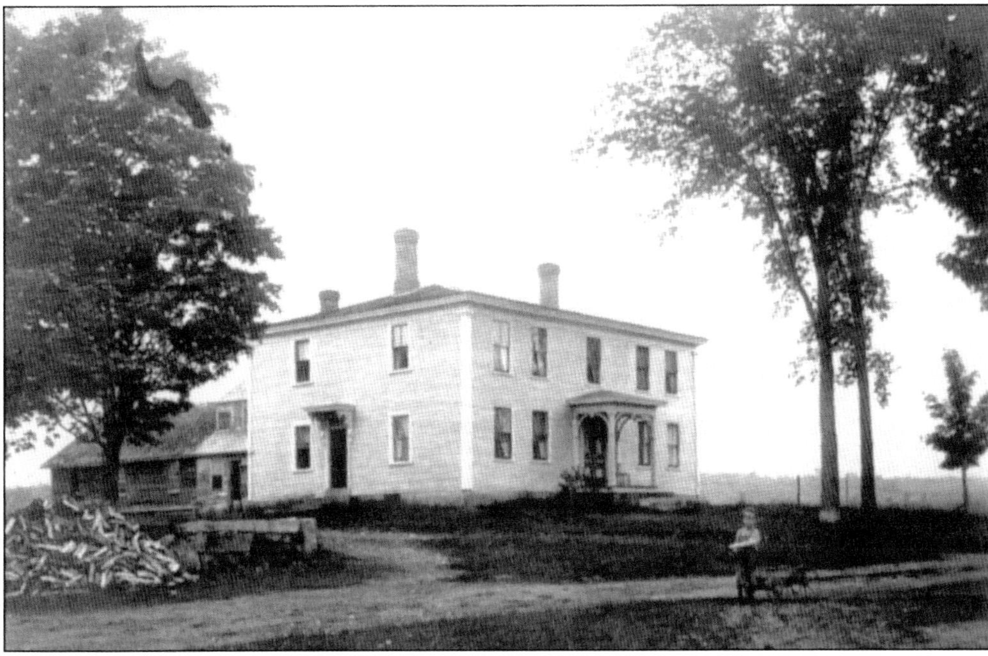

Nathaniel Pease built this large, handsome home on South Road around 1800. Nathaniel was the son of Zebulon Pease, an early settler in this area. This home has always remained in the Pease family and is occupied by one of his descendents today. The boy in the foreground is Ray Gibson. An earlier home built by Zebulon Pease was located across the street but the house burned around 1952.

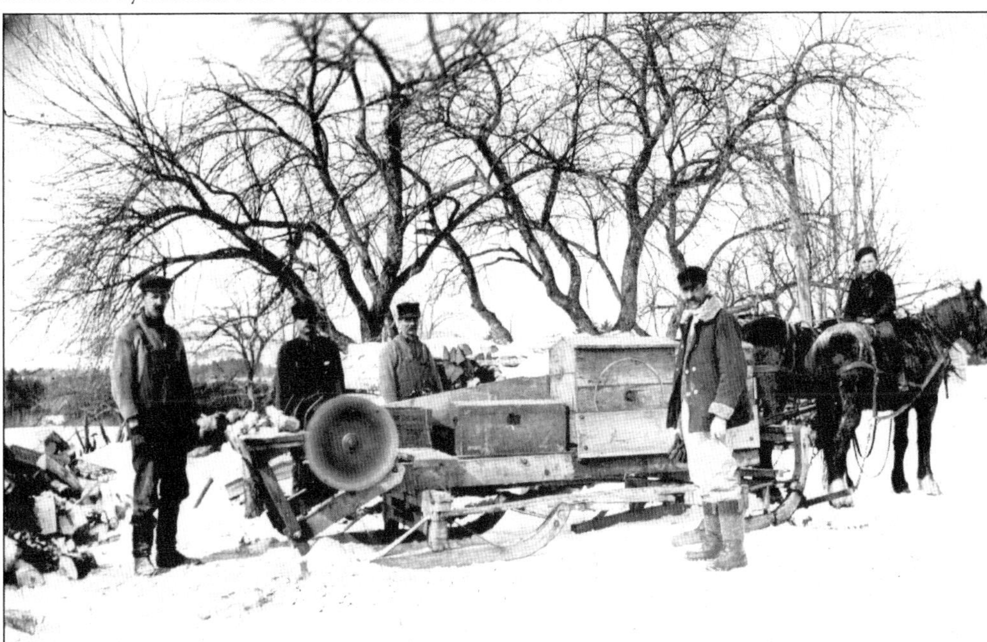

This was a portable sawmill owned by Edward Pease. It is shown here being put to good use, probably sawing wood to replenish the winter fuel. The sawmill was being operated by the Pease family. Seen here, from left to right, are Arthur, Charles, Frank, and Edward. Phil Gibson is the boy on the horse. The horses' names were Ben and Chub.

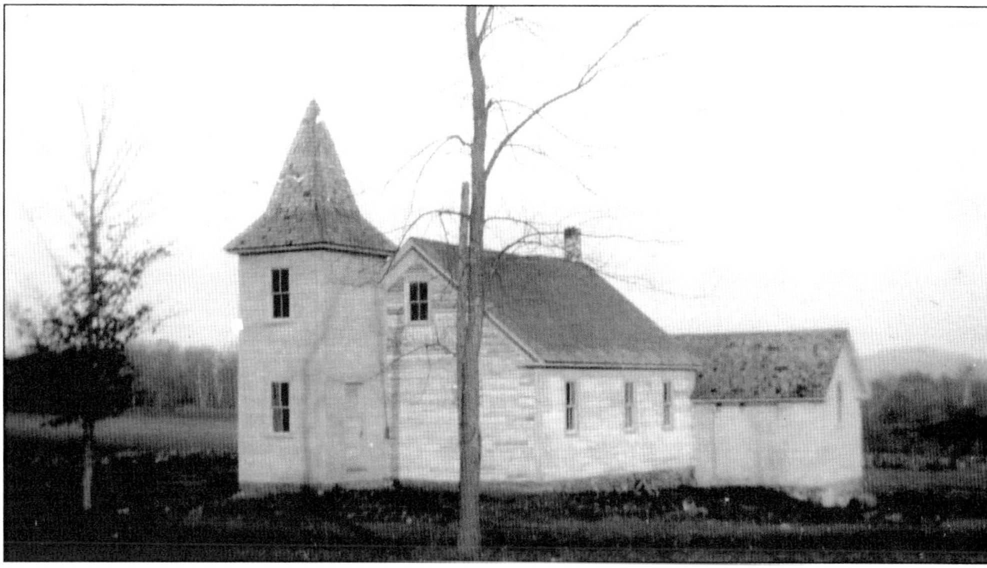

This picture of the Maplewood School, located on Maplewood Road near the intersection of Mountain Road and the Newfield town line, certainly does not show the beautiful trees typical of Maplewood. The neighborhood streets are lined with majestic maple trees planted by Dr. J. W. Dearborn in 1882, when Maplewood was considered part of North Newfield. The building is now a private home, identified by the unusual tower-like structure.

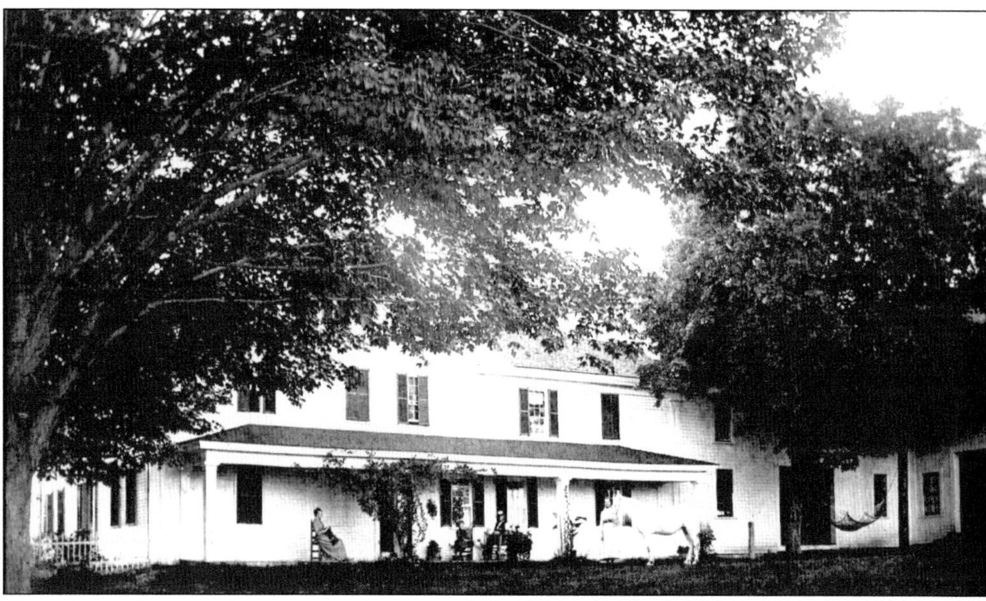

The Honorable Charles Sanborn homestead, built in 1797 by John Sanborn, was one of the earliest homes in the neighborhood of Maplewood. It is still located on Mountain Road on the Newfield town line. The people in the picture are members of the Sanborn family. Charles Sanborn was among the few prominent people instrumental in producing the *History Of Parsonsfield, Maine*, which was spearheaded by Dr. Jeremiah W. Dearborn in 1888.

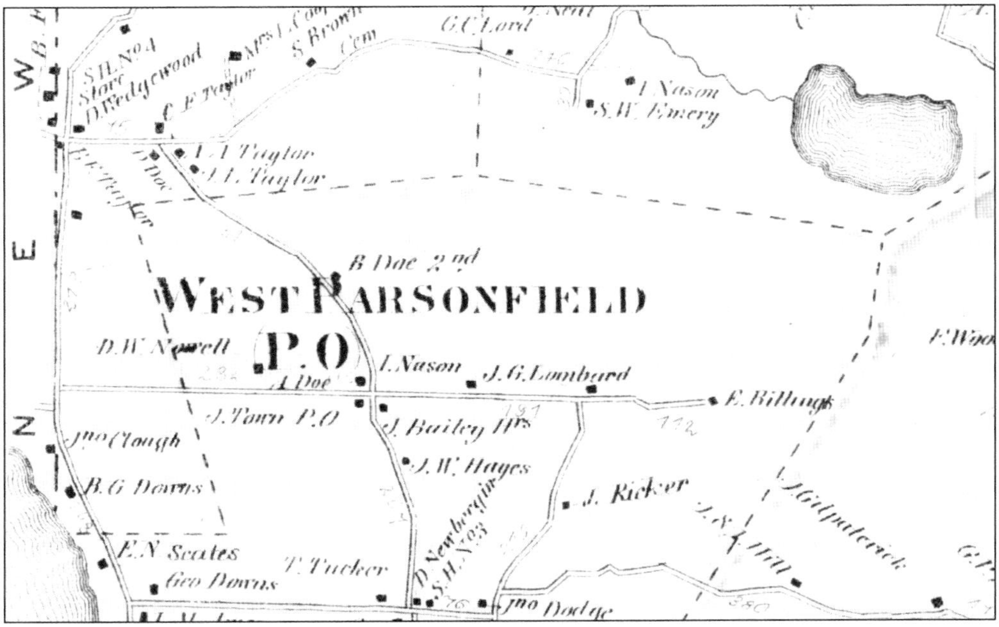

West Parsonsfield Village was located near the New Hampshire border and Province Lake, with Roberts Corner at the center and Taylor City on the state line a short distance above. A little farther north, just off Middle Road in the area now known as the Leavitt Plantation, is the Parsons' family cemetery. Across from the cemetery once stood the first frame house in Parsonsfield built by Thomas Parsons in 1784.

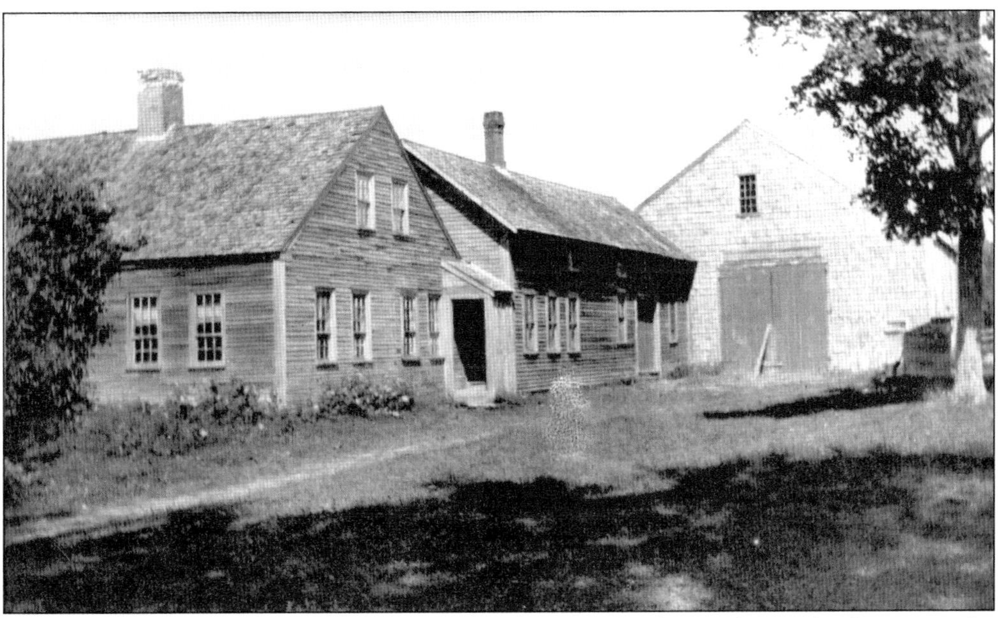

This 1905 photograph shows what was once the home of Joshua Roberts, also known as the Tristram Hurd Doe homestead. It is still located at Roberts Corner, the intersection of Stagecoach Road and Mountain Road. The house was remodeled between 1915 and 1917. In 1971, it was the home of Harrison Doe and his sister Ethel Leavitt. The District No. 3 Doe School House still stands to the right of this building.

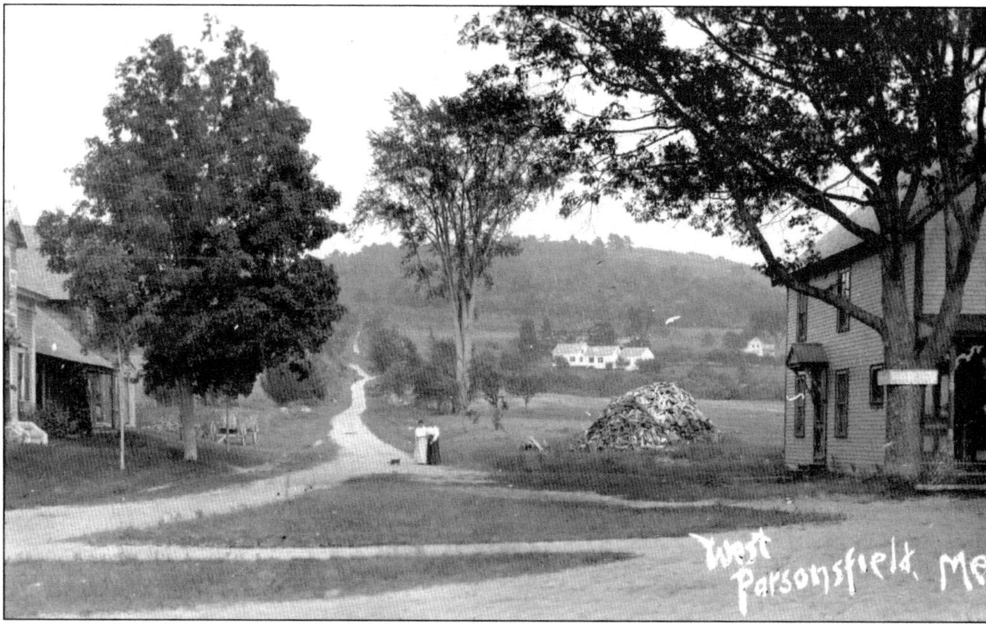

This is Taylor City around 1900, looking up Stagecoach Road from the state line. The building (left), built around 1878, once belonged to George and Rose Beal, and is now Alice and Earl Taylor's home. The center house belonged to the Thomas Henderson family. In the distance to the right was originally the home of Dr. William Taylor, and later Thomas Taylor. Taylor's Store is on the right.

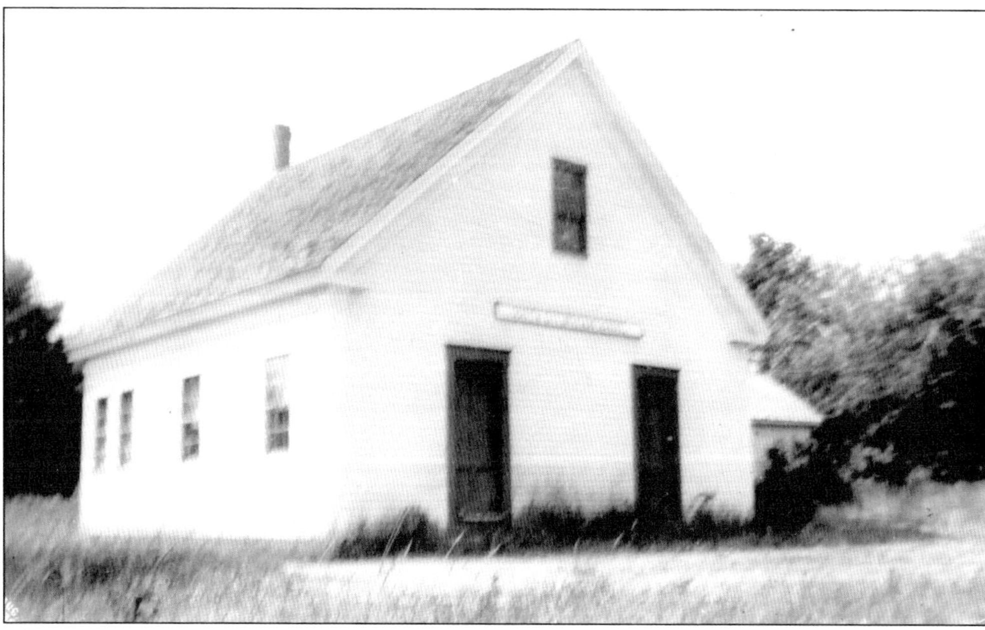

The New Hampshire and Maine state line went through the District No. 4 City or Line school house on Hasty Road, a short distance from Taylor City. Being located in two states, two towns, and two counties, the school was attended by children from Effingham, New Hampshire, and West Parsonsfield, Maine. The town of Effingham paid for the teacher and Parsonsfield maintained the building. Only rubble remains where the building once stood.